The Anatomy of
Industrial Decline

Recent Titles from Quorum Books

THE ANATOMY OF INDUSTRIAL DECLINE

Productivity, Investment, and Location in U.S. Manufacturing

JOHN E. ULLMANN

with the participation of William K. Bradshaw,
Bill Edmonds, Barbara Franco, Christopher Gary,
Lydia J. Goutas, Paula Gullo,
Donna Hoppenheim, James P. Kehoe, Jr.,
Barry Lituchy, Leslie Millman, Richard Nota,
Clifford Pincus, David Straus, Lloyd Straus,
Caryn J. Tobias, Robert A. Walz,
and Eric Williams

Quorum Books New York • Westport, Connecticut • London

Library of Congress Cataloging-in-Publication Data

Ullmann, John E.
    The anatomy of industrial decline : productivity, investment, and
location in U.S. manufacturing / John E. Ullmann ; with the
participation of William K. Bradshaw . . . [et al.] .
        p. cm.
    Bibliography: p.
    Includes index.
    ISBN 0-89930-244-0 (lib. bdg. : alk. paper)
    1. United States—Manufactures—Capital productivity.   2. United
States—Manufactures—Finance.   3. United States—Manufactures—
Location.   I. Title.
    HD9725.U43   1988
    338.4'767'0973—dc19   88-3097

British Library Cataloguing in Publication Data is available.

Library of Congress Catalog Card Number: 88-3097
ISBN: 0-89930-244-0

First published in 1988 by Quorum Books

Greenwood Press, Inc.
88 Post Road West, Westport, Connecticut 06881

Printed in the United States of America

∞™

The paper used in this book complies with the
Permanent Paper Standard issued by the National
Information Standards Organization (Z39.48–1984).

10 9 8 7 6 5 4 3 2 1

CONTENTS

TABLES

PREFACE

In recent years productivity trends in American manufacturing have been studied with rising alarm, as the realities of industrial decline, as well as the resulting domestic economic problems and international trade gap, have become too clear to ignore. The present volume examines these trends in relation to capital investment by different industries and analyzes whether geographic shifts of industries have had significant effects on their performance.

This book results from the continuing series of M.B.A. research and thesis seminars at the School of Business of Hofstra University. For each of these seminars, a director chooses a topic and is subsequently responsible for editing a volume and presenting it for publication. The topic is then divided into individual assignments, which are carried out by the participating students.

In past volumes of this kind, this has meant, in effect, that each student drafted a chapter. In this volume, the approach was slightly different. The assignments consisted of certain forms of analysis that were common to all industries. Thus, except as noted below, each student was given the task of examining one or more major (i.e., two-digit) industry groups as defined in the U.S. Department of Commerce's *Standard Industrial Classification* (SIC), except where these were too large or heterogenous. This was then followed by a detailed examination of the individual industries at the four-digit level. Finally, the individual topics of the analysis were consolidated on a cross-industry basis. Thus, for example, our study of locational trends in chapter 4 covers all industries.

The industry groups that were covered by each student are listed in the accompanying table. Each student is responsible only for the draft of his or her industry analysis, as submitted to and accepted by the project director. The general reviews of the methodology of productivity analysis and of the public policy issues associated with them, as well as much of the discussion of individual industries, are the work of the project director alone. Past or present employers of the participants were in no way involved in the study, which neither sought nor obtained additional outside support.

I am very much indebted to my colleague Dr. Lonnie K. Stevans for his assistance with the computer analysis presented in chapter 3.

Authors of the Industry Analyses

Industry	SIC Numbers	Author
Food, tobacco	20, 21	Caryn J. Tobias
Textiles	22	William K. Bradshaw
Apparel, leather	23, 31	Eric Williams
Lumber, wood, furniture	24, 25	Donna Hoppenheim
Paper, printing, publishing	26, 27	David Straus
Chemicals	28, except 282	Lydia J. Goutas
Petroleum, rubber, plastics	282, 29, 30	Paula Gullo
Stone, clay, glass	32	James P. Kehoe, Jr.
Primary metals	33	Richard Nota
Fabricated metals	34	Barry Lituchy
Machinery, except electrical	35, except 357	Barbara Franco
Electrical machinery, except electronics	361, 362, 363, 364	Clifford Pincus
Electronics	357, 365, 366, 367, 369	Leslie Millman
Motor vehicles	371, 3751, 379	Bill Edmonds
Other transportation	372, 373, 3743, 376	Lloyd Straus
Instruments	38	Christopher Gary
Miscellaneous manufacturing	39	Robert A. Walz

The Anatomy of
Industrial Decline

PRODUCTIVITY

1

Issues and Problems

ANALYTIC OBJECTIVES

Productivity is one of those comprehensive societal measures that constantly engage the concern of politicians, business leaders, and academics. The issues involved relate not only to the measures themselves, to what they say and what they do not say, but also to the general state of the society that turns them out.

This volume deals with productivity in manufacturing, that is, in a business sector that has attracted the most worried kind of attention without much in the way of success in curing its problems. Short-range disturbances aside, manufacturing employment grew steadily in absolute numbers from the time the United States became a major industrial power in the last century. However, in the period covered by this study, it reached its maximum and has since declined. Employment was 16.8 million in 1960, 19.3 million in 1967, a peak of 20.3 million in 1980, and back to its 1967 level of 19.3 million in 1985.[1]

Consumption of manufactured goods kept increasing, however. The difference was made by the excess of imports over exports which developed during the period of this study. Although the United States was running a deficit in its balance of payments in 1967, this was largely due to its military expenditures abroad; the merchandise account was still in surplus. Accordingly, this book also deals with the international aspects of the problem. In the final chapter, a detailed industry-by-industry review of the realities of the import problem is presented. Productivity and industrial performance, in short, can no longer be assessed merely in domestic terms, but rather must take into account the reasons for the takeover of the markets of many products by imports. These reasons in turn require qualitative assessments of products and industries that go beyond quantitative results.

Because one major measure of commitment to any business is what people want to invest in it, volume of capital investment will also receive attention, especially in relation to productivity. Nevertheless, a straightforward presentation of the numbers would be insufficient. Rather, the format of the study is to look at each industry in detail and thus provide further physical explanations of what has happened, beyond the numerical results. At bottom, industrywide statistics stem from the collective decisions of the managements of the firms involved, the performance of its technical and other professionals as well as of its workers, the nature of the markets and their interpretations by managements, the feasibility of product or process innovation, and a host of other factors. Much as one might wish for a simple world in which overall economic measures are fully reliable, as well as infallible, guides to action, such does not correspond to reality.

For these and other reasons, productivity is an important issue in any society and a crucial one in an industrial society. As Kendrick and Pech put it in their 1961 book on the subject, "The story of productivity, the ratio of output to input, is at heart the record of man's efforts to raise himself from poverty."[2] This broad definition, however, immediately suggests that productivity is a derived effect, resulting from the application of human, technical, and financial resources to tasks that society wishes to have carried out and supports in some way, whether by paying directly or by some variant of social cost. Nowadays, there are few areas of endeavor in any human society where someone does not question productivity, using or sometimes proposing methods for its measurement.

This volume offers an analysis of productivity measurements in particular manufacturing industries. It does so at a time when the general area of manufacturing in the United States has been especially troubled, as more and more industries cease to be viable and abandon their traditional roles in favor of imports or at least major imported components. For this reason, the presentations in this volume rely not only on traditional quantitative measures but also on qualitative assessments of individual industries. A major set of problems is posed by the need, under present circumstances particularly, to call the traditional measures into serious question, both as to what they measure in general and as to how they deal with the problems of specific industries.

The succeeding chapters of this volume, therefore, start with a review of methodological problems that defines what is known and what still remains to be measured in ways beyond the scope of this volume and, indeed, beyond practicality. In the present troubled state of manufacturing, the traditional measures often do not reveal very much in the way of significant progress in the direction of better performance, and they are even less impressive when their significance is assessed in detail in relation to particular industries.

Another issue addressed in this volume is that of the location of manufacturing. Although the political controversies surrounding this subject have subsided somewhat and some areas that had been hurt, like the Northeast, have recovered in some respects, the issue is still relevant. Plant closings have reached epidemic proportions in some areas of the country, but as will be shown in detail, the jobs tend to vanish altogether rather than move to some other domestic locations. The reason is simply the protracted American industrial decline. It has drastically changed the makeup of different industries, how they are financed or, as is more common in many cases, how much disinvestment they have to sustain as their managements buy and sell what are quite often the spavined remains of once viable enterprises.

Clearly, these are very broad areas of public policy and, in many respects, are beyond the scope of this volume. Nevertheless it is necessary to draw attention to them, not only because it is essential to be aware of all the major problems before one can analyze what went wrong, but also because major socioeconomic trends ultimately determine what can be done politically. For example, agendas for further research must obviously take these parameters into account.

Such possible actions are, of course, political and in part eventually resolve themselves into settling what parts of society will bear the principal burdens of difficult times ahead. This point has been clear for a long time, certainly for as long as the industrial decline of the United States has been going on. Specifically, the most contentious issues are over allocating social costs so that much of the cost of the damage to the industrial structure will be borne by individuals and groups other than those who were directly involved in the affected industries—or those who had mismanaged them in the first instance. In this volume, such issues regularly underlie the analysis of the fortunes of particular industries.

The decline in manufacturing has now gone on long enough to permit at least some generalizations as to the changes in American industry. Broadly speaking, it has gone through three periods since World War II.

The first was a time of postwar reconversion, as American industry prepared to meet an enormous pent-up demand for goods backed by substantial personal savings. Moreover, as the only former belligerent whose country had emerged without physical damage, the United States had the largest functioning industrial sector by a very large margin. And in a reversal of political attitudes, involving the needs of the then new Cold War and the rejection of traditional isolationism, the United States accepted a responsibility for international relief work in such initiatives as the Marshall Plan and the beginnings of the American aid program to what was then first called the Third World.

It is important to recognize this international dimension because it occurred at a time when American industrial supremacy was virtually complete. However, to respond to a point often made in connection with the current increasingly troublesome issues of international trade, it is not true that the United States put its defeated enemies together again industrially. Marshall Plan assistance to West Germany was approximately $1.6 billion, and economic assistance to Japan was about $21.8 million, but those countries invested their own internally generated funds in enormous multiples of these very small U.S. amounts.[3] Private American investment in the industries of these countries was negligible; indeed, as opportunities arose in the 1950s some long-held minority interests of U.S. companies were sold, such as General Electric's share in A.E.G. of Germany and Hitachi of Japan.

In retrospect this period was a high point in American industrial development, even apart from its international stature. Investment in plant and machinery was ample, and so was product innovation. Some bad mistakes were made, notably by the steel industry which chose to use 1890s technology for its huge new plants instead of the new processes then being installed by its competitors in Europe and Japan. Still, it was a successful period—in retrospect almost a golden age. As to productivity, teams of managers and technicians came from all over the world to try to learn American methods then, even though it has generally been true that, looking beyond the technical details, industrial attitudes are so culturally specific that they cannot be readily transferred to other societies. It was just as true then of American experiences as it is now of Japanese ways of doing things, which have also had their share of would-be imitators.

American industry's second period began in the 1960s, when certain influential rationalizations for industrial decline, such as the "postindustrial" theory and the so-called information age, first surfaced. The former theory was the view that an industrial society could progress beyond such mundane matters as making the things needed in favor of merely managing their manufacture elsewhere. The latter theory held that concern with making things had been, or should be, superseded by the processing of information.

Such formulations could be readily debunked on internal grounds. It was easy to see how the United States would come to depend on foreigners for its goods: foreign countries would not hold still long as mere hewers of wood and drawers of water for the United States and would strike out on their own industrially, without limits set by anyone else. As to the information age, it was clear that information, however defined, is not a free good and therefore must be justified just as much as any other cost of a business; otherwise processing information only results in a further increase in already excessive overhead.

Whatever the defects of these views and similar ones,[4] there is no question that they set the stage for some not altogether benign neglect of manufacturing in general and its technological underpinnings in particular. Another crucial ingredient was the escalation of the arms race during the Kennedy Administration which followed the "missile gap"—later found to have been spurious. Nevertheless, together with the moon shot, preparations for which were also then getting under way, and soon afterwards the Vietnam war, it set the stage for an ever increasing technical content of weaponry. That, in turn, began to make ever greater demands on U.S. technical skills and related capital.

One consequence of the diversion of capital and of technical effort was a growing inability of American manufacturing industries to follow their traditional practice of using improved methods and equipment to make up for their own rising costs and foreign competition, especially that due to cheap labor. In earlier times, productivity had been improving fast enough for U.S. manufacturers to pay the highest wages in the world and to lower the price of many products in current and often constant dollars.

However, as B. Y. Hong has shown, when this improvement slowed down as the result of technological and managerial neglect, manufacturers had to pass along their increased costs as increased prices and began losing their markets, as well as triggering inflation.[5] Indeed, the result was not only inflation but stagnation as well, that is, what came to be called "stagflation." As a further result, "foreign sourcing" and direct foreign investment by U.S. corporations grew rapidly; it was the time of "exporting jobs."[6]

The third and current stage began around 1980; it is a combination of escalating industrial decay, trade gaps of unprecedented size, and the huge debt, domestic and foreign, to which the Reagan budgets have led. The slow collapse of the dollar had to be engineered to try to stem the rise of imports. A second and obvious consequence of that kind of currency devaluation is that a country begins to sell cheap and buy dear, but an even more far-reaching result is that the United States and its tangible assets have become a bargain. Foreigners, flush with otherwise unusable dollars, were not slow to reduce the United States to the state of a net debtor for the first time since the early 1900s. Exports have not picked up enough, however, and the trade gap has remained bad; there simply are not enough exportable products, and the skills to create them have vanished amid the recent industrial and economic distortions.

Lacking exports, the United States has one remaining choice: selling assets. Thus, Japan bought more than a quarter of all U.S. government securities issued in 1986. Its automobile industry established branch plants in the United States, to take advantage of costs that had become lower than at home. An attempt by Fujitsu (a principal robot maker) to buy Fairchild Semiconductors was blocked by the U.S. Department of Defense, but, as we will note later, there have been many other joint ventures in other parts of the electronics industry. There have also been huge British acquisitions of service businesses, as in banking and advertising, and many German ones in retailing and publishing. All this is certainly a far cry from earlier and more opulent times.

As noted in more detail below, the statistical analysis of this study mainly relates to the period 1967–82, that is, to the second period described above and the beginning of the third. However, it must inevitably take note of subsequent developments as well; if there is one clear aspect of current difficulties, it is that they have not so far proved easily or significantly reversible.

PRODUCTIVITY AND ITS CAUSATION

It was noted earlier that productivity is a derived effect. Since it is the ratio of output to input, it immediately raises the question of what goes into the numerator and denominator of this fraction. These factors will be examined in detail later, especially in relation to changes in production systems, product quality, and the structure of the industrial labor force. But there is, in addition, the issue of the actual relationships between the factors that go into production or, more exactly, the issue of causation. On this subject, Frederick C. Mills correctly states the main problem:

Measures of productivity carry no causal imputation . . . a measure that sets output against volume of invested capital is not to be taken to mean that the capital factor is responsible for the changes that may occur in the ratio. Again, if an advance is shown by a productivity ratio that sets output against man-hours of work done, this is not to be taken to mean that the gain is to be attributed to the labor factor in production. In all cases the actual factor input is a composite of all agents of production. The human factor uses power, capital equipment, and organizational devices of various sorts in exploiting natural resources to produce economic goods. It is convenient, and meaningful, to measure changes in output with reference to changes in some one component of the factor composite, but it would be a great mistake to assume that this factor operates alone in bringing about a gain or loss. . . . [Thus] the effectiveness . . . varies not only with the intensity and skill, but also with the number and quality of the tools employed, the amount of power utilized, the nature of the productive organization, and other features of the production process.[7]

It is important to set forth Mills' caveats in detail because in the kinds of conflicts that now surround productivity measures, especially those relating to labor, causality is assumed, when in fact it is highly questionable. Thus, in a crude example of wrongly imputed causality, labor productivity is taken as an indicator of how hard people work, instead of being considered as the result of a broader range of input factors, as Mills correctly advocates. There are other elements as well; thus, as will be shown later, such issues as product innovation, design, and quality, not explicitly mentioned by him, become crucial factors, particularly in an industrial structure in decline.

This volume deals only with labor productivity and the volume of invested capital. For reasons that will be explained in the appropriate chapters, no attempt has been made to measure capital productivity nor has productivity been related to other factors such as energy input. It is also important to make the general point that productivity measures are not per se measures of efficiency. Strictly speaking, a measure of efficiency in a technical or industrial context must have a measure of a potential maximum before any losses, because an efficiency measure basically is the ratio of what a system actually produces divided by what it could produce if there were no losses and if it worked perfectly.

This is done, for instance, by engineers in measuring the efficiency of certain mechanical, electrical, or thermal devices, as in the performance ratings of air conditioners. On the other hand, car miles per gallon of fuel, which might also be thought to be a measure of efficiency, is meaningful only in relation to what other cars can do and sometimes, as indicated over time, the increasing frailty of a given vehicle. Similarly, productivity (i.e., output/input) ratios are useful mainly for comparing to past trends, or to what competitors can do, rather than for setting some absolute standard or defining some ultimate performance potential. Moreover, as the next section indicates, there are even more basic problems with what goes into defining productivity ratios.

DEFINING INPUT AND OUTPUT

One would suppose that, whatever the other problems of interpretation, it would at least not be too difficult to define without argument what is input and what is output in a production process and thus come up with a productivity ratio once these are measured. There are, however, certain other issues that must be addressed in presenting a productivity analysis, especially when, as in the present volume, problems of particular industries will be held to the fore.

The problem essentially resolves itself into what effects certain inputs have had on productivity when they had to be provided not because they were primarily required by the product itself, but rather due to other necessities. Perhaps the most controversial of these relates to environmental protection, which became a progressively more important matter in the 1970s. One study that endeavored to isolate the effects was that of Edward F. Denison who, in 1978, concluded:

By 1975, . . . output per unit of input in the non-residential business sector of the economy was 1.8% smaller than it would have been if business had operated under 1967 conditions. Of this amount 1.0% is ascribable to pollution abatement and 0.4% each to employee safety and health programs and to the increase in dishonesty and crime.[8]

Denison's analysis combines all input factors—which is not what is done in this volume—but apart from that, such a statement taken alone would ignore the fact that previously the costs of pollution had been borne by society at large and so too, in essence, had many of the consequences of workers' ill health and injuries. Denison, of course, was aware of this and added the disclaimer that "the purpose of this article is to aid analysis of growth and productivity; it is not to judge the wisdom of government programs which have benefits as well as costs." Unfortunately, when environmental protection was much reduced in the subsequent conservative drive for deregulation, such disclaimers did not find many listeners among those who sought to reverse the trend.

In a second article Denison considered over one hundred different analyses of productivity change and concluded that they failed to make a significant dent in a large, unexplainable residual.[9] He finally decided that "everything might have gone wrong at once" among major determinants. Still, no doubt such other factors as the decline of technical innovation in the nonmilitary sector of U.S. manufacturing might have offered explanations. Unfortunately, such considerations, which will be duly noted in the industry analyses of this volume, do not lend themselves to cross-industry generalizations but rather are peculiar to the industries involved.

The issue of social costs and consequences of industrial activity has in fact been raised in even broader form. In Denison's analysis, he is essentially dealing with the effect of turning social costs into direct business costs, that is, he is concerned with what industries must themselves spend in order to take better care of their employees, their environment, and in issues of product safety, their customers. Note that where this results in extra costs, these are passed on to the firm's customers or, perhaps, are in part absorbed by lower profit rates. However, the new expenditures are *added* to what has been produced, that is, the value of output increases.

It is exactly that kind of social bookkeeping that is now being questioned. At present, this mainly affects discussions of how to measure gross domestic product (GDP) and its growth rates, but quite obviously it has major implications for productivity measurement as well. The point is simply that a rapidly rising proportion of economic activity now has to do with repairing environmental damage, removing wastes more carefully (or, distressingly often, merely more expensively), dealing with environmental health problems, and providing much else in remedies for the dysfunctions of modern life.

According to Christian Leipert, who has done such an analysis for West Germany, some 10 percent of all economic activities are a reaction to already incurred damage and to the stresses to which both nature and society are increasingly subjected.[10] In a sense, these are what are sometimes called "defensive" activities and should not be regarded as further perking up the GDP and its growth rate. In other words, not all activity deserves to be counted as a gain or profit when it is actually a cost or loss because it only enables some other activity to be carried out or, so to speak, picks up after it. The value of the goods or services actually delivered to society is therefore reduced by the costs of such remedies, however society tries to do (and pay for) the job. Pretending that such an activity is not an input factor to industrial work and measuring it, if at all, as part of the output can thus result only in growing self-deception in social accounting. This potential misjudgment of economic performance would become more severe as the defensive activities themselves increased in importance, the degree of which is set by social necessity, public health, and political pressures.

Studies of such effects in the United States have not yet been done, and the present volume can rely only on data bases as currently available. What is clear, however, is that conventional analyses necessarily overestimate any "progress" that has been made in productivity. Accordingly, for example, the very modest rising trends of labor productivity described later would have to be deflated much further (if indeed, they are statistically significant in the first place), because the true magnitudes of societal repairs should be considered a burden rather than an asset and should serve to reduce the value of output rather than increase it.

PRINCIPAL SOURCES OF DATA
AND PLAN OF THE STUDY

The basic idea for this volume resulted from a preliminary survey conducted in 1980 titled "Regional Changes in Manufacturing Productivity."[11] This was a thesis project written by Jeffrey Wenzel, under the supervision of the director of the present study. It was a topical theme because at that time industrial decline was having a particularly strong impact on the traditional industrial areas of the Northeast and Middle West, and migration to what had come to be called the Sunbelt was widely being considered to foreshadow a profound change in the economic and, eventually, the political geography of the United States. The study, which will be described in more detail in chapter 4, indicated that there were no statistically significant regional differences and that the often considerable variation among the major industry groups was largely sui generis, that is, due to factors within the industry groups themselves.

Reviewers at the time, however, made the point that it might have been more useful to look at individual industries, that is, to go from the SIC 2-digit major groups in the original study to individual 4-digit industries. One reason was that the major groups encompass great variations in the products, processes, and eventually health and prospects of the industries that make them up. The present volume attempts to deal with this problem by looking at the individual industries, and eventually by combining some of the results within the major groups in connection with the relationships between investment and productivity. It was also decided to combine the regional analysis with a review of the investment record of manufacturing and to examine particularly the nature of statistical relationships between investment and labor productivity.

The above pilot study was done using only the 1967 and 1977 Censuses of Manufactures. In the present volume, the basic data set is that of the U.S. Censuses of Manufactures for 1967, 1972, 1977, and 1982, with intermediate annual reports. This naturally was a much more formidable task, but it allows a clearer assessment of industrial conditions in a time when, in general, the industrial decline continued, as noted earlier in this chapter. Unfortunately, in recent years U.S. censuses of all kinds have had increasingly long lead times, as well as data processing difficulties, in the wake of widespread cuts in information gathering and processing after 1981. As one result, data on value added by manufacture for 1982 were incomplete in the preliminary census reports that were used for the major analysis, and rates of change had to be based on the period 1967–81, rather than 1967–82. Still, the information was sufficient to do the bulk of the productivity analysis and its relation to investments and location.

The plan of this volume is that the next chapter will deal with labor productivity, and the following one with investment trends and their interrelationships. The subsequent chapters deal with the significance of locational changes in relation to productivity and with the effects of international trade. Each chapter commences with a discussion of the issues in general substance and methodology and proceeds with a presentation of the numerical results and commentaries for the various industries.

NOTES

1. U.S. Department of Commerce, *1987 Statistical Abstract of the United States* (Washington, D.C.: Government Printing Office, 1987), 394.

2. J. W. Kendrick and M. Pech, *Productivity Trends in the United States* (New York: National Bureau of Economic Research, 1961), 1.

3. S. Melman, *Profits without Production* (New York: Knopf, 1983), 205.

4. J. E. Ullmann, *The Prospects of American Industrial Recovery* (Westport, Conn.: Quorum Books, 1985), 130-36.

5. B. Y. Hong, *Inflation under Cost Pass-Along Management* (New York: Praeger, 1979).

6. Melman, *Profits without Production*, 17-39.

7. F. C. Mills, *Statistical Methods* (New York: Henry Holt, 1955), 502-3.

8. E. F. Denison, "Effects of Selected Changes in the Institutional and Human Environment upon Output per Unit of Input," *Survey of Current Business*, January 1978, 21-44.

9. E. F. Denison, "Explanations of Declining Productivity Growth," *Survey of Current Business*, August 1979, Pt. 2, 1-24.

10. C. Leipert, "Bruttosozialprodukt, defensive Ausgaben und Nettowohlfahrtsmessung" (Gross Domestic Product, Defensive Expenditures and the Measurement of Net Welfare), *Zeitschrift fuer Umweltpolitik*, April 1984, 229-55.

11. J. Wenzel, "Regional Changes in Manufacturing Productivity" (M.B.A. thesis, Hofstra University, 1980).

LABOR PRODUCTIVITY

2

OBJECTIVES AND INTERPRETATIONS

Labor productivity is essentially the quantity of a product turned out for each unit of labor expended. This seems simple enough, but actually the formulation and measurement of labor productivity present considerable practical difficulties which define and circumscribe the usefulness of this measure. The overall measures presented in this chapter must therefore be interpreted in the light of these restrictions and in relation to the purpose for which they are to be used.

Specifically, there are two sets of questions. First, what is the purpose of such an overall measure, especially when it results in an industry-wide index of some sort, or even a transnational one? Second, how should the numerator and denominator of the productivity fraction be measured, that is, how are product output and labor input defined?

As to the first question, measures of labor productivity could have two kinds of interpretation. The first is simply that they estimate how much labor a given industry expends in order to fulfill a given *product function.* Note that this is not the same as the output of a specific product, such as a barrel of cement, or a pair of shoes, even though output might in practice be measured by the quantities of each. Rather, these items and all other industrial production are goods that do something or furnish a service for which society has created a demand. Whether this demand is met by any particular kind or design of a product is not a primary consideration in this view of labor productivity. Rather, an index of labor productivity is an essentially *macroeconomic* measure, that is, one that relates the effort expended by that industry to the economy as a whole.

Thus, for example, when the old electro-mechanical calculating machines were replaced by ever smaller and cheaper electronic ones, the social purpose of having an aid to calculation was served by a technically completely different product. As it happens, it also was an enormously more convenient and versatile product, as well as one that quickly became very much cheaper. One should not, of course, take such progress as a frequent result, let alone as an inevitable one. This example, however, also makes the general points that product design, in all its aspects, must be central to the definition and measurement of output and that the import of productivity statistics cannot be judged without considering major qualitative changes in the industry.

This is particularly important in connection with the second use to which productivity statistics are often put. There is a tendency in other contexts, notably in wage setting, to regard such indexes as *microeconomic* measures as well, that is, ones that relate to individual industries and, within them, to individual enterprises. The purpose is to have an indication of how hard or effectively people work, so that wages can in some way be negotiated on the basis of such a measure. In the last chapter, it was shown that this is a much more questionable interpretation. It makes an assumption of causality in judging productivity levels and trends that should not be made without a detailed examination of the industrial operations involved. It thus cannot a priori justify giving credit, or blame, to any single input factor for the results. There are, quite obviously, enormous differences in labor deployment and in managerial and other support in different enterprises.

The distinction between the macroeconomic and microeconomic interpretations is also a centerpiece of this study. The major trends in labor productivity presented here are meant to be interpreted in a macroeconomic sense. The quantitative measures are supplemented by qualitative assessments of what is happening to products, factories, and workers. Only in this way can the managerial and other problems of particular industries be effectively addressed.

OUTPUT

The definition of output is simple only when it is a highly homogeneous product, and in manufacturing there are very few products that fit this bill. In fact cement, lime, and gypsum are the principal single and more or less homogeneous products that define the output of manufacturing industries of significant size. The output here would simply be the tonnage produced. For just about all other industries, the heterogeneity of product requires methods of measurement that must necessarily remain approximate and that, especially when used for microeconomic reasons, require an understanding of the sources and implications of product diversity.

The present study uses constant dollar value added by manufacture (CDVAM) as a measure of physical output. Value added by manufacture is industry volume less cost of raw materials, fuel, and contract work. It thus essentially consists of the contributions of labor and capital in the firm and its profit. Although the inclusion of the latter has sometimes been criticized, it is clearly related to the other two ingredients, and the measure is thus accepted as an indicator of the impact of a given establishment and, when added to the others in a given industry, of the industry as a whole. Value added by manufacture is deflated by using the price index for the industry's product or, in a few cases where not available directly, for a broader but closely related group of products. As will be noted later, price indexes have problems of their own, but the method is the only practical one in heterogeneous industries.

Value added by manufacture has also been chosen for this volume because it is part of the same data base in the Census of Manufactures as the statistics used for investment in plant and equipment; since their relationship is a central topic of this volume, the use of a common source of data was considered advisable. Moreover, since other quantity indexes are not available for all industries, this method was the most generally applicable.

Of such other quantitative indexes, the principal ones are those of the Federal Reserve Board (FRB). Its method of computation is described as follows in an article on recent revisions in the series which, incidentally, turn out to involve only minor changes in the results:

For industries in which direct measurement [of output] is not possible, output is inferred from production-worker hours and the use of electrical power. Periodic revisions benchmark the individual industrial production series to more comprehensive data sources. One of the major sources for benchmark revisions is the Census of Manufactures which is undertaken every five years.[1]

The census is supplemented by the data from the Annual Survey of Manufactures which is done for the intervening years. In effect, what the FRB does is also to use deflated value added by manufacture. A different set of statistics is prepared by the Bureau of Labor Statistics (BLS), but these are now in the process of being revised to harmonize with the FRB indexes.

The microeconomic aspects of the analysis, those most closely related to the actual functioning and prospects of the industry concerned, are of course a function of what has been happening to the industry's product line. There are three areas of interest here: product diversity, product design, and of increasing concern in recent times, product quality.

There are many industries in which both changes and diversity are inherent in the product itself, are long familiar, and are thus implicitly recognized by anyone looking at the industry's productivity statistics. Clothing, footwear, steel beams, and light bulbs are but four examples among hundreds of products that, by their nature, must at least be made in different sizes. In practical market terms, they must also be made in different shapes and designs. In its effect on labor productivity, there is then a possibility that the product line may be fragmented to such an extent that production quantities of single items fall to uneconomically low levels; yet they must be made in order to maintain a full line.

At times, moreover, the total output of an industry is affected not so much by any sudden changes as by a slow shift in industry markets that ultimately brings about a substantial rearrangement of the industry's segments. Thus, the steel industry now has a much greater share of its market in alloy steels and reinforcing bars, relative to its staple carbon steel items, than it did thirty years ago. These new major products require different kinds of production facilities and therefore have quite different labor requirements. This also has implications for economy of scale, which will be discussed in the next chapter dealing with capital equipment.

When a product has to be made in many versions, it also requires substantially higher total inventory because stock of one size or type cannot make up for shortages in another one. An early classic case of this occurred in the late 1940s, when manufacturers of bathroom fixtures decided to make them in many colors, rather than in the previous ubiquitous white, and there have been many other instances since. Extra inventory means extra storage facilities and extra order processing; the effect may not be significant in most cases, but it should be recognized as a possible factor.

The case of the bathroom fixtures was a single policy decision; in a sense it was a discontinuity in the business. In many other cases, however, change is regular and institutionalized. Examples are the periodic model change of cars and appliances and, in apparel, the long established need to come up constantly with new items. The point here is that the products still are of a similar kind year after year, so that this does not necessarily mean a major change in production methods and facilities.

There is also a product policy called line extension, in which it is hoped to tap additional markets by making the product in several versions even when the distinctions are not great and when neither the nature of the product nor established industry practice demand a new version. Such a change occurred in cigarettes, for instance, of which there are now some 175 brands, a far cry from the time some thirty years ago when 6 brands accounted for much of the market. Another example is that of soft drinks: Pepsi-Cola and Coca-Cola may now be had in eleven versions, depending on whether they contain sugar or caffeine or new or "classic" syrup. In fact, it may even be difficult in such cases to come up with advertising messages for one version that does not damage another; presenting sugar and caffeine as grim poisons in one may not do much for the sales of the other versions that still contain them. Perhaps, in practice, the giant musical numbers and the sex fantasies that seem to be the staple of soft drink commercials tend to blur such contradictions. In any event, the differing versions do add to the costs of the business, albeit probably not significantly at the actual production end.

The foregoing sources of product heterogeneity are prompted by market necessities, traditions, and new strategies. There are others, however, that have to do with product design itself. In one way or another, that kind of product change is the result of innovation and may or may not represent major changes in production methods. Only if such changes are required can one expect significant discontinuities in the productivity statistics. Otherwise the change may well be insignificant in relation to the fluctuations in output that occur for any number of reasons in any production system.

There are three ways such new concepts may manifest themselves. First, the technology of the product may be improved or, in fact, changed entirely. The above example of the calculators is a clear case of this. It may be viewed as part of the tendency in machine design of all sorts, observable from at least the 1920s onwards, of replacing

mechanical parts and subassemblies with electrical and later electronic components that do the same job. Speed regulation of electric
motors, for instance, which was once often done by mechanical gear-
boxes, is now done almost universally by electronic methods.

Second, product change may be prompted primarily by cost considerations. At any time, a variety of possible changes in a product is
available to designers and their managements. In studies done by the
principal author of this volume, it was shown that reduction of production costs was a prime criterion in selecting new design features
from among the possible choices. There was, in short, a good deal of
economic determinism in the applications of new technology and
product designs.[2] It is noteworthy that the concerns of other parties
at interest, like users, were not consistently considered; sometimes
they were affected favorably, sometimes adversely. Lower production
costs, however, proved the most powerful criterion of acceptance in
product change, except in such cases as automotive safety devices
like seat belts, which had to be legally mandated before they were
adopted.[3]

A third source of change, at times related to the second, is simply
the routine work of product engineering departments, other product
designers for manufacturers, and industrial engineers. They have to
justify their existence and budgets by regularly coming up with improvements and cost reductions in both products and processes.
When done competently, this merits the term *value analysis*. This is a
set of skills and practices, originally presented in the late 1940s by
Lawrence D. Miles, that, as its motto put it, sought to "omit, combine, make cheaper." However, as carefully noted in Miles' seminal
work, the first need is to maintain or improve product function and
other characteristics.[4] This in turn requires broad and up-to-date
knowledge of functional analysis, materials, processes, and costs,
and is thus far removed from mere cost cutting for its own sake,
regardless of the consequences.

One particular trend, which may or may not affect the performance of the product, should be mentioned in this connection. It is
the growing practice of manufacturers of durable goods—from furniture to metal products and appliances of many kinds—to make them
"knocked down" (KD) and let customers do the assembly. The work
may often be troublesome and time consuming; there are few more
dubious, not to say ominous, phrases in commercial speech than
"some assembly required" or "simple assembly required." In some
cases, as in complex installations, there are in fact services that do

the job for an extra charge. From the viewpoint of measuring labor productivity, this practice may have significant impact. It means that the manufacturer's assembly labor is not required and therefore not counted as part of making the quantity of product turned out. It is not counted at all when done by the customer and not counted in the manufacturing sector when done by some service business. Either way, the practice overestimates the amount of product turned out per unit of labor at the factory. Furthermore, assembly operations in manufacturing still are highly labor-intensive compared with the rest of the processes.

One such case is that of automobiles where dealers have long complained about defects and omissions in car assemblies which they must then remedy as part of their dealer preparation for which, incidentally, they levy an increasingly substantial charge. Again, whatever the details, the work done under this rubric should really be part of the manufacturer's work and not that of the dealer whose activities are counted in the service sector and not in manufacturing.

These considerations lead directly to product quality. There are three effects here. The first is that of the price indexes used to deflate the value added by manufacture. The ones used here are the usual BLS indexes, which again are unexceptionable when used for macroeconomic evaluations but which must be looked at in more detail when considering the specifics of product lines.

Price indexes are based on market baskets of products. It has, of course, been long accepted that when the usage of products changes drastically, a discontinuity is introduced that makes the index unrealistic as a measure of the kinds of prices that must be paid for the industry's products. In fact, this has been one of the most serious problems in index number theory from its beginnings. However, a secondary problem, not generally discussed, arises when the quality level of the product changes. When it declines, more of the product must be used; in effect, the output needed to satisfy a given societal need becomes inflated. Increased volume for an industry thus not only infers expanding markets but also may reflect poorer quality which causes the product to wear out faster. The opposite is obviously the case when quality is improved.

There is a second difficulty that arises from the price indexes themselves. Here, declining quality may have the effect of driving more people toward what had been the high end of the product line. Specifically, since it is impossible to include every item in the market basket used for computing the price index, it must be based on some sort of sampling or other judgment. The Bureau of Labor Statistics specifies the products it uses, in considerable detail.[5] When, due to its quality decline, such a product can only fulfill the need of an ever shrinking portion of the industry's market, and causes a shift to higher-priced versions, the effect is the same as a price increase.

For example, when a decent pair of trousers once cost $17.99 and now can be had only for $29.99, there is a price relative there of 166.7, that is, a dollar is worth only about 60 cents. Yet trousers are still available at $17.99, and if these are part of the market basket, they would remain there to contribute to the price index. But if more people have to buy trousers at $29.99 because the cheaper ones are no longer to their liking, the price index becomes understated and the output overstated, unless the more expensive ones are likewise part of the market basket and, as noted, there are practical limits to the number of items that can be included.

The third quality effect lies in the kind of remedial actions a manufacturer must, or chooses to, take in response to quality problems. These actions may have different results, depending on their specifics, and may affect the *quantity* as well as the nature of the output, as is the case with the other product diversities discussed above. In what follows, it is important to note that it is output that is being measured; whether a given enterprise can or cannot get away with any of the following practices or whether the market eventually does or does not exact retribution for bad service are separate issues. Profitability, growth, or demise of individual businesses are not part of data collection for labor productivity.

There are at least four possible strategies: First, a manufacturer may essentially decide to let customers fend for themselves and to take whatever market or business chances are involved. This may be a viable strategy for such items as novelties or disposables of all kinds, where any corrective action would be infeasible, and in fact for many products in which quality expectations by consumers are not high, brand consciousness or loyalty are limited, or breakdowns are expected as part of the general scheme of things.

Second, the manufacturer may simply decide to *replace* any items that customers find defective or that break down during a warranty period. In that case, the numbers of units produced must be increased to compensate for the defectives returned, but one should note that the social purpose of the product is only served by the net usable units. In other words, what might be called the effective output is overstated. As to the labor component, it is increased by the work time needed to make the replacement units. Thus both numerator and denominator of the labor productivity fraction are increased. One cannot say a priori what the final effect of this would be on the firm's or industry's viability, but one is faced with the curious phenomenon that as long as a manufacturer turns out junk and replaces it afterwards, the productivity fraction might not be affected too much, depending on the numbers.

Third, returned units may be *repaired* by the manufacturer. In that case, the total number of units will remain the same, but the labor is increased by whatever is needed to make the repairs.

Finally, the repair or adjustment may be done by an outside service business, for example, by an authorized dealer, in which case the extra labor is not counted at all at the manufacturing end, any more than it is with outside final assembly, as discussed above. It is quite obvious, therefore, that for a given amount of final product, these four methods would give different results, probably drastically so in the case of replacement vs. repair or inside vs. outside service.

LABOR INPUT

Statistics on labor input are collected in two ways. Input may encompass all employees or only the number of production workers or their work hours. In this volume, the analysis is based on all employees, that is, the measure used is constant dollar value added by manufacture per employee (CDVAM/E).

The reason for this is twofold. First, a pervasive factor throughout this century has been the ever increasing proportion of nonproduction employees in manufacturing, comprising more engineers and technicians, administrative and clerical workers. This represents not only an obvious and quite considerable shift in the skill mix but one that has served to blur quite directly the lines between production and nonproduction employees. For example, when machines are no longer set up by the workers operating them, but rather, in the ever increasing proportion of computerized machinery, by means of software coming out of the engineering department, then the people doing the programming must be added to the production operatives themselves in order to have a realistic measure of labor input. One should note that this phenomenon particularly has given rise to considerable operating problems, as well as to political controversy, for example, unionized workers vs. nonunionized office employees.[6]

More broadly, the growth in administrative overhead is part of a given industry's labor input and both its size and its hierarchical structure have come in for their share of criticism in analyses of American productivity problems. The varying overhead proportions among and within industries would, in any event, introduce yet another difficulty in measuring productivity and interpreting the results.

The second issue is in part related to the first and has to do with the degree of responsibility of production workers and employees generally for the work they do. It is thus the central issue whenever measures of worker productivity are used for justifying or denying wage increases, or for changing work rules and other conditions of employment.

Yet the degree of worker responsibility is anything but clear. What to make, how to make it, in what quantitiy, at what price, and with whose invested money are still the classic decisions of management and generally define the nature of private business. Thus, when these decisions are made by the Department of Defense and not by private managements, a military contractor is distinguished from other private businesses.[7]

At the level of production workers, their task is to turn out the product specified by management and by the engineers and technicians who have settled on the particular design details and production methods. Unless the work is predominantly worker-paced, meaning that workers control both rate and nature of the jobs they do, their responsibility for the results, though always present, must nevertheless be modified.

In modern manufacturing, in fact, truly worker-paced operations are becoming increasingly rare. Rather, the production machinery cycles through its operations automatically, and the pace, and thus the productivity, are set by what the machines can do. Workers may eventually be reduced to loading the machines or orienting the workpiece, or even mainly to minding the machines—coping with problems or providing maintenance. The jobs are then machine-paced rather than worker-paced and may, in the case of maintenance, become demand-paced, just like a service business where employees have to wait for customers to show up.

There is, in fact, a central paradox in the measurement of productivity in any service industry or similar operation. In the above case, having a large maintenance staff in relation to the demand makes for speedy action when problems arise but, on the other hand, costs more too. Thus, striking a reasonable balance between too much and too little has long been a problem in operations analysis, for which various mathematical models have been found useful.[8] The quality issue also has an obvious effect here; the better the product or production system, the fewer the problems for which a system must be designed. Declining product quality can have a major downward effect on productivity in such systems.

Finally, there are aspects of labor input that affect certain industries, at least on a short-run basis. It is for this reason that labor productivity statistics are best viewed on a longer term basis, rather than as a quarter-to-quarter fever chart in which short-term fluctuations are accorded major significance. The reason is that in many manufacturing systems, there is a built-in damping mechanism that comes into play in industries given to sharp changes, such as major cyclical ones, as well as in those that are highly automated. When business declines, firms often hang on to workers because a certain number is needed to staff a production unit, even when it is working below capacity. It is not until business gets bad enough to shut down entirely that major layoffs occur. Similarly, there is a time lag when business improves; firms then make do with overtime at least initially, rather than put on new employees.

Layoffs also impair the experience ratings of firms for unemployment insurance, resulting in higher taxes later on. This may be a significant consideration in industries in which feast or famine conditions are not endemic and the highest bracket in unemployment insurance taxes is not accepted as inevitable.

It is for these reasons that the following discussion of the quantitative results against a background of industry conditions focuses on long-term trends in productivity and, in the next chapter, on capital spending. The comments on the general fortunes of various industries are drawn from the observable trends of constant dollar value added by manufacture (CDVAM) from which CDVAM per employee (CDVAM/E) was computed, as well as from the other sources cited.

THE RESULTS

As noted, the principal indicator of productivity will be constant dollar value added by manufacture per employee (CDVAM/E). To allow a comparative evaluation, *rates of change* rather than absolute values will be considered. Absolute values are specific to the industries involved, to the need for machinery and other capitalization; what is of interest here is the rate at which the productivity ratios have increased or decreased from 1967 to 1982 or, in some cases, 1981. It is recognized that, by picking one's first and last years, such rates can vary widely. Still, the use of identical, or almost identical, periods makes comparisons within the data set acceptable. Moreover, the rates are based on least squares analysis of the logarithms of the data and not merely on last year/first year ratios. Thus all intervening years have been duly considered in arriving at the final result.

The general results for the analysis appear in the first column of the table in the book's Appendix. As is immediately evident, there are considerable variations in rates, both within and between the major groups. In evaluating the results, two points immediately become clear. First, a not inconsiderable number of industries have negative trends, that is, their labor productivities have actually been declining.

Second, there is the question of what positive values can be considered at least reasonably good. There is, of course, no practical way of showing how the industries could perform if everything in their products, processes, and managements were done at some unspecified (and probably unspecifiable) optimum level. Still, there is something to be said for a benchmark of economic performance against which these results can be set. For this comparison, we have chosen the growth rate of constant dollar gross national product for the period 1967–81, which is found to be 2.8 percent, and for 1967–82, which turns out to be 2.5 percent. The lower value for the latter comes about because GNP declined by 2.5 percent in real terms between 1981 and 1982.[9] This comparison has the advantage of introducing a standard that varies with overall economic conditions. It thus reduces the effects that might be present in using some arbitrary constant value as a sort of passing grade.

Beyond these general observations, there are the specifics of the industry results which are presented below for each major group. They include evaluations of market trends and industry volume drawn from the value added statistics in the raw data that were used to compute productivity, as well as from other published sources. They are intended especially to draw attention to individual readings and, where possible, to offer explanations for the numerical results and the changes that have taken place in the product structures of the various industries.

Food and Kindred Products (SIC 20)

This major group consists of forty-four individual industries. Eight of them, or 18.2 percent, had negative change rates for 1967–81. A further seven (15.9 percent) had rates of increase below 1 percent a year. At the other end of the scale, nine industries (20.4 percent) had rates higher than the 2.8 percent trend in real GNP.

An examination of the specific industries in this group indicates that market success is not necessarily associated with high productivity growth. Thus, the red meat sector of the meat products group (SIC 201) has not had significant growth, basically because of high red meat prices and consumer concern with health. The aging of the population is also a factor because older people tend to consume less red meat. Higher cholesterol levels in beef and pork, compared to other meats and fish, and some epidemiological evidence linking high consumption of beef and pork to a higher incidence of certain cancers have been the main focus of concern over health.

Reduced demand for red meat has been offset by rising demand for poultry (SIC 2015). This is based in part on new products, such as boneless chicken breasts, finger-sized poultry products, chicken entrees, chicken hot dogs, and other processed poultry products that were introduced and accepted by the market. A further factor in this expansion is that poultry producers have been making strenuous efforts to create individual brands in the industry, following a very different strategy than the meatpacking industry. Brands such as Perdue, Cookin' Good, or Holly Farms have been fighting advertising battles not much less sustained than those of the fast-food chains and have not shied away from knocking each other's products—which is usually the final stage of escalation in advertising wars. This expansion of markets has not, however, resulted in much improvement of productivity. Although poultry producers have been building larger and more automated facilities, the rate of increase in CDVAM/E has remained at little more than zero.

It should be noted that in spite of the industry's ability to take advantage of health claims that favor poultry products, these products are by no means immune from health problems of their own. The most serious is the frequent contamination of poultry products with salmonella and campylobacter which, according to the National Academy of Sciences, altogether are responsible for four million cases of food poisoning a year.[10] Not all of these are poultry related, of course, but even so, the precautions for handling raw poultry that are regularly recommended in the press involve the most elaborate sanitary routines; they certainly are no less so than those for handling raw pork to avoid the risk of trichinosis. Furthermore, practices such as impregnating turkey with a basting solution mainly of oil introduce fats not naturally present and thus reduce the advantage of low fat content. Making smoked or cured cold cuts out of turkey still involves the use of nitrites which have caused much concern and controversy when used in beef or pork products.

The dairy products group (SIC 202) has experienced relatively high productivity growth (3.5 percent) in the cheese industry (SIC 2022). The industry has also had a rising volume, since consumers perceived cheese (especially natural cheese) as a healthful dairy product and a good source of protein and calcium; it has also had growing use in fast-food products. Further, the varieties available increased, even though many new products are imported, and prices also did not rise as much as red meat. Butter (SIC 2021) did not fare as well, as a result of public fears of high cholesterol. Although reduced of late, there is a global oversupply of butter, and stories on the size of the surplus mountain appear in news reports from time to time.

As to milk itself, in spite of strenuous advertising efforts that present milk as the source of the same kind of frenetic jollification usually found in soft drink commercials, milk consumption per capita has declined greatly. The reasons are again health concerns over cholesterol—to which the industry has responded with a variety of low-fat milks—shifting product preferences, demographic changes (aging of the population), and the low price of substitute beverages. In the future, the cheese industry will probably also see its gains eroded, as a result of concern over cholesterol, sodium, and caloric intakes.

The preserved fruits and vegetables group (SIC 203) has experienced substantial productivity growth in its pickles, sauces, and salad dressings industry (SIC 2035, 3.49 percent) which is probably mainly related to much larger volume in such items as bottled salad dressing and, again, to a broadening of the product line into ethnic and gourmet items. Canned goods (SIC 2033) still have twice the volume of shipment of frozen foods (SIC 2037), but the industry has not experienced significant growth because consumers increasingly tend to prefer fresh and frozen foods.

Although many of the frozen food industry's traditional products stagnated, there was rising demand for tomato products, single-serving soups, aseptically packaged juices, and low-sodium canned foods. Tomato-based products made their way into pasta dishes which have become very popular. Single-serving soups can be prepared in micro-wave ovens, as can single-serving meals with fewer than three hundred calories. These appeal to working couples, one-parent families, and the elderly; the latter had not been targeted much by food manufac-turers until recently, but low-sodium products and smaller packages are designed in part for that market segment. So far, however, these new and diversified products have not resulted in major growth for the frozen food industry. This is believed to be due to greater pro-duction costs and especially to greater energy costs, compared to the other food industries, which in turn caused prices of frozen foods to rise faster than those of food generally.[11]

In the grain mill products group (SIC 204), wet corn milling (SIC 2046) had the highest rate of increase of CDVAM/E (5.1 percent) of any food industry. This exceptional rate was associated with major technological improvements in its production processes (see chapter 3 on its capital investment rate). On the other hand, cereal and break-fast foods (SIC 2043) has not had either high productivity or high market gains. The main reason appears to be the declining age cohort of young children (age 5–14). Thus the use of relatively more expen-sive presweetened cereal is falling, and in response to dietary con-cerns, manufacturers stress convenience, vitamin fortification, fiber content, "natural" ingredients (or at least claims), protein content, and other appeals to an older set of customers.

The sugar and confectionery group (SIC 206) has had mixed re-sults. Cane sugar (SIC 2062) and beet sugar (SIC 2063) refining have both experienced negative rates of change in CDVAM/E, the latter the second worst of any food industry. Beet sugar is an important product in other countries, but in the United States it is a standby and has, in the past, mainly been a factor when cane sugar supplies were disrupted in some way; even for that, corn syrup would now be a decisive competitor. Dietary concerns have also exacted downward pressures on consumption of sweets generally.

Nevertheless, confectionery products (SIC 2065) and chocolate and cocoa products (SIC 2066) have had high rates of productivity improvement of 3.51 and 3.02 percent respectively. A growing taste for more sophisticated chocolate products may have introduced the kind of upscale bias in that industry which was described earlier in this chapter and in turn tends to inflate output and thus overstate productivity.

In the fats and oils group (SIC 207), cottonseed oil mills (SIC 2074) have the second highest rate of growth of CDVAM/E (4.28 percent) among the forty-four food industries. The reason appears to be related both to markets and to methods. For health reasons, notably worries over cholesterol, vegetable oils have greatly cut into the market for animal-based fats like butter and lard, even though total per capita fat intake in the United States is still considered much too high by the preponderance of expert opinion.[12] The change, however, appears to have affected only cottonseed oil in a positive way. By contrast, soybean oils (SIC 2075) and vegetable oils, n.e.c. (SIC 2076) both show a declining CDVAM/E.

In the beverages group (SIC 208), bottled and canned soft drinks (SIC 2086) have had appreciable growth in CDVAM/E (2.93 percent). The biggest influence here has no doubt been the rise of products sweetened with aspartame or aspartame and saccharin; the latter is expected to be phased out in the next few years. Other changes were the caffeine-free varieties and, also with profound implications for production methods, plastic bottles. So far, consumers do not appear to have realized that plastic bottles can withstand only about half the gas pressure of glass bottles, so that carbonated drinks go flat soon after the bottles are opened; one would have supposed this to be a negative factor, especially in the case of the widely used two-liter bottles.

Compared with the upward trend of the soft drink industry, alcoholic beverages have fared materially worse. The CDVAM/E rates for beer (SIC 2082) and for distilled liquor, except brandy (SIC 2085) have risen at low, almost equal, positive rates; wine and brandy (SIC 2084) have a slight negative result. In general, per capita consumption of beer and liquor has been flat or declining for some time, as a result of shifts in age cohorts (e.g., young males, who are the prime beer drinkers, were declining in number for most of the study period), health consciousness, campaigns against drunken driving, raising of the drinking age to a uniform twenty-one years, and other factors. As to U.S. wine makers, they have been much beset by imports and have thus not benefited as much as expected from a significant rise in wine consumption, at least early in the period of this study.

As to the remaining parts of the food industry, they include roast coffee (SIC 2095), which had a high CDVAM/E growth rate (3.23 percent), perhaps again due to an upscale bias in the product line in favor of instant and decaffeinated products and various specialties. The popularity of pasta dishes has made the manufacture of macaroni and spaghetti (SIC 2098) into a substantial growth industry, and this in turn has encouraged new and more fully used facilities. The result is also a relatively high rising trend in CDVAM/E (2.99 percent).

In summary, changes in this greatly varied group have been widespread enough to activate some of the difficulties in data interpretation described in the introduction to this chapter. Among the major market changes in this group, the principal ones appear to be a move away from foods implicated in the cholesterol health problem, such as red meat, dairy products, and animal fats. By the mid-1980s, there was growing pressure to restrict fat and salt intake in general, but by early 1988, this had not yet taken on the same urgency as the cholesterol-related concerns. There has always been public controversy over health claims for foods and the nutritional information to be listed on the labels. It continues unabated, having become embroiled in the ideological commitment of the Reagan Administration to "deregulation," with constant pressures to tell the public ever less and to allow ever more additives and other questionable practices.[13] The relationship between diets and health is evidently highly complex, and the public is regularly warned against an increasingly wider array of foods. It has been suggested that if someone wrote a new diet book called *What You May Have*, it would fit on a mimeographed sheet.

This confusion is also reflected in eating out. The fast-food industry, as well as restaurants in general, which had been most seriously implicated in feeding people too many fats and too much salt, went into salads and similar products, but at least in the case of restaurants in general, that was no longer a drastic departure from accepted practice. Indeed, in a frequently fad-ridden industry, trend-setting articles in various media noted by late 1987 that *nouvelle cuisine* (i.e., using less fat), which had arisen in the 1970s at the beginning of the "light" foods trend, was considered no longer "in."

As to food intake in general, whatever the effects of the exercise craze and the continuing proliferation of light foods, general observation of the populace shows obesity to be as common as ever. Certainly, there is little evidence that light versions of a product have fatal effects on the market for its traditional forms. Rather, the whole line coexists. Indeed by 1987 light beers, which had enjoyed a rising trend, were beginning to meet consumer resistance.

Fashion is also evident in a second diversifying trend, that of ethnic foods. Thus Mexican food appears to have peaked, just as the quiche wave had passed somewhat earlier. Creole dishes also appear to have settled down to a finite niche in the market. Still, they all continue to exist and new ideas are constantly reported. There is no question, therefore, that the food industry will face demand for an ever more diversified product line that involves changes in basic approaches, and not just the by-now traditional decisions on how far to go in processing foods, in response to convenience needs and most recently to microwave cooking.

Compared with these pressures, such other trends as concern over fiber intake are likely to have less effect on the industry's production systems. Fiber content may be improved merely by varying the recipes for various foods, such as cereals, breads, and pastas, without material changes in the production systems themselves.

In general, the effects on labor productivity of all these expected changes are not likely to be significant compared to the great diversity that now exists in the food industry with regard to capital equipment, scale, and production methods.

Tobacco Products (SIC 21)

This industry group is very much dominated by its largest component, the cigarette industry (SIC 2111). Its troubles and the continuing downward pressures on its markets are too well known to need detailed review here. Of all legally manufactured products, cigarettes face the most concerted legal restrictions, with the prospect of more to come. The pressures toward outlawing smoking in more and more environments, such as airlines, offices, restaurants, and elsewhere, have sparked controversies in areas beyond the immediate issue. Thus, for instance, black and Hispanic minorities smoke at greater rates than others and their absolute consumption is still increasing. The tobacco industry has therefore persuaded some of their community leaders to oppose further restrictions on the grounds that their impact falls disproportionately on these groups.

Similarly, civil libertarians are sharply divided over whether to ban advertising altogether for what is, after all, a legal product. Proponents are concerned over the sophisticated messages of the tobacco industry, especially those directed to getting the young to start smoking and thus become sufficiently habituated to make quitting later difficult, if not impossible. This is a serious problem in the light of medical evidence that nicotine addiction is a physiological as well as psychological problem. Opponents fear that once censorship of a legal activity, even an increasingly unpopular one, is established, it will be difficult to prevent the application of the precedent else-where, especially given the current political and legal atmosphere.

The industry has also had to face a loss of social status. Among men particularly, smoking is increasingly viewed as a habit of lower socioeconomic groups; the division is less sharp among women, who also seem to have more difficulty stopping once they have started. Either way, however, it is a far cry from the image of sophistication and high living that cigarette advertising sought to project for genera-tions; its advertising now concentrates on blue collar media, some homemaker magazines which still accept the ads, billboards, and sports events. About fifty-three million people, or 32 percent of the adult population, still smoke, down from 42 percent in 1967, and most of these are blue-collar workers and the poor.[14]

However, in spite of these adverse changes in the market, the long-known and well-documented disastrous effects of cigarettes on pub-lic health, and the warning labels, total cigarette consumption rose steadily, though at a declining rate, throughout the period of this study. Per capita use declined beginning in the 1960s, but a growing population and new smokers—mainly minorities—kept total consump-tion rising. Still, it peaked at 635 billion in 1981 and fell to about 582 billion by 1986. Sales have been falling at an accelerating rate, from 2 percent for 1985 to 1986, to expected rates of 3 to 5 percent a year for the period 1987–92. Meanwhile, retail prices per pack, including federal tax, almost doubled between 1980 and 1986.[15]

This price increase is a not unsurprising consequence when a highly automated and capital-intensive industry must face the added costs of declining capacity utilization. Another result to be expected from this is that the rate of increase in CDVAM/E for the cigarette indus-try would be low; it is found to be only 1.47 percent a year.

The cigar industry (SIC 2121) also has a stagnant market; if it were not for increased sales of small cigars (cigarillos) it would be declining. Cigar smoking has long been forbidden in aircraft where cigarette smoking was permitted, and is also subject to the downward pressures of the "no smoking" movement. At first, cigars were impli-cated less in lung cancer causation than were cigarettes, but they have since been found to promote other cancers, notably of the mouth and bladder. The cigar industry also has low growth in CDVAM/E, as does tobacco stemming and redrying (SIC 2141), which essentially services the other parts of this major group.

By contrast, the remaining industry, chewing and smoking tobacco (SIC 2131) had a relatively high rate of increase of CDVAM/E of

4.91 percent. For a time during the study périod, it benefited from increased sales as smokers believed pipe smoking to be less harmful than cigarettes. However, like cigars, pipe smoking is implicated in mouth and bladder cancers. It has since declined as well.

Chewing tobacco and snuff, which are also included in this industry, likewise benefited from increased consumer interest, though they are a very small product, used in 1983 by no more than 3.2 percent of male smokers and hardly at all by women. The once frequently seen cuspidor (still found until recently in sizeable numbers in the halls of the United States Congress) had long been relegated to the barbaric past, but young people had taken up snuff and chewing tobacco in some places, again instead of cigarettes. However, a flurry of industry advertising and promotion of the product to that market was countered rather effectively by some television shows in 1986. They depicted rather graphically the terribly disfiguring results of operations for cancer of the mouth and nasal passages which may be the result of using snuff or chewing tobacco; they also chronicled the long suffering and eventual death of some young athletes who had taken up the habit. Current trends, therefore, are to restrict all tobacco products, or at least make the warnings ever stronger and more explicit.

Textile Mill Products (SIC 22)

The textile industry is a large and diverse group. Broadly, it consists of industries that make fibers and those that weave or knit them into fabric of some type. It is a very important manufacturing industry; together with apparel (SIC 23) it employs one out of ten American workers in manufacturing and has by far the largest proportion of women and minorities.

The record of growth of the entire textile group is lackluster; from 1972 to 1982, its volume grew by only 0.3 percent a year in real terms.[16] The individual industries have had sharply differing fortunes, and these are reflected in comparably wide swings in productivity, that is, in CDVAM/E. Indeed, in a number of them the upward and downward movements are so violent that the "long-term" trends computed by the usual least squares methods lack statistical significance. The specific reason is that for these industries the trend during the study period (1967–81) was an initial rise, followed by a protracted decline.

The general results show eight industries out of the thirty (26.7 percent) with increases in CDVAM/E greater than the 2.8 percent annual rise in real GNP. These industries are mainly in broad woven fabrics, and in such special areas as processing of textile waste (SIC 2294), and tire cord (SIC 2296). Yarn spinning, other than wool (SIC 2281), also did slightly better than 2.8 percent.

On the less favored side, four industries had increases from 0 to 1 percent a year. They include lace (SIC 2292) which, at that time, was not too fashionable (it was to make a small comeback later), upholstery padding (SIC 2293) which had to compete with foam rubber, and coated fabrics, not rubberized (SIC 2295) which also had rising competition from other materials. In addition, two industries have negative rates. They are knitting mills, n.e.c. (SIC 2259), and carpets and rugs, n.e.c. (SIC 2279).

The varying fortunes of the textile major group come about because it is buffeted not merely by one but by two sets of profoundly disturbing factors. The first of these is fashion. Certain kinds of materials for clothes have gone through fashion cycles, with favorable as well as dire consequences for their industries. An example is the increased use of natural fibers following the energy crunch of the early 1970s which altered the balance between them and man-made fibers. This was a matter not only of technological competition, as in some high and low growth industries mentioned above, but also of fashion—garment makers began to use some fabrics intensively and others less. Since the industries dealing with each kind of fabric are, in part, classified separately, the changes show up quite clearly. Another industry, this one adversely affected, was that of circular knit fabric mills (SIC 2257), which benefited from the fashion in double-knit garments but lost out when the fashion faded.

The second source of crisis is imports. The textile industry was one of the earliest developed during the Industrial Revolution. It is fair to say that from those earliest times on, in addition to creating some of the most miserable industrial working conditions in its home bases, it has always searched for cheaper labor wherever that can be found. As a result, it has shifted both its locations and its product sources, with often drastic consequences to whatever region or working population was left behind. It is therefore the unfortunate case that the troubles of the industry with cheap labor competition from other regions and countries have ample historical precedents. The problems of imports will be discussed again in chapter 5, and the implications for location within the United States in chapter 4.

It is also noteworthy that in the period of study in this volume (1967 to 1982) and, for that matter, since then, there has been no product innovation that compares even remotely to the time in the late 1940s and 1950s when the new man-made fibers were introduced. Nylon, dacron, and orlon, and some lesser polyolefins like polypropylene, revolutionized the industry's product line and enormously expanded the product possibilities. The Italian pioneer in the field, Giulio Natta, received the Nobel Prize in chemistry for discovering the extensions of polymerization that were at the root of this work; he was one of the very few scientists in textile-related fields ever to have received this honor. An important application of the new textile chemistry was in various elastic or stretch fibers, and these too became the ingredients of new materials.

By contrast, in more recent times the industry has worked with the set of raw materials that existed in 1960. Changes have been mainly in market shares of these fibers. Thus, one observable change, especially in women's clothing but also in such products as men's trousers, is a comeback of viscose rayon, which at the time when nylon, orlon, and especially dacron were first introduced was expected to fade from the scene. Yet it did not, and after the oil shock it began to make a real comeback.

The reason is that its raw material is cellulose in general and, particularly in the United States, cotton linters; these are the very short fibers left over after cotton ginning and are therefore, in a sense, waste materials. In this respect, rayon had an advantage over the other man-made materials that derived from oil refinery coproducts and thus became much more expensive.

Rayon was also able to capitalize once more on its familiar ability to take color especially well, better for instance than orlon. At the same time, cotton itself became more fashionable which in turn prompted an expansion of cotton acreage and a greater supply of linters as well. One result, however, was that many garments, especially for women, wound up with care lables that read "dry clean only," rather than the "wash and wear" instructions of other times. In that sense there was a product change that some might, and do, consider regressive.

The textile industry has tried to counter its difficulties by appealing to patriotism but also, and more concretely, by emphasizing specialty fabrics of high quality, rather than mass-produced items where the importers would have a greater advantage. However, trying to specialize in small lots has its own pitfalls. It is one thing, as we noted earlier, to be aware that economy of scale has its limits; it is quite another to pretend that it does not exist and to follow a strategy that requires constant and usually expensive new setups for small batches of product. Computers, of course, have made some of these practices much more feasible. Still, textiles are made on large, high-output machines, and thus small lots must overcome a high cost disadvantage. The belief that U.S. industry can save itself with small specialty businesses is, in any case, something of a delusion, even though it has been advocated, notably by Robert D. Reich, as one possible answer to American industrial decline.[17]

Meanwhile, the strategy of concentrating on small specialized business has certainly not been followed consistently. Whether they are high fashion or mass-market items, one sees not only clothing items entirely imported or entirely domestic, but also items labeled "made in the U.S.A. from imported materials" and "made in country X from U.S. materials." Both cheaper and more expensive items may be found in any of these categories, thus indicating that imports seem to have their impact on much of the product range.

Apparel and Fabricated Textile Products (SIC 23)

Apparel shares with the textile industry the two major problem areas of fashion and imports and thus shows similar characteristics of volatility and decline; indeed, a discussion of the apparel industry is naturally linked to the textile group. The apparel group as a whole did somewhat better than textiles, with a growth rate in volume in real terms from 1972 to 1982 of 1.1 percent, which compares with 0.3 percent for textiles but which still is markedly lower than that for real GNP.[18]

This major industry group consists of thirty-three individual industries; complete data were available for thirty of them. Again, as in the groups previously presented, the Appendix reveals the industries whose rate of productivity improvement exceeds the growth rate in real GNP for 1967–82 (2.5 percent a year). There are nine such industries (30 percent of the thirty industries with complete data). The ones with the highest rates are heavily concentrated in nonapparel producing industries, for example, house furnishings other than curtains and drapes, n.e.c. (SIC 2392), textile bags (SIC 2393), and canvas and related products (SIC 2394), and in industries performing specialized services and operations for others in the major group, such as pleating and stitching (SIC 2395), the highest one, and automotive and apparel trimmings (SIC 2396), the second highest. Other higher readings are evident in producers of men's and boys' separate trousers (SIC 2327) and, marginally, work clothes (SIC 2328), in women's and misses' blouses (SIC 2331), as well as in fur goods (SIC 2371) and apparel belts (SIC 2387).

There is one industry with a growth trend between 0 and 1 percent: women's and misses' dresses (SIC 2335). Also, 4 industries have negative rates, including one, leather and sheep lined clothing (SIC 2386), at a rather steep 3.35 percent.

The group as a whole is highly labor intensive. Capital equipment has seen only limited change, as noted in the next chapter, and mainly because its mainstay in many areas is still the individually operated sewing machine, opportunity for economy of scale is likewise very limited. As a result, the industry is particularly vulnerable to imports from cheap labor countries, and perhaps even more than in the textile industry, its managements are constantly on the lookout for cheaper sources. Clothing factories may be quickly established, and as long as there is an ample supply of cheap labor, new players in the apparel game constantly appear. Certainly, clothing labels show ever more varied and farflung countries of origin. Increasingly, these new producers of clothing are in Third World countries where labor safeguards are minimal, and laws and practices in labor relations are repressive in the extreme.

One consequence for the United States has been that an industry never noted for its kindly treatment of employees has become the locus of a new generation of sweatshops. This has always been a problem in the industry, whether, in earlier years, in the form of home work under miserable conditions or in equally miserable factories. Thus, a good deal of the industrial history of New York from 1890 to about 1950 consists of accounts of these abuses; later the virtual outlawing of industrial home work came about primarily because of abuses in these industries. Just as in textiles, this industry group has always employed a large proportion of women and minorities. Child labor, too, was rife in earlier times in the United States, and still is in some of the present importing countries. Opportunities for exploitation are thus both traditional and ample.

The present-day American sweatshops are often located in immigrant communities where workers are unlikely to complain over working conditions, especially when their own immigration status is questionable. During the protracted controversies that preceded the Simpson-Mazzoli immigration legislation of 1986, such practices received much attention; illegal immigrants were frequently caught in Immigration Service raids on garment factories, especially in the Los Angeles area.

As to markets for the industry, fashion in clothing affects single product lines or single firms within a given industry much more than other products or firms whether favorably or unfavorably; some damping effect for the industry as a whole then results when one firm's good fortune comes at the expense of another firm's disaster. Still, the industry is sufficiently specialized so that when one kind of garment becomes less fashionable, the ill effects may be quite widespread, and the zero-sum criterion does not hold within individual industries. Blue jeans, for instance, have passed their peak and, though still a very important product, have passed well beyond their stage of incessant promotion and almost universal wear by major market segments.

Nevertheless, one notes that even major fashion changes are seldom universal. For men, despite occasional promotions of different garments, very little has changed over the years. Leisure suits and double knits came and passed from the scene during the study period, but otherwise most male fashions continue with only minor changes. Widths of lapels and ties are hardly the stuff of great product change.

Women's fashions are, of course, subject to much greater variation, encompassing colors and styles. One may, in fact, hypothesize that the present tendency to loose fitting garments may stem from a need to have these items made by minimally qualified work forces abroad or in the United States. Yet, for instance, different skirt lengths or other major fashion features coexist. Whatever desires for frequent generalized obsolescence of clothing may be present in the industry, reality and the customers' resources create limits.

As in much of the U.S. economy, moreover, there appears to be a widening gulf between the most and the least affluent market sectors. In apparel, especially, it has shown itself in the eclipse of many clothing stores and chains that had catered to a middle market; with the decline in well-paying blue-collar and lower level white-collar jobs, especially, this market eroded badly enough for several major department store and retail chains to go out of business. The apparel industry thus mirrors the increasingly bipolar trends in the general economy.

Lumber and Wood Products (SIC 24)

This major group primarily serves the construction industries, especially in home building, and thus mirrors the ups and downs of its
principal customer. The industries within the group have shown quite
similar patterns of variation in volume and thus in value added by
manufacture.[19] From its level in 1967, activity began to decline
throughout the early 1970s; by the late 1970s there was an upswing,
resulting in peaks around 1976–79. Then a steep decline followed
which, in every case except wood kitchen cabinets (SIC 2434) in
which there is a substantial replacement market, resulted in constant
dollar volumes in 1982 below those of 1967. For such industries, the
cyclical nature of their business makes uniform statistical trends over
fixed periods not very useful for forecasting purposes that would
have to take the ups and downs into account. Indeed, after the 1981
cutoff of the data, the industry had a modest upswing again, albeit
not as ample as in the past. Rather, the industry has had to contend
with strong competition from imports, predominantly Canadian, to a
far greater extent than ever before.

In one industry in this group, that of nailed and lock corner wood
boxes (SIC 2441), there was a secular decline that put value added in
constant dollars in 1982 at only 40.1 percent of its 1967 value. That
industry is not dependent on housing, but it was especially hard hit
by the replacement of its product by cardboard containers of ever
greater strength and versatility and, to a lesser extent, by plastic products.

In general, however, this is an industry group whose product has
not greatly changed. Except for particle board (SIC 2492), which in
its present form goes back to the late 1940s and which has made considerable inroads in markets for plywood, product instability is not a
major problem. The industry's raw material supply is, however, still
controversial, centering on the need for more effective conservation
of forest resources and the watersheds they often protect. These have
become urgent problems as the result of the "deregulation" atmosphere of the 1980s and the protracted attempts on the part of the
Reagan Administration to increase lumber output from the national
forests.

The constituent industries of this major group were extensively
redefined in 1972, so that consistent results for the entire study
period of 1967–81 were available for only nine out of the seventeen
in the current SIC. Of these, four had negative rates of change of

CDVAM/E and three more were between 0 and 1 percent. The highest, logging camps and logging contractors (SIC 2411) only had a rate of 1.5 percent. Certainly, on the basis of the data available, one could characterize this group as having a relatively low rate of improvement.

The poor overall result for this major group is, however, not unexpected for an industry that combines highly cyclical markets with rather high capacity specialized production systems. Such circumstances create major problems in assuring sufficient utilization of capacity.

Furniture and Fixtures (SIC 25)

The thirteen individual industries of this major group have had varying fortunes. Statistics on value added by manufacture in constant dollars indicate an almost flat trend for its largest sector: those industries making household furniture of wood and metal, including upholstered (SIC 2511, 2512, and 2514). Industries serving the burgeoning market for office furniture did much better. Wood office furniture (SIC 2521) tripled its constant dollar VAM; metal furniture saw a 58 percent increase from 1967 to 1982. Specialized furniture for public buildings (SIC 2531), however, also stayed flat.

Another industry, making wood television, radio, phonograph, and sewing machine cabinets (SIC 2517) declined by 1982 to about 38 percent of its 1967 constant dollar VAM. This was because of major changes in the products it served, notably the extinction of most manufacture of consumer electronics products in the United States, as well as the increase in the use of plastics and metals instead of wood.

The remaining industries in this major group had modest rises in constant dollar VAM, except for mattresses and bedsprings (SIC 2515), which had an increase of about 50 percent, and the very much smaller household furniture, n.e.c. (SIC 2519), which rose by about 75 percent.

Turning now to the productivity measures, the industry did slightly better than lumber and wood products. As the Appendix shows, two industries, mattresses and bedsprings (SIC 2515) and household furniture, n.e.c. (SIC 2519), had rising trends in excess of 2.8 percent a year; these, as noted above, also had substantial increases in activity. However, six industries had negative rates of change in CDVAM/E. They are upholstered furniture (SIC 2512), metal office furniture

(SIC 2522), furniture for public buildings (SIC 2531), wood and metal partitions (SIC 2541 and 2542), and drapery hardware, window blinds, and shades (SIC 2591), the latter very close to zero. Between 0 and 1 percent, there is furniture and fixtures, n.e.c. (SIC 2599).

The above record is a consequence of a continuing shift away from traditional wood furniture. Nevertheless, the furniture industry has managed to maintain something of a craft tradition provided one is willing to wait out what often are protracted delivery times. On the other end of the product scale, however, is the growing tendency to let customers take care of the assembly themselves; this is found even in rather complicated and large pieces of furniture where the job might take hours. Such products are shipped "knocked down" (KD), and the purchaser must manage with wood (usually particle board with vinyl "veneer") cut to size, with the requisite holes drilled, and some plastic bags full of hardware. As noted earlier, output per unit of labor is overstated when assembly labor is sloughed off on others in this manner.

Paper and Allied Products (SIC 26)

Paper is largely derived from wood and thus shares some of the problems of SIC 24 above. This applies most directly to products linked to the building trades, as is the case with lumber. The most obvious example is the building paper industry (SIC 2661), whose products are used most extensively in home building. It is crucially affected by the cyclical nature of that industry, ending the study period with a 1982 CDVAM only 30.5 percent that of 1967.

It applies even more to the pulp (SIC 2611), paper (SIC 2621), and paperboard (SIC 2631) industries. All of them have similar environmental problems, linked not merely to the issues of forest conservation and sustenance generally, but to air and especially water pollution as well. These are major problems, in view of the wide use of potentially very damaging chemicals and the fact that much of privately owned forest land belongs to paper companies rather than to firms primarily selling lumber and related products.

These three industries are also highly capital intensive with huge production units, often built around only one or two actual papermaking machines of the Fourdrinier type. They thus share the kinds of problems noted previously when cyclical or secular declines happen in industries with that kind of built-in inflexibility. Meanwhile, complete new paper mills cost at least $500 million to build.[20]

As to the specific record of CDVAM for these industries, pulp mills (SIC 2611) had sharp fluctuations, ending in 1982 slightly on the positive side. Paper (SIC 2621) did much better, recording a 30.8 percent gain from 1967 to 1982. Paperboard (SIC 2631), on the other hand, declined somewhat by about 16.5 percent. In the paper fabricating industries, results were likewise mixed. Sanitary paper products (SIC 2647) showed very high growth, with VAM for 1982 at 2.3 times the 1967 level. Bags, except textile bags (SIC 2643), converted paper and paperboard products, n.e.c. (SIC 2649), and corrugated and solid fiber boxes (SIC 2653) showed modest growth. On the other hand, four industries showed declining trends, including pressed and molded pulp goods (SIC 2646), which are another product beset by competition from plastics, and stationery tablets and related products (SIC 2648), which since they include a substantial consumer line, shared in the eclipse of personal correspondence in relation to telephone use. Set-up paperboard boxes (SIC 2652) declined by 50 percent as their markets were increasingly taken over by folding boxes (SIC 2651). Building paper (SIC 2661) also declined, sharing in the downturn of the building industry and the other industries that provide it with materials, as in major group 25. The remaining industries in the paper making or using industries show little or no change in their CDVAM readings over the study period.

It must be noted, however, that this major group as a whole had much better results from about 1971 to 1975. It was only during later declines in the economy that the changes took place that produced the lackluster record described above. This is also notable in the productivity measures of CDVAM/E for this major group, which in general show very little change when the entire study period is considered but which show an up and down cycle when the trends are examined in detail.

As to the overall record for the study period, data were available for fifteen out of the seventeen industries in the group; redefinitions in 1972 of two of the industries prevented their comparable analysis. Of the fifteen, eight had rates of change between 0 and 1 percent per year. A further four had negative rates, one of them, paper coating and glazing (SIC 2641) at a substantial 2.28 percent. Paper mills (SIC 2621) alone had a positive rate of change exceeding the 2.5 percent rate of constant dollar GNP.

Printing, Publishing, and Allied Industries (SIC 27)

This has been a growing industry group. Out of the seventeen constituent industries, there were only three small ones that showed a decline. They were establishments specializing in bookbinding (SIC 2789), photoengraving (SIC 2793), and electrotyping and stereotyping (SIC 2794). Other than these, growth was recorded all round.

For some observers of the media scene, the general growth record of this industry might be unexpected. This is because, in the wake of writings by Marshall McLuhan and others, it was widely expected that the printed word would give way to electronic messages and that therefore those industries specializing in printed output would fare poorly. This, however, did not happen. Media, old and new, went on coexisting, even though there were shifts among them. As always, advertising made enormous use of printed media and accounted for about 40 percent of total receipts in printing and publishing.

Even newspapers (SIC 2711), which were really expected to suffer, managed to post a gain in CDVAM of 24.6 percent from 1967 to 1982. Their circulation in 1985 stood at 62.6 million and there were 1,676 newspapers, compared with 1,749 newspapers with a circulation of 61.6 million in 1967.[21]

As discussed further in the next chapter, one crucial factor in the newspaper industry was technological change, especially in typesetting of all sorts. In 1967, the time-honored linotype machines were still working away; photo-composing, word processing, and other modern methods were still in their early stages. By 1982, electronic composing and computerized word processing were firmly established, and by 1987, desktop publishing, once mainly for computer hobbyists, was becoming very noticeable, amidst expressed views that this would greatly expand public access to getting things published. Of course, for anything to succeed, distribution and effective publicity are key; the means and resources for both are still concentrated in the larger organizations.

These changes were not without protracted struggles, especially in newspaper publishing. This is an industry with long established and strong trade unions that are organized along the old craft lines. When electronic methods made their inroads, there was grave distress, as jobs and whole trades were automated out of existence. Those affected could not hope to practice their old occupations again. Coming at a time when the number of daily newspapers in given cities and areas was shrinking drastically as well, the effect was devastating. In the later 1970s and the 1980s there were many strikes over issues of job security and the rate of introduction of the new methods. Indeed, this was a global phenomenon, with long strikes over similar issues taking place in other countries, such as Britain. One of the worst involved the British papers of Rupert Murdoch who, at the time, was also establishing his business in the United States by acquiring several media properties, including newspapers, one of which, the *New York Post*, he was forced by law to sell in February 1988, in order to be able to retain his New York television station.

This major group has another noteworthy characteristic in its labor force: an important part of its input consists of creative work in the humanities, by the many writers and artists that serve it. Although there are many industries with large professional components in their work force, they are predominantly technical and scientific.

One result is an input more difficult than usual to quantify. Advertising itself is, of course, a business service and, as such, is not classified under manufacturing, but magazines and newspapers, for instance, employ photographers and layout artists, even though they buy much of what they need from outside services as well. Certain kinds of printing also require significant artistic input.

More extensively still, any industry with "publishing" in its title has staff writers, reporters, editors, and others whose output is not conventionally measurable. In fact, some cultural historians would argue that an attempt to do so would be both futile and conceptionally undesirable. Even in a business setting, marketing experts would have to concede that a cause and effect relationship between advertising and business results is notoriously difficult to analyze in detail.

In the creative area, therefore, the work follows traditional patterns, even though here too new products have been of great benefit, such as new printing and reproduction methods, and word processing. For the more technically dependent parts of this major group, the ways of doing work changed drastically during the study period. The productivity measures, therefore, reflect macroeconomic efforts rather than internal performance measures to an even greater degree than is the case in most other industrial groups or individual industries.

Consistent trends in CDVAM/E for 1967–82 were available for thirteen of the sixteen industries of this group (SIC 2793 and 2794 were combined for this purpose). As the Appendix indicates, only one industry, that of greeting cards (SIC 2771), came even close to the 2.5 percent constant dollar GNP standard adopted here for comparisons. Two industries, book publishing and printing (SIC 2731) and manifold business forms (SIC 2761), had levels between 0 and 1 percent, and six industries, or 46.1 percent, are in the negative column. The remaining four have levels very near 1 percent, which is also unimpressive. This record, as discussed in more detail in chapter 4, may be due to the fact that this is a very widely dispersed industry and even though it has seen much technological change, quite often little more is needed to start an establishment than a few machines which thereafter may only be required for particular jobs and thus not see too much capacity utilization.

Chemicals and Allied Products, Except Plastics (SIC 28, Except 282)

In discussing the trends in the very large and heterogeneous major group of chemical and allied products, we decided to omit SIC 282 which makes plastic resins and related materials. Plastics manufacture is closely related to its raw materials and therefore more appropriately combined with its fabricators in the major group rubber and miscellaneous plastics products (SIC 30). How to define the various chemical industries has in fact long been something of a problem. As a result of redefinitions in the SIC, notably in 1972, several data sets were incomplete, requiring estimates in some cases and limiting the results in others.

It has actually been suggested that all industries employing predominantly chemical processes should be lumped together as "chemical process industries"; the group would have to include all of SIC 28, as well as pulp and paper (SIC 26), petroleum products (SIC 29), rubber and miscellaneous plastics products (SIC 30), some basic metal processes (SIC 33), and a few others. This reformulation received much attention, especially in the 1950s, among industry managements and educators. There can be little argument that there are common technological and scientific foundations of all these activities and that professionals trained in chemistry and chemical engineering can make contributions to all parts of the group. The Census of Manufactures, however, did not adopt it because the resulting group would have been excessively large and would have created too many discontinuities in the data series.

The group, as defined here, includes both growth industries and stagnant ones, industries that are truly at the scientific frontier as well as those making products that have changed little since antiquity, except for some newer instrumentation and packaging processes. More than any other, it is health related, not merely in obvious cases like pharmaceutical preparations, but in others, such as agricultural chemicals where the use of the product creates hazards as well as benefits. In developing its products, therefore, the industry must contend with extensive government regulations; in some cases, these virtually determine the future of any given item.

As to specific performance, CDVAM data indicate that the basic inorganic chemicals group (SIC 281) has declined over the study period. Medicinal and pharmaceutical products (SIC 284) have exhibited substantial growth, as did soap and related products and toiletries (SIC 284) and adhesives and gelatin (SIC 2891). Fertilizers (SIC 287, except 2879) tend to fluctuate in line with agricultural activity, but agricultural chemicals (SIC 2879) show a clear upward trend. Explosives (SIC 2892), which do not include ordnance, declined and so did carbon black (SIC 2895), a product that has been much beset by competition from substitutes. The pattern that emerges from this record is that industries with intensive new product development and significant research related to it show an upward trend, whereas the traditional ones referred to earlier tend to be stagnant or in decline.

Turning to the productivity statistics in the Appendix, the results for CDVAM/E show quite different variations. Of the twenty-four industries for which consistent results could be obtained, seven (29.2 percent) had rates of increase exceeding 2.5 percent. They are alkalies and chlorine (SIC 2812), medicinals and botanicals (SIC 2833), surface active agents (which are the active ingredients of detergents) (SIC 2843), industrial organic chemicals (SIC 2869), fertilizer mixing (SIC 2875), agricultural chemicals (SIC 2879), and explosives (SIC 2892). It is not easy to postulate a common cause for these higher than average rates.

Another seven industries wind up in the negative column including, most prominently, pharmaceuticals (SIC 2834), phosphatic fertilizers (SIC 2874), and carbon black (SIC 2895). The latter two have had flat or declining values added and thus probably reflect lowered capacity utilization in a highly capital-intensive and automated industry. As to pharmaceuticals, soaring research costs have no doubt been instrumental in this result. Of the remaining ten industries, six have trends in CDVAM/E between 0 and 1 percent. In short, the performance is highly uneven, reflecting equally uneven trends in the markets for the industry's products as well as variation in its production systems.

Petroleum Refining and Related Industries (SIC 29)

This industry group is dominated by its largest constituent, petroleum refining (SIC 2911). As a whole, it is highly capital intensive and has relatively low employment in relation to the value of its output. It is also most seriously dependent on raw materials costs, the more so since these were in turmoil for much of the study period.

The industry has experienced major changes from 1967 onwards in product demand and crude oil prices and supply, as well as changes in regulation affecting both its products and its production facilities.

Before the oil price shocks of the 1970s, the use of oil in the United States had been increasing at rates of about 6 to 7 percent a year, which means a doubling of demand about every 10.7 years.[22] Until the embargo of 1973, the domestic industry was protected by import quotas, but these ended in the growing energy shortage. The OPEC price increase of 400 percent was followed by another doubling of the price of crude oil in 1979. Until that time, domestic prices were controlled, but they were then allowed to rise to world price levels.

In response to the high prices and shortages, there were major changes in demand for the industry's products. Gasoline consumption by cars was cut considerably, mainly by getting people to buy smaller and lighter cars and by recognizing that, for most of the driving done in practice, the engines in the older cars were too big and too wasteful. A fifty-five-miles-an-hour speed limit also encouraged these trends. It must be noted, however, that as the price of oil fell in the 1980s to about half its maximum levels, the trends were reversed; it remained to be seen whether technical improvements in the engines, leading to greater fuel efficiency, would mitigate a sharp rise in fuel consumption.

Other refinery products were also affected by conservation efforts. Thanks to price control, natural gas became cheaper to use in parts of the country with distribution networks, and many oil furnaces were converted to gas. Another very important development was energy saving by businesses, especially by heavy fuel users. To be sure, such techniques as cogeneration (the use of waste heat for power and other purposes) were not implemented in the United States as much as in other industrial countries, but the effort was considerable and in view of the new equipment installed largely irreversible. In other words, there could not be the industrial equivalent of a return to large gas-guzzling cars. The conservation efforts caused a drop in demand of over 20 percent between 1978 and 1983.[23]

Nevertheless, the United States remained vulnerable to disruptions in energy sources. The almost complete elimination of conservation efforts and related incentives by the Reagan Administration thus appears to be highly irresponsible, to say the least. So did its long refusal to fill the National Petroleum Reserve; it conspicuously failed to do so when oil prices were at their lowest and only bestirred itself when OPEC had managed to stabilize them again at a higher level. Yet a national goal of energy independence could be attained, without significant decline in the quality of living.[24]

As to the other industries in this major group, lubricating oils (SIC 292) are closely linked to refining and are often made in or near refineries. Their markets tend to follow fuels and general industrial activity. Paving mixtures and blocks (SIC 2951) and asphalt felts and coatings (SIC 2952) are related to the construction industries and thus tend to move with them; these markets have also had their share of volatility in the study period and since then.

The CDVAM/E statistics reveal negative trends for all but one of the industries. The exception, at a level of only 0.7 percent a year, is petroleum and coal products, n.e.c. (SIC 2999). It is a small industry, making waxes, packaged and powdered fuels, and fuel briquettes. Some of these attracted attention when fireplaces became more popular during the oil shortages.

Rubber and Plastics Products (SIC 282 and 30)

This industry group, as presented in this volume, combines fabricated rubber and plastics products with the raw materials industries of the latter. The plastic industries have, of course, been among the major growth sectors of business, but plastics and synthetic rubber depend on petroleum feedstocks and so were badly affected by their price escalation in the 1970s. The growth rate of usage declined from 12 percent a year in 1960–70 to 7 percent in 1971–81. This put the producers under severe economic strain, in addition to competition from imports, but this was moderated as petroleum prices fell again.

The industry is also a relatively capital-intensive one, so that a downward trend in capacity utilization served to reduce the value added by manufacture. Because of the operating rigidities built into the production systems, this could not be reflected in proportionate cutbacks in employment, thus leading to declines in CDVAM/E. A consistent series of CDVAM/E for 1967–81 is not available for the leading industry in the plastics material group, plastics material and resins (SIC 2821), but data for 1972–82 show a decline of 3.8 percent a year. A full series was available for synthetic rubber (SIC 2822); it also showed a negative result, as did cellulosic fibers (SIC 2823). Other synthetic fibers did better, posting a rising trend in CDVAM/E.

Turning to the fabricating sector, we again are lacking data for some SICs for the whole period, but tires and inner tubes (SIC 3011) rose at a very slow average rate whereas reclaimed rubber (SIC 3031) did rather better. This was a busy industry, using most of its capacity, because during the energy crunch reclaiming rubber became more economic than it had been. The other industries all showed declines on a 1972–81 basis.

The industries in this group have always tended to be innovative in their products, especially those working with plastics both at the resin and fabricating stages. The period from about 1945 to 1965 especially brought an enormous increase in the kinds of plastics and fibers available. This unparalleled spate of innovations was therefore largely complete by the beginning of the period of the present study. Some of these materials were elastomers (i.e., synthetic rubbers) which had been a high-priority item ever since the well-remembered dislocations in the rubber supply during World War II.

However, rubber tires, which might be considered relatively staid products irrespective of their raw materials, saw perhaps the most extensive changes. First, as tubeless tires became almost universal in the early 1960s, the industry soon lost almost the entire inner tube business. Then came the development of steel-belted radials, which required much product and process innovation but which eventually caused a large drop in volume because the radials lasted twice as long as the nylon or rayon cord tires. One effect was wide turmoil in the industry that eventually led not only to extensive corporate reorganizations but also, and more immediately, to widespread shutdowns of tire plants.

As they have done from their beginnings, plastics continued to make severe inroads on other products, notably on metal and glass. The latter came about especially in the development of plastic bottles. These, however, have been challenged on environmental grounds because they are quite permanent and are not biodegradable. Pressures on the industry have come from advocates of biodegradable materials; they exist, albeit at greater cost. Other steps have been the state requirements of bottle deposits, but unlike at least some glass bottles, plastic bottles cannot be reused and are therefore ground up in the refund automats.

The proper disposal of plastics is, in fact, one of the major technical-economic problems of waste disposal generally and of this industry in particular. Plastics generate toxic fumes when burned; some of the early materials particularly were highly flammable, and others burn only when exposed to direct flame and do not support combustion otherwise. One particular difficulty is that several major plastics produce dioxin when burned together with paper. This is one of the greatest impediments to resource recovery schemes and power generation from waste.

Leather and Leather Products (SIC 31)

This is by far the smallest of the major industry groups in terms of volume of shipments, but its troubles are such that they merit special mention. Like no other, this industry is beset by foreign competition to the extent of having parts of it virtually eliminated or reduced to marginal existence. The Trade Reform Act of 1973 included adjustment assistance clauses which provided for special economic assistance for communities whose major industry had been put out of business by imports. For years, the shoe industry (SIC 314) in particular was the main beneficiary qualifying for that kind of assistance.

Unfortunately, however, that assistance mainly took the form of transfer payments for retraining and help for displaced workers rather than for technical and managerial assistance to the industry to help it become more widely competitive again. That, of course, would have been the most appropriate action and could have set a welcome pattern for industrial recovery in general.

Productivity statistics are not available for the whole study period in the form of CDVAM/E because of product redefinitions in 1972, but from about 1958 onwards, the Bureau of Labor Statistics shows an essentially stagnant trend in its index of output per production worker hour.[25] A similar situation holds in the rubber and plastics footwear industry (SIC 3021) where CDVAM/E statistics also show no long-term improvement.[26]

Although imports are central to the footwear industry's problems, they are only one of several factors that have hindered the improvement of productivity. Another is the impact of fashion on the size of production runs. A given batch of identical shoes rarely accounts for more than 5 or 6 percent of a factory's daily output and is usually less than 1 percent. There are some three hundred different size combinations and typically over ten thousand styles, in addition to an endless variation in quality, color, and patterns of raw materials.

Raw materials have, in fact, had troubles of their own, as leather has steadily become more expensive and as man-made substitutes have had their own share of troubles. The use of DuPont's Corfam for uppers, for instance, ended in spectacular market failure. The material could neither "breathe," nor stretch to fit, the way leather uppers could.

The great growth in athletic footwear as a result of the exercise boom has affected the relative standing of leather and other kinds of footwear, and of style groupings within them, but the production problems seem to have caused the same kinds of trouble to all parts of these industries. For example, the elaborate design of running shoes compared to that of old-fashioned sneakers has caused a major increase in the number of production operations and has thus narrowed the gap between the complexity of dress shoes and rubber footwear.

Finally, in spite of the variety offered, there seem to be major problems in footwear design, especially for women. Whether the designs themselves or their execution are at fault, there are widespread complaints of inability to find shoes that give proper support and do not cause back problems and other orthopedic difficulties. Suffering for the sake of fashion is not, of course, unusual, but in footwear that can create clinically definable conditions. The above health problems are manifestly on the upswing; it is not yet possible to determine whether shoe design or the effects of such stressful new activities as jogging or running are responsible. This is an industry whose products are, despite constant fashion changes, based on very old design concepts. Still there clearly are major problems outstanding in product design and thus in the general conditions in which the industry operates and seeks to cope with its operational problems and international competition.

Stone, Clay, and Glass Products (SIC 32)

This major group consists of twenty-seven constituent industries, of which twenty-two make what are largely products used in con-

struction. The other five are consumer products, mainly eating uten-
sils and ornamental goods for the home. The two groups are thus
very different in character. The former ranges all the way to what is
usually called heavy industry, meaning capital-intensive production
of standard products that often have bulk characteristics even though
they may actually be piece parts.

Bricks (SIC 3251), ceramic tile (3253), and concrete products
(SIC 3272) including concrete pipe, would be examples of this category; other products like cement (SIC 3241), lime (SIC 3274), and
gypsum (SIC 3275) are simple bulk products. Abrasive products (SIC
3291) combine the two sets of product characteristics; the industry
turns out both bulk grinding compounds and abrasive wheels and
stones. Another industry, ready-mixed concrete (SIC 3273), almost
has the character of a service business along the lines of wholesalers
or jobbers that serve the contractors in building projects, except for
its need for mixing and batching plants and specialized delivery
equipment which put it in the manufacturing category.

The dependence of many industries in this group on construction
necessarily causes them to share its fluctuations in activity. To a degree, the products of this group are more involved in heavy construction, including roads, and commercial and office buildings, than in
home construction, as is the case, for example, with lumber. Still,
vitreous plumbing fixtures (SIC 3261) or ceramic tile heavily depend
on home building as well, and houses too have concrete foundations
and concrete or concrete block basement walls.

The study period saw rising and falling trends in construction, as
detailed earlier. The industries in this group thus follow the same
trends. When interest rates rose to historic highs in the late 1970s,
building slumped, even though there was countercyclical activity in
the public sector. The record of value added in this group reflects
that movement, as well as a subsequent partial recovery. Such trends
make for major problems in what are often rather capital-intensive
industries, and therefore vulnerable to the ill-effects of reduced
capacity utilization.

Whatever the ups and downs in business activity of these industries, their trends in productivity, as given by CDVAM/E, show conspicuously little change. Four of the twenty-six industries for which
complete data could be obtained had negative rates, and fifteen
others had growth rates between 0 and 1 percent. None increased at
rates greater than the 2.8 percent rate of constant dollar GNP from
1967 to 1981.

Although this group turns out many products that are the staples of an industrial society and that have changed little or not at all, it has its share of turmoil in its markets. First of all, it includes the industry with what is undoubtedly the most controversial major industrial product: asbestos (SIC 3292). Although the first concern over the health hazards of asbestos was recorded as early as 1907, it was not until the 1960s that increasingly severe restrictions were imposed on the industry.[27] The details are too well known to be recounted here; suffice it to say that the hazards are reflected in a 50 percent decline in constant dollar value added in the industry between 1967 and 1981. The filing for bankruptcy by Johns Manville, the largest company in the field, in response to billions of dollars claimed in lawsuits, was another result. At present, the careful removal of existing asbestos content in buildings has become an industry at least as prominent as new installations, which are now restricted almost out of existence.

Compared with problems such as these, those of other industries in this group are minor. Yet, in their own way, they caused considerable dislocations. A case in point is that of glass bottles, the principal product of SIC 3221. The inroads that plastic bottles have made on the market of this industry, in spite of the disadvantages of plastics, were described above under rubber and plastics products and earlier under beverage products.

Before plastic bottles, there had been a market struggle within this industry between deposit and lighter disposable ("one way") bottles. The latter, of course, are needed in much greater numbers and thus create added industry volume and the jobs that go with it. This point was a major factor in the struggle for state bottle deposit laws, especially in states like New York, where there was a sizeable bottle-producing industry. Eventually, of course, plastic bottles engulfed them all.

In addition to wine and liquor, where the reuse of bottles has been prohibited for good reason ever since Prohibition, beer is the last major holdout for glass bottles rather than plastic ones; even there, however, aluminum cans have steadily increased their shares. Plastic bottles for some liquor brands have also made their appearance. The final result in the study period was that constant dollar value added in SIC 3221 rose about 27 percent from 1967 to the peak year of 1973 and then declined by 1981 to slightly below its 1967 level.

Primary Metal Industries (SIC 33)

This major group encompasses the production of ferrous and non-ferrous metals in forms suitable for further manufacture, although it includes end-use products like nails and even consumer products like aluminum foil. Its markets are similarly diverse, but the important ones are related to capital goods and construction (especially heavy construction), which are highly cyclical, and to automobiles, which have been a declining market as imports have increased and cars have grown smaller, with a greater plastics content.

These features in themselves do not, however, pose the main problems. This is a troubled industry group whose problems are both general to all its constituents and particular to major sectors. The first of the general problems is that the group has been suffering from major cost disadvantages that beset not only the industry of the United States but of Canada as well. Mining industries in North America have been much beset by lower cost producers elsewhere. Their competitors were favored by lower labor costs and in many cases by geology that gave them more easily worked deposits or, as in iron ore, deposits of a high quality that have essentially been depleted within the United States.

The result has been an enormous proliferation of steel capacity, especially as the producing countries wanted to add further processing capabilities to their extractive industries. Steel mills are also industrial status symbols, clearly identifying their owners as industrial countries. The whole process has been badly overdone, however. It is now estimated that there is excess capacity of 200 million tons a year; until recently, it was estimated at 300 million tons, but this was reduced by widespread demolitions of steel plants in the United States and some European countries. To put this in perspective, at its peak around 1960 when it was the highest in the world, the maximum U.S. capacity was about 135 million tons a year; it has declined since then to about 85 million tons. There likewise is overcapacity in aluminum and other nonferrous metals.

A second general problem is that plastics have made severe inroads on the markets for both steel and nonferrous metals. Not even aluminum has shown itself to be immune after a long history of displacing other metals. Having, in the course of the study period, displaced steel in cans, aluminum was soon widely replaced itself by plastics, for example, as in tubes for toothpaste and ointments.

Finally, progress in design of many products and some other basic changes in the way materials are used have led to great reductions in the amount of metal required to sustain a given physical volume of production.

The foregoing troubles appear to fall with particular virulence on the steel industry. First, thanks to some major discoveries, notably in Australia and South America, iron ore is extraordinarily plentiful and available in many places in good run-of-mine quality. In the United States, however, the best direct-use iron ore is gone, and the once fabled Mesabi range of Minnesota must resort to pelletizing, a process of concentration that involves grinding, removing the iron by magnetic methods, forming the material into pellets, and sintering them. The result actually is an excellent product with high iron content that saves more energy in subsequent processing than is expended in the beneficiation process. The costs are, however, higher than those of simply scooping the stuff out of the open-pit mine and sending it on, even if long sea transport is involved.

The American industry, in fact, has a second problem. The current ore is primarily taconite, which comes in both magnetic and nonmagnetic forms. At present, magnetic taconites are the main ones exploited, but they too are running out; as that happens nonmagnetic taconites must be used, and their iron cannot be removed by simple magnetic separators. This removal requires more complex processes, notably froth flotation, which is a much more expensive process first developed for copper sulfide ores.

As to better design and resulting lower usage, the amount of steel required to sustain one point in the Federal Reserve Board Index of production of durable goods fell from 1.68 million tons in 1950 to 1.04 in 1965 and 0.61 in 1980. These are declines of 38.1 percent in the fifteen years from 1950 to 1965 and 41.3 percent in 1965-80.[28] The foregoing statistics are based on domestic production; actual usage was higher after the United States became a net importer, beginning about 1960. Still, the percentage declines in needs were about the same.

Certain product lines were especially hard hit. For example, in the late 1950s, long after sophisticated techniques for using reinforced concrete had been developed in Europe and in research establishments in the United States, the U.S. construction industry began to use it more extensively. This cut into the market for steel framing shapes, such as girders and columns, in favor of reinforcing rods.

These could be made in what came to be called minimills, which using mainly scrap metal could turn the rods out in good quality with minimal investment compared to integrated steel mills.

These problems of overcapacity and of market disturbances are extremely serious but are, the former especially, in large measure beyond the control of the American steel industry. It is in the management of its own technical-economic future, however, that the steel industry has been most seriously remiss, as in its handling of the major technical innovations that have revolutionized the industry. These are issues of capital input and thus are discussed in detail in chapter 3. Here, however, it should be noted that these problems have had a major, if not almost fatal, impact on the market and volume trends of this industry; they have had their impact not only on raw steel (mainly SIC 3312), but also on some of the fabricated items such as sheet and tube.

The various castings industries have also had varying degrees of trouble from imports, new technologies, and substitution. The basic metals industry supplies not only construction but also automobile and machine builders of all kinds. To the extent that these customer industries are badly beset by imports, the basic industries suffer as well. An imported machine tool does not use American castings, and an imported car does not use American sheet steel.

Insofar as they express themselves in the CDVAM/E statistics, the twenty-two industries in this group for which complete data were obtained have had poor productivity growth. Twelve of them are seen to have negative rates of change, and another seven are between 0 and 1 percent a year. Only three nonferrous processing industries do better. Moreover, the whole group was hard hit in the period after the end of this study and has seen much further retrenchment and reduction in capacity.

These retrenchments have also been associated with mergers and acquisitions and with a desire of major producers to get out of the steel business. One of the more graphic examples of the futility of trying to get the American industry to remain committed to its original purpose occurred in 1982 when the U.S. Steel Corporation used the tax advantages in the 1981 Revenue Act to buy Marathon Oil instead of to build a new and fully up-to-date steel mill. In all, this is a troubled industry group, a situation made worse by the obvious fact that it is a central ingredient of any significant industrial system.

Fabricated Metal Products (SIC 34)

This group comprises fabricated metal products except machinery and transportation equipment. As the listing in the Appendix indicates, it is a diverse group which, just like primary metals, again includes products used in the manufacture of machinery and other items that find their main use in construction. The health of their customers is thus of prime concern to this group. It also includes hand tools of all sorts and many items that are not only used in original equipment manufacture (o.e.m.) but also in maintenance and restoration jobs for buildings of all kinds and in replacement parts. Clearly, these are very basic products, but as noted in more detail in chapter 5, some parts of the group especially have had their share of import trouble.

With minor exceptions, the products of this industry are not among the most innovative. Many of them have to be made in standard sizes or to standard specifications to satisfy building codes or standards long established by ANSI (American National Standards Institute) and its predecessor ASA (American Standards Association), or, at times, those of their foreign counterparts. Details of screw threads, for instance, are standardized, and so are many other products of this group, especially SIC 3451 and 3452. This means that opportunity for innovation in products is limited except in new designs for appearance's sake, as in the industries primarily making building products (SIC 344). In others, designs are furnished by the customers, as in the case of forgings and stampings (SIC 346). Plumbing and heating items (SIC 343) are determined by building codes as well as proprietary designs. For metal cans (SIC 3411), new materials and production methods are the focus; some 60 percent of that industry now furnishes aluminum cans for beverages. Ordnance is related to the military, and its product too is largely standardized.

The industry group is thus an old and somewhat hidebound one, as reflected in its record in productivity change. As the Appendix indicates, only two constituents, metal cans and nonferrous forgings (SIC 3463) have rates of increase in CDVAM/E greater than 2 percent. Of the thirty-five industries for which complete data are available, eighteen have negative rates and twelve more have rates between 0 and 1 percent.

Machinery, Except Electrical (SIC 35, Except 357)

As modified here, this major group excludes office machinery, which though originally mechanical, has gradually acquired enough electrical and electronic features to warrant its inclusion in electronic products, below. What remains runs the whole gamut of industrial machinery, that is, of the machines that turn out much of what has been described in other parts of this volume.

Together with parts of electrical and electronic machines, this major group is therefore at the center of any industrial society and, in many ways, determines its degree of industrial success. Being forced to use somebody else's machinery in an industry removes a great deal of decision power from the users. As was noted in the discussion of the steel industry, not participating in process and machine development makes the users essentially dependent on designs for other needs and resources and, worst of all, lets foreign competitors get the initial benefits of the new concepts.

These points are important in connection with this industry because it has become increasingly troubled. One by one, the constituent industries of this major group have been affected by imports in an ever rising and disastrous way. Yet, as noted in more detail in chapter 5, this was once an epicenter of industrial competence where, in many areas, the U.S. manufacturers were virtually unchallenged and unchallengeable. The declining health of this industry group is thus an uneven one, but the sectors of it that are still successful, or just viable, are becoming fewer. What makes this record so deplorable is simply the fact that the major inventions and improvements that provided the original foundations long ago were either made in the United States or else were first commercially developed by American firms. Their very names long echoed the history of their products and of their inventors.

The machine tool industries (SIC 354) are a particular case in point because their products are used to make other machines and because their deterioration became something of a paradigm and forerunner of troubles elsewhere in the group.[29] In no other large industry group was American pioneering effort more strongly evident than in machine tools. Americans not only invented some of them, like the milling machine, the turret lathe, and various gear-cutting machines, but also invented the tooling that made them usable. Most important perhaps was the concept of interchangeable parts in which tolerances in manufacturing were made tight enough to permit easy assembly of the parts without individual fitting. Applied to manufacture in other metalworking industries, the methods and machines made possible the widespread use of complicated machinery in the form of domestic appliances and mass-produced industrial machinery. Mass production itself, with its integrated manufacturing systems and process layouts, was the logical next step and soon followed.

It was in their ability to carry out the commercial development of their products—to make a product whose purchase could be readily justified by potential customers and that worked well when bought—that the American makers were preeminent.

Much of the inventive work, however, happened long ago. The rise of the industrial age approximately coincides with the existence of the United States. Before 1776, machines available for manufacturing operations differed little from those in the Middle Ages or earlier. A century later, nearly all the principal types of machine tool had been invented. However, progress continued, mainly by making the machines larger, more powerful, and more reliable. Another approach to design change was to replace what had once been mechanical linkages with electrical ones, or separate electrical drives. This became feasible as soon as electric motors themselves could be made small and cheaply enough to permit that kind of redesign.

The industry prospered greatly in the years after World War II when its products were indispensable to industrial reconstruction. The United States was the only major industrial society that had emerged undamaged from the war and was therefore able to take advantage of new business opportunities resulting from new inventions and design changes. Nevertheless, there were shortcomings that were to prove forerunners of much more severe troubles. First, the industry signally failed to keep its own production systems up to date. Its managements appeared to take an almost perverse delight in not using the prescriptions for success that they constantly urged on their own customers. The machines used to make the machine tools were increasingly antiquated, as the stock of operating machines in the United States became steadily more ancient. That meant that productivity improvement largely ceased and that the industry therefore became ever more vulnerable to the labor cost differential of American workers relative to their foreign competitors. Much of the machine tool industry itself became a small-volume handicraft operation; even the excellent skills of much of its work force could not prevail with the kinds of equipment and production systems that had become generally prevalent.

Such design alternatives as modular construction were proposed but largely ignored, alternatives that would have meant assembling machines from standardized subassemblies, each of which could then be made more economically in larger quantities and could be speedily assembled into units of flexible performance to suit what customers wanted. Aside from lower production costs, the prevalent delivery times, which had stretched into many months, could thereby be shortened dramatically.

A particular case was that of transfer machines, which are large units that consist of work heads performing various machine operations and special conveyors that transport the work pieces automatically from one station to the next. Obviously, this was an area in which modulization and standardization would have been very beneficial. Yet the makers of that kind of equipment responded only when their principal customer, the automobile industry, threatened to make its own equipment unless the industry could rearrange the parts of its existing machines and some new ones to create a production system for new models. Before then, a model change had invariably meant scrapping many otherwise perfectly usable pieces of equipment.

The deterioration of this industry towards handicraft status was exacerbated as soon as its customers began to buy imports and volume began to fall. One would have supposed that this would create serious pressure towards technical and managerial reform, but that was not generally the case. Rather, the industry began to buy foreign subassemblies, or entire machines, made by foreign subsidiaries or contractors. This process was well under way by the mid 1960s and was almost universal by the end of the period of this study.[30]

A second response was created for the industry by a new direct customer, the U.S. Department of Defense. Beginning in the 1950s, it supported the development of new machine tools, and in the 1960s, of the numerically controlled units. This had two effects. First, the creation of these units was surrounded by the secrecy and red tape of most military work, and second, the cost of the units was no longer a consideration.

That in turn had the effect of restricting the market to military contractors who could charge to their contracts what in commercial work would have been unacceptably high machine costs. In effect, a two-tier market was created, one for the Pentagon, where high price did not matter, and one for the industrial customers, where it did. The response of the latter, quite obviously, was to buy the imported machines that were available much more cheaply and quickly.

The machine tool industry has, ofcourse, been decimated by these developments. The departures of the once famous major companies continue. For instance, the sturdy factory building of the bankrupt Bullard Machine Company in Bridgeport, Connecticut, where the vertical lathe had been invented long ago, was turned into high-priced condominiums. Two contenders were fighting over the remains of the Morse Cutting Tool Company of New Bedford, Massachusetts, which had been founded in 1864 by Samuel A. Morse, the inventor of the twist drill. One possible buyer hoped to keep things going, but the other wanted to salvage the name, describing the machines as obsolete—as "greasy antiques."[31]

In the once great machine tool center of Springfield, Massachusetts, the large companies are mostly defunct or have turned themselves into agents for imported machine tools and occasionally make extra-specialized tools for military contractors, where costs and quick delivery are secondary. Others have been bought by conglomerates, only to be disposed of later. Small shops have been more successful, doing high-quality precision work for customers around the United States, but surviving only as job shops in the interstices of an industry the core of which is gone.[32]

Machine tools are the key to much of machine manufacturing in general, and the rest of this major group has experienced its share of troubles. Succeeding in the capital goods market requires a product whose purchase can be justified by the potential customer; it must offer a return on investment by way of cost savings that put it ahead of alternative investments in the customer's expressed or implied list of priorities. Quick delivery and reliability are also clearly important.

When the improvements of a machine come in slow increments, if at all, it is hard to make much of a case, unless the customer has to expand operations or has an old machine that has irremediably collapsed. Major technical progress—a technological end run—offers a quick advantage; it is the kind of "threshold" that makes life pleasant for marketers of any product. To achieve it, however, requires concentrated and persistent research as well as careful commercial development. In the current state of affairs, those resources are in short supply. An indication of the truth of this assessment is offered by the fact that for decades the Inventories of Metalworking Equipment, which the *American Machinist* conducts about every five years, has shown a steady aging of the dwindling number of machines that are still around. Replacing them with what passes as new ones these days is clearly not very inviting.

As a result, machine tools are not the only part of this industry group that is in difficulty. The first stage of trouble for these industries, many of which had once had substantial export markets, is that they lose third country markets; later they have to contend with imports on their home ground.

This has happened in several other industries; textile machinery (SIC 3552) is a sad example in which American manufacturers failed to introduce innovations, such as shuttleless looms and ringless spindles, and failed to respond to the need of its customers for easier setups for a more flexible production mix. The offshoot is that the American textile industry now largely relies on foreign suppliers.[33]

Construction machinery (SIC 3531) still has an export surplus, but it is shrinking, and the industry is saved in its third country markets primarily by the fact that the large American companies have foreign subsidiaries that can still supply it competitively. This industry still shows a substantial growth in CDVAM/E for the study period.

The highest rate of increase in this measure for the study period 1967–82 is shown by oil field machinery (SIC 3533), which had a great boom after 1973. When oil prices fell again in the 1980s, the industry suffered greatly. Mining machinery (SIC 3532) also had an upswing in connection with the opening of new coal fields at that time, and that too showed itself in higher productivity. The widespread reequipment of the printing trades discussed earlier showed itself in higher growth rates for CDVAM/E in printing trades machinery (SIC 3555).

The statistics for this group must be read with caution, however. A shift toward simpler equipment, the use of more imported subassemblies, and above all, design changes, can make the determination of physical output very difficult indeed. For this reason, price indexes suitable for deflating raw VAM data are particularly questionable. BLS data for the few industries for which they are available show little or no growth in worker productivity and negative readings for machine tools.[34]

Electrical Machinery, Except Electronics (SIC 361–364)

The industries in this group comprise electric transmission and distribution equipment (SIC 361), electrical industrial apparatus (SIC 362), household appliances (SIC 363), and electric lighting and wiring equipment (SIC 364). Their constituent industries are listed in the Appendix. Most were relatively stagnant during the period of this study.

The reasons are not difficult to discern. SIC 361 did poorly in part because of its bellwether industry, the makers of transformers (SIC 3612). That in turn partially resulted from the sharp reduction in the growth of electrical consumption following the oil shock, which left manufacturers of the equipment working way below the 80 percent capacity that they had maintained throughout the 1960s and on into the early 1970s. Some major makers, like General Electric and Westinghouse, suspended manufacture of certain kinds of equipment.[35]

The principal threat to both SIC 361 and 362, which between them account for the bulk of electrical power equipment used by industry, came from imports. Much of this equipment is of traditional design, although very important innovations in insulation and especially in magnetic steels were made in the late 1940s and 1950s. This eventually led to such actions as the reduction by the National Electrical Manufacturers' Association (NEMA) of standard motor sizes for given power output and to a general trend toward smaller dimensions.[36] Though the major actions along these lines had been taken before the study period, there was still ample opportunity for more compact redesigns and these, apart of course from lower prices, proved to be potent advantages of imports.

This meant that innovation in these industries began to have a heavy foreign component. Yet here too Americans had made many of the major discoveries that had established the whole electric power industry and the equipment of its users. Around the beginning of the century, Thomas Edison, B. G. Lamme, George Westinghouse, Frank Sprague, and many others laid at least the product foundations for industrial firms that soon attained world fame in their fields. Yet with the advent of electronics, as discussed further in the next section, interest in the whole field faded, especially after power consumption was scaled back in the late 1970s. Even the teaching of power-related electrical engineering took a back seat.

Household appliances had similar product problems. Not only were most of them also invented in the United States, but in more ample times American manufacturers had pioneered the mass production of what must have seemed rather complex pieces of machinery.

This, however, is also an industry that depends heavily on housing starts and thus on interest rates as well as consumer confidence. The major appliances such as refrigerators, home laundry equipment, dishwashers, etc., depend on new housing; people buy these high-priced items and expect them to last, so that the replacement market is relatively much smaller. Small appliances are more often bought and may even be impulse items, but that tends to make them more sensitive to price competition. Apart from microwave ovens, which really are electronic devices, there have been few significant new product entries in this industry. At any rate, it has proven to be much at risk from foreign competition as far as small appliances go. Some firms that had entered the field at times of better markets left it. This included even Westinghouse, which sold its appliance business to White Motors (now White-Westinghouse), and General Electric, which sold its small appliance business to Black & Decker while retaining the large items.

Electrical lighting and wiring equipment again includes many standard items that are particularly vulnerable to low-cost imports, as well as lighting fixtures (SIC 3645), in which high-quality imports also play a significant part, along with low-priced items. These industries also are sensitive to building needs because, perhaps even more so than appliances, they may seldom be replaced after they are installed at the time the structure is built.

The CDVAM/E statistics show low rates of increase for the principal parts of the industry groups discussed in this section. It is noteworthy that sewing machines (SIC 3636) show a negative rate; their manufacture in the United States has almost ceased, and yet these were invented in the United States and also were the first complicated machines to be turned into domestic appliances (purely mechanical ones at first, of course) in the nineteenth century. This, in short, is yet another set of industries that appears largely to coast on past achievements.

Electronic Products (SIC 357 and 365–369)

Electronic products would surely qualify as the most important industrial newcomer, if not of the century, at least of the second half of it. Even air transport, which might qualify as a runner-up, makes use of electronics to such a degree that aircraft are to a large extent flying computers and other electronic packages. Electronics have, in fact, taken over much of the functions of some equipment that was once done mechanically, if it could be done at all. That is why office machines (SIC 357) are included in this discussion. They include computers, which would be enough reason for including them, but other machines like typewriters and copiers now have enough electronic content to make their continued presence in machinery, except electrical (SIC 35), somewhat anachronistic.

One would think, therefore, that this should be an industry in which the United States would be preeminent without any question. After all, many of the basic discoveries were made in the United States, including the most basic and portentous of all, the solid state circuitry.

The industry is, however, deeply troubled. Its problems are well known, but it is important to set them forth at least in outline because they are an object lesson in industrial decay. A particularly sobering aspect is that they clearly show that such decay is not self-limiting and that it is not readily reversed. What is disheartening is that the illusions that have brought about the present conditions are still firmly held, albeit perhaps with a greater sense of doubt and worry than heretofore.

The first illusion is that successful commercial development would more or less inevitably follow scientific pioneering. The transistor, the first solid state device, was invented for the Bell System in 1946. In the early 1950s, AT&T was required to license the technology freely, as part of a deal with the antitrust authorities that allowed it to keep Western Electric as a wholly owned subsidiary (aside from a very small minority interest) with a monopoly in providing equipment for the telephone system. In return, the Bell System had to license solid state technology to nontelephone applications.

It is important to be aware of this because at the time of the very first revelations in connection with the enforced licensing, there were two major parties at interest. The first was the U.S. Department of Defense, which immediately realized the military potential of solid state technology and proceeded to support it by research grants and product development. Thus, military electronics have played a powerful, if not dominant role in the development of the U.S. electronics industry; but solid state technology and the products it has spawned are in no way a result of spinoff from military technology.

The commercial development of the new technology was left to the second major party at interest, the Japanese. American makers of radios and television sets showed some interest, but they had just equipped large new factories for making tubes and were not keen on having them become speedily obsolete. It has been duly noted in the discussion of other industries that the United States has progressively lost out in industries where the basic inventions were made by Americans, but solid state electronics is one in which commercial and military development parted company almost from the start.

It was soon noted that this was happening, and research managers in some industries, as well as some outside observers, noted that the objectives of military and commercial development were so different that the products could not fail to be largely useless in the other sector. Change from military to commercial applications would be particularly difficult.[37]

It is manifestly *not* true that money does not count at all in military work; one does, however, deal in what seems to be a different currency, with costs "orders of magnitude" (itself a military phrase, meaning powers of ten times) greater. A second point is traditionally made with weaponry: it simply has to work, no matter what the cost. That is also nonsense; the history of weaponry that failed to work proves the point amply, and in 1987, in the era of $300 claw hammers and $640 toilet seats for the military, of the Shuttle disaster and the Star Wars illusions, no one need be instructed that the military use of technology is often disastrous.

It is, to say the least, poignant that the commercial development of electronic products went in exactly the opposite direction. Price of commercial products does count, of course, but quality must also be maintained. That proved to be particularly important in a technology of which it may be said that it almost does not work. At least rearranging atoms was a very different procedure from the usual industrial tasks.

It was the Japanese who largely managed to make solid state circuitry into a mass product; there were few American firms that were able to do the same. IBM and Texas Instruments stand out as the most prominent ones. They, however, developed their commercial products in their own right and on their own; it was becoming plain that even where a given military product might have some commercial applications, it would have to be practically reinvented before it could be sold at reasonable, rather than Pentagon, prices.

By the beginning of the period of this study (i.e., by 1967), the production of radios had, for practical purposes, ceased in the United States; television sets made entirely of domestically produced components were soon to follow. Computers presented a brighter picture, but calculators soon moved to the Asian producers. As the 1970s went on, the chip problem moved to the forefront of concern, and therein lay another bitter lesson.

There was an axiom that prevented many a management from taking effective action earlier. It was that no matter what else happened with products, the "high end" of technology would stay in the United States. It was evident from the start, of course, that one could not keep competitors in their places that way. From the very beginning of modern technology two hundred years ago, there had always been a symbiosis among members of given industries in given regions. They learned from each other, and most of all, there was constant feedback from users and competitors to basic research. This feedback then led to more basic discoveries and caused a leapfrog effect that circumvented attempts at outside control.[38] In this way, for example, as random access memories (RAMs) went from 64K to 128K to 256K and on up, Japanese shares of the market increased rapidly a development called "chip wars."[39]

The offshoot was that soon there were virtually no electronic products made in the United States that were not based on imported chips. It then was no wonder that "clones" of American standard computers appeared in Asia and were soon made available in the United States as well. Countries that were producing what one might call the "active ingredients" of computers felt entitled to make the rest as well. The rest consisted of items like keyboards, printers, and other partly mechanical items; that part of the manufacturing industry in the United States had itself fallen into disuse. The domestic manufacture of office machinery, especially typewriters (SIC 3572), had likewise ended, again with the almost sole exception of the IBM line.

The decline of the fine mechanical industries in the commercial sector thus made itself felt once again; its nature and causes were discussed in the last section. The effect was a direct one in the chip controversy. These circuit boards cannot be made except by extremely high precision machines and are then made very quickly, often involving mere seconds of labor per unit. Even if that labor cost nothing, it would not make a decisive difference. Where the difference does come in is in the cost of the machinery and tooling required; the loss of competence in much of the relevant technology, or rather its preemption by high-cost military work, effectively shut out American producers.

One ultimate effect was to prevent any American entries, let alone competitive ones, in an increasing range of electronic products. By the end of the study period, video recorders were available. None have ever been made in the United States for consumer use. Neither have compact disk players, the new digital tapes, or digital television sets, the last two made by both European and Japanese firms.

Meanwhile, military-industrial approaches to work, with all their secrecy, bureaucracy, and endless red tape, have not brought the kind of technological end runs that were promised by the spinoff arguments. The case of radar is especially instructive. It is really the only electronic technology that can truly claim direct military ancestry, the beginnings of which are now some fifty years in the past. Yet whatever spinoff it has ever produced consists of consumer items like small boat navigation aids or police radar-trap detectors, virtually all imported and commercially redesigned to the point of reinvention. Such urgently needed systems as those for effective and safe air traffic control and for detection of windshear and clear air turbulence have never issued from the makers of radar equipment, or from anyone else. So far, at least, the disasters and near-disasters constantly being reported have not brought any answers. Yet such systems would be the most logical extensions of radar technology.

Whenever something new comes about, whether it be optical fiber cable or superconductivity or supercomputers, there is now immediate concern over Japanese end runs, rather than those of American competitors. There is nothing less than an ongoing preemption of technical progress. True, new and successful computers are still being introduced by American producers, but the business has been much shaken out, as in the withdrawal of Texas Instruments from the computer business in 1983. Even IBM has had to face major problems in its products and organization.[40] There is at least some concern among marketers that the sales of the most recent models will have to be in a replacement market that may prove rather more resistant than expected.

It is also to be noted that the business is not without its fads, meaning product lines that have a rapid rise, followed by a rapid fall. During the period of this study, electronic games were a particular case in point. They were touted as very much a wave of the future. For example, Atari, Inc., was singled out as having a particularly bright prospect because for a time it was successful in producing both its hardware and software in the United States. Indeed, when a group of Democrats proposed a recipe for industrial recovery that combined high-tech manufacture with intensive militarism and a macho foreign policy, they soon were styled "Atari Democrats." When Atari went into a tailspin in 1982, it took with it the fortunes of its parent company, Warner Communications. Most significant for the present discussion, it moved what was left of its manufacturing to Taiwan.

The CDVAM/E statistics for this group do show forward movement, but compared with what they could have been, they seem modest indeed. In fairness, of course, one must note that there have been few industries in which economy of scale has shown itself more rapidly, especially with computers. Costs per kilobyte of memory, for instance, have plunged steadily. This means that the nature of output has changed so drastically that comparable products for a price index would be hard to define, especially for the particular period of this study, when enormous changes took place.

Motor Vehicles (SIC 371, 3751, and 379)

At the beginning of the study period, in the mid 1960s, motor vehicles and automobiles in particular had a generally rising trend of sales, interrupted only when the economy was affected by significant recessions. The industry was one of the principal players on the American industrial scene, and its future seemed secure. Imports were little more than nuisances, even if they had moved somewhat beyond the stage where imported cars were looked upon as curiosities. At the end of the period, imports were steadily progressing toward a one-third share of the U.S. market. American-built cars had acquired a reputation for poor design and poor quality, with several major model failures as a consequence. A major maker, the Chrysler Corporation, was near bankruptcy and had to be bailed out by government action. Sales of domestically produced units reached a peak of 9.3 million units in 1973 and declined to about 7 million by 1987. Sales for 1988 were projected at only 6.5 million units.[41]

Moreover, "domestic" was becoming a somewhat flexible concept; where once only the United States and Canada had been looked upon as a single economic unit by virtue of special agreements between the two countries, now U.S. manufacturers were buying large components abroad for their cars, including engines. Furthermore, major makers were importing entire cars from their own foreign subsidiaries or, as with so many other products discussed earlier in this volume, acting as sales agents.

The industry has, of course, been affected by factors other than imports. The automotive safety laws enacted in the 1960s, after much trouble and intensive opposition from the automobile industry, clearly required some reworking of designs. Far more sweeping was the effect of the oil crisis, which first had its impact in 1973 and which led to a requirement for more fuel-efficient cars. Yet U.S. makers did not have many such cars to sell; they were essentially the small models, and American makers had stayed away from these since the very beginning. The obvious reason was that the profit was less, but at times there seemed to be almost an ideological commitment to large cars. For example, a particularly insistent advertising campaign by General Motors in spring 1974, just after the crisis, extolled "full-size" cars as the only seemly vehicles around.[42]

Customers, however, evidently thought otherwise. The push from imports that followed, costing the American industry a huge share of its market, was primarily in small cars. When the American industry finally introduced small models of its own after what seemed a remarkably long gestation period, even for an industry not noted for quick action, they were, as noted above, of poor quality and no match for the imports.

It is instructive to observe that the industry seems to be about to make the same mistake a second time. When the imposition of quotas on Japanese imports, as well as the beginning appreciation of the yen relative to the dollar, caused Japanese cars to rise in price well above even American-made models of similar size, Japanese makers responded in part by using their quotas on higher priced and more profitable models. That left an opening at the lowest end of the market which was quickly filled by other makers, such as Hyundai of South Korea, and which introduced the prospect of many other entries. Hyundai's market success has been quite impressive. Meanwhile, however, the American industry was hailing the return of the big car in the wake of reduced gasoline prices and was looking forward to a rise in gas consumption. In this it reversed some of the conservation progress that had been put together in the wake of the oil crisis.

At the same time, one market sector that had been increasingly attracting major European and Japanese makers was that of luxury cars, but the stock market crash of 1987 did not augur well for the sale of Porsches, Audis, Jaguars and Acuras. It is noteworthy that there were no American entries in that particular market niche. U.S.

sports cars have a different image, as do large U.S. cars generally, like Cadillacs, Lincolns, or the top Chryslers.

The reponses of the U.S. firms include plant closures and large lay-offs of both production workers and white collar staff, as well as very large investments in new plants.

Meanwhile, in trucks (SIC 3713) a certain amount of downsizing was also in progress, but this was halted when, under pressure from trucking interests, the Reagan Administration required all states to permit "double bottoms," meaning trucks pulling trailers, on at least some of the interstate highways.

Small trucks, however, had a great boost in sales in the 1980s, al-though here imports from Japan and later Korea reduced the share of U.S. makers. This was a good business, however, even though by 1987 saturation was being forecast.[43] Here, incidentally, some old safety battles looked as if they would have to be refought. It was disheartening, for example, to have Lee A. Iacocca, in a segment of *60 Minutes* in early 1987, defend the absence of head rests for pro-tection against whiplash in almost the same terms an earlier genera-tion of Chrysler executives had used in opposition to seat belts and other safety devices in 1961.[44]

Real innovation in this industry seems to be hard to come by. There is, for example, nothing very concrete on the horizon with respect to new propulsion systems, such as engine-electric drives or battery-powered vehicles. Yet such major changes are the kinds of technological end runs that might put any company able to imple-ment them, decisively ahead. The industry has always relied heavily on outside sources for its real innovation, as in the development of the fluid drive based automatic shift in the 1940s.

Finally, foreign makers have been establishing branch plants in the United States that are much beyond mere assembly shops. Indeed, some of the Japanese cars made by the American plants of their producers have higher domestic content than do some of the models sold by American makers. Volkswagen, of course, failed in its U.S. effort, but that was because, in the United States and some of its other major markets, it was never able to repeat the success of the long-lived Beetle.[45] The Japanese makers have done very much better.[46]

The other industries in this group have had comparable difficulties; motor vehicle parts and accessories (SIC 3714) depend on the auto industry for much of their design work and take little independent action, apart from specialty and add-on items. Others reflect a failure by domestic suppliers to meet the desires of customers, as well as an inability to meet import competition. This is true of bicycles (SIC 3751), which had benefited a great deal from the exercise vogue. The American motorcycle industry (the other part of SIC 3751) was reduced to a single maker, Harley Davidson, and that firm was rescued only by protectionist measures as well as by the redesign of its models to incorporate some of the features of their foreign competitors. Motorcycles have also been hard hit by the decline in the principal age cohort of their users, mostly young men. Comparable saturation is to be recorded for campers and travel trailers (SIC 3792); their bulk, however, makes them essentially proof against significant imports. The last commercial industry is SIC 3799, which deals with such items as snowmobiles and snowbikes. These vehicles are also still largely domestic, though inroads have been made by imports in the former.

Lastly, there is tank production (SIC 3795). This industry is, of course, dominated by the military. Its output has included the M-1 tank and the Bradley vehicle, both of which have been widely reported to be of poor design, of very poor quality, and indeed downright dangerous to their users. The waste and scandals related to their production put them in a class by themselves.[47] The M-1 tank was produced by Chrysler during the study period, but the division had to be sold by Chrysler as part of its government-sponsored rescue package.

The rate of increase of 11.4 percent in CDVAM/E for this industry must, moreover, be seriously questioned. There are no price indexes for weapons as such, as noted in more detail in the next section, but it is known that the price of weaponry has been rising at very high rates that grossly exceed those for the producer price index for durables. Thus the value added by manufacture in constant dollars is very much overstated by using this price index, and so is CDVAM/E.

As to the reading for the other industries in this grouping, CDVAM/E has increased greatly for automobiles and for motor vehicle parts and accessories, reflecting a sharp increase in automation as well as in capacity utilization relative to the much reduced capacity of the industry. Others, as shown in the Appendix, have fared less well, with travel trailers and campers, and truck trailers (SIC 3715), in the negative column.

Other Transportation Equipment (SIC 372, 373, 374, 376)

This grouping consists of four sets of industries at the three-digit SIC level with sharply differing fortunes. The aircraft industry (SIC 372) is divided into two distinct market segments, the military and the civilian. The latter is further divided into aircraft for airlines and those for general aviation (i.e., private planes). American firms are very active in all these areas, with varying success. Military aircraft, like all weapons, have had their share of malfunctions and troubles. Two aircraft are particularly germane to this study because their troubles essentially took place during the study period. The first is the F-111, once called the TFX, a very problematic aircraft whose troubles date back to the award of its original contract and extend through to the Libyan raid when one-third of the planes failed to work properly. The second plane is the C-5A transport, a huge craft that had great problems in cost overruns and deficient quality, ably chronicled by A. Ernest Fitzgerald, a principal whistle-blower in this case.[48] The tradition continues with the F-16, the F-18, and many others.

Commercial aircraft owe their origins in part to the technology of military jets, but their method of construction had to be very different and, above all, had to satisfy very different criteria. The U.S. builders, however, have had their share of difficulties. During the study period, first General Dynamics and later Lockheed had to abandon the market, the latter after failing to make money with its trijet L-1011. Aircraft builders work with a very real break-even point in that they must sell a minimum number of each model in order to recoup development costs. Boeing and McDonnell-Douglas are the sole survivors.

Since the 1940s, the United States had something of a world monopoly for large passenger planes, but this has now been eroded in third country markets as well as by some imports bought for domestic flights. The reason is the rise of Airbus Industrie, a French-German-British consortium that has produced the highly successful wide-bodied twin jet A-300 and its later models, the A-310 and A-320. The American makers were tardy in responding to the threat from this type of aircraft, which is much more economical than the heavy trijets. The competing Boeing 767 has had only limited success, the more so because the deregulation of the industry in recent years has brought considerable financial and operating turbulence.

American makers also have largely left aircraft suitable for small or commuter airlines to imports. Britain's de Havilland, the Dutch firm of Fokker, and others have captured the market, even though U.S. makers of private jets might have done better than the foreign makers actually did. As to small aircraft, such famous American firms as Piper, Cessna, and Lear are still potent factors, even though they too face competition from an increasing array of international competitors.

In shipbuilding (SIC 373), U.S. yards have ceased to be factors in anything other than naval construction (i.e., as part of the military sector), a process that was virtually complete by the beginning of the study period. Shipbuilding was, in fact, the first large technically oriented industry to go into a decline compounded of effective and more advanced foreign competition (first from Germany and Sweden, later from Japan and Korea) and military dependency. This brought about the usual tolerance of managerial incompetence and eventually its share of scandal-ridden projects. The most noteworthy is the Aegis cruiser program, in which falsification of time records, cost overruns, intimidation of inspectors, and other tactics brought about a temporary suspension of General Dynamics, the principal contractor. Yet it hardly need be recalled that the United States once was one of the great shipbuilding nations of the world, including among its achievements such production oriented successes as the mass production of Liberty ships in World War II by Henry J. Kaiser.

Small boats have done perceptibly better but are very much discretionary items, with a large second-hand market. Still, it is an industry where, generally, U.S. equipment is still paramount.

The railroad equipment industry (SIC 374 and its sole member, 3743) is, for practical purposes, limited to two producers of diesel locomotives and two builders of freight cars; all other needs are now met by imports. Although electric traction was, for practical purposes, invented in the United States, there are now no builders capable of producing transit equipment or electric locomotives. The United States has, in any case, the lowest proportion of electrified mileage among all major railroad countries, which is itself a calamity from the viewpoint of energy economy.[49] When it tried to reequip its sole mainline, the Northeast Corridor line from Washington, D.C., to New Haven, Connecticut, General Electric built a totally unsuitable locomotive which had to be replaced by a model built under license from Sweden's ASEA.

Finally, missiles and space products are military items, subject to the characteristics of military-industrial operations. Their costs and reliability have been seriously questioned, especially in connection with the feasibility of even more ambitious projects like Star Wars.[50]

This group of industries includes several important activities related to military procurement making the determination of constant dollar value of central importance. The problem is that the market basket for a price index is almost impossible to devise because of the rapid design changes. At any rate, no consistent index is available, but some estimates have been made from time to time. Thus, of interest in the study period, the Senate Armed Services Committee estimated inflation in weapons costs at around 15 percent a year in 1970.[51] In 1980, an estimate by the Defense Science Board put the annual rate at 25 percent.[52] Certainly, the repeated cutbacks in the numbers of weapons that can be produced with a given amount of money suggest that whatever price escalation takes place must be very substantial. Basing an intended constant dollar growth of military budgets on the producer price index is certainly far off the mark.

The CDVAM/E readings for industries with large military markets, where available, must therefore be regarded with much reserve.

Instruments and Related Products (SIC 38)

This is a highly diverse group in its markets, combining small-scale makers of instruments and medical specialties, with much larger ones making standardized products in quantity. The largest constituent industry is photographic equipment and supplies (SIC 3861), which is a very large, true mass-production industry; where once there were many American suppliers, the industry has now been reduced to Kodak, Polaroid (who are both greatly troubled) and a few small makers of specialty equipment. The manufacture of cameras in the United States has come to a virtual end. The photographic industry, in short, is subject to what in this volume has been called broad-gauge competition, meaning competition that extends from the cheapest items to the most expensive. Thus the cheapest cameras are imported from the Far East and so are advanced instruments such as single-lens reflex cameras, auto-focus cameras, and in general, all cameras based on advanced electronic controls. The American photo industry thus has become, to a large extent, like a chemical process industry, turning out film and photo papers rather than cameras and other equipment.

Electronics has, in fact, played a principal role in the changes in the products of this industry group. The basic principles of several major ways of measuring pressure, temperature, and flow were established long ago. Miniaturization of instruments was the first major change in recent times, but that was to a large extent accomplished by the early 1960s. What was then undertaken was the telemetering of much information and its integration into computer systems. This happened in industrial applications as well as in medical and other scientific instrumentation. An important element was the improvement in accuracy that was made possible by digital means of measurement and by digital readouts that could be directly translated into written records where needed. That kind of redesign also made still further miniaturization possible.

One constituent industry was, in fact, changed entirely by the advent of electronics: watches and clocks (SIC 3873). The industry had, of course, long been dominated by imports, but it was possible, at least for a time, for American producers to make the electronic movements, both of the digital and the quartz analog types. That, however, was a temporary achievement. Imports again took center stage. It is noteworthy that Switzerland, which was badly hurt by the advent of electronic clocks with movements mainly from the Far East, took successful steps to develop a capability along these lines for itself and managed to rescue its famous watch industry from what might well have been its termination. The United States was less successful; there are, for practical purposes, no watches made in the United States on a scale comparable to that of the major importers.

The CDVAM/E statistics show wide variation, ranging from high rates of increase in engineering and scientific instrumentation (SIC 3811) and optical instruments and lenses (SIC 3832), with rates over 5 percent a year, to negative performers like dental equipment and supplies (SIC 3843) and ophthalmic goods (SIC 3851), where the switch to plastics may have had a decisive influence, and finally to the ever more constricted photo industry (SIC 3861).

Miscellaneous Manufactures (SIC 39)

This group does not lend itself to generalizations, including as it does industries with very different products, processes and markets. Several of the largest, however, have in common that they are badly beset by imports. Games and toys (SIC 3944) and sporting, amusement, and athletic goods (SIC 3949) are cases in point, but here, as in other industries in this group, some American makers have been able to retain and even expand traditional export markets. This is discussed further in chapter 5. Games and toys have seen an appreciable increase in electronic content, and that in itself was responsible for a major increase, at least in imported components.

Some industries depend rather strongly on others and thus share their fortunes or misfortunes. Buttons (SIC 3963) and needles, pins, and notions (SIC 3964), for instance, have seen downward trends, as both the apparel industry and home dressmaking have declined. Feathers, plumes, and artificial flowers (SIC 3962) have lost out due to fashion changes; the latter are largely supplied by Asian imports. The use of carbon paper (SIC 3955) has declined as copiers have taken the place of multiple-copy typing.

The CDVAM/E statistics show an industry group that largely has negative or low positive rates of change. Of the twenty constituent industries listed, eleven have negative rates, and a further four are between 0 and 1 percent. There were some higher rates, however. Games and toys, dolls, sporting goods, and linoleum all show increases at or above the constant GNP rate of 2.5 percent.

A CONCLUDING NOTE

The foregoing summary of conditions in the various industries has attempted to describe the major changes in products, both in their nature and in their trends within those industries. In so doing, this chapter has not explicitly dealt with what should really be a leading issue in productivity statistics, the human factors. To a large degree, however, these are similar. The same laws apply to all manufacturing, modified in some cases for reasons of safety and environment. What must be inferred from the foregoing is that many industries are in trouble, and this in turn has inevitably led to a decline—a disappearance in some bad cases—of job opportunities. For literally millions of workers in manufacturing, the period of this study (1967–82) was a time of declining morale, as workers and other employees of the troubled industries could see the end approaching. That part of the national economic problem is beyond the scope of this volume. Productivity statistics, like history, are necessarily written by the survivors, even if these are ever fewer.

NOTES

1. J. D. Hosley, et al., "A Revision of the Index of Industrial Production," *FRB Bulletin*, July 1985, 487.

2. J. E. Ullmann, "Criteria of Change in Machinery Design" (Ph.D. diss., Columbia University, 1959).

3. J. E. Ullmann, "Some Economic Aspects of Automobile Safety Devices," in Consumers Union of the U.S., *Passenger Car Design and Highway Safety* (Mt. Vernon, N.Y.: Consumers Union, 1962), 248.

4. L. D. Miles, *Techniques of Value Analysis and Engineering*, 2d ed. (New York: McGraw-Hill, 1972).

5. Bureau of Labor Statistics, *Handbook of Methods*, Bulletin 2134-1 (Washington, D.C.: Government Printing Office, 1982).

6. D. F. Noble, *Forces of Production* (New York: Knopf, 1984).

7. See, for instance, J. F. Gorgol and I. Kleinfeld, *The Military Industrial Firm* (New York: Praeger, 1972).

8. For theory and examples, see J. E. Ullmann, *Quantitative Methods in Management* (New York: McGraw-Hill, 1976), chaps. 13 and 14.

9. U.S. Department of Commerce, *1987 Statistical Abstract of the United States* (Washington, D.C.: Government Printing Office, 1986), 456, 699, and earlier issues.

10. Reported in "Handle with Care: This Bird Can Make You Sick," *Consumer Reports*, October 1987, 602. This article also gives instructions for the safe handling of poultry products.

11. D. Hodgen, "Processed Fruits, Vegetables and Specialties," in U.S. Department of Commerce, *U.S. Industrial Outlook 1985* (Washington, D.C.: Government Printing Office, 1986), 40.9.

12. This point is made in almost all books and articles on diet: for a trade view, see K. Bunch and J. Hazera, "Fats and Oils: Consumers Use More but Different Kinds," *National Food Review*, September 1984, 18.

13. For a report on this, see J. E. Ullmann, "Science and the Regulation Bogey," *Annals of the New York Academy of Sciences*, vol. 403 (1983), 69.

14. "'No Smoking' Sweeps America," *Business Week*, July 27, 1987, 40.

15. "Big Tobacco's Fortunes Are Withering in the Heat," *Business Week*, July 27, 1987, 47.

16. *U.S. Industrial Outlook 1985*, 44.8.

17. For a general discussion of this point, see J. E. Ullmann, *The Prospects of American Industrial Recovery* (Westport, Conn.: Quorum Books, 1985), 85, 88-90. A more central role for specialty products was advocated particularly in R. B. Reich, *The Next American Frontier* (New York: Times Books, 1983).

18. *U.S. Industrial Outlook 1985*, 45.7.

19. *U.S. Industrial Outlook 1985*, 27.1.

20. *Industry Survey* (New York: Standard and Poor's, 1985), B65.

21. *1987 Statistical Abstract*, 536, and 1969 edition, 507.

22. G. M. Keller, "Streamlining the Oil Industry: Cash Flow More than Reserves," *Financier*, March 1985, 33.

23. Ibid.

24. For a discussion of the feasibility of energy independence for the United States, see Ullmann, *American Industrial Recovery*, 184–91.

25. Bureau of Labor Statistics, *Productivity Indexes in Selected Industries*, Bulletin 2003 (Washington, D.C.: Government Printing Office, 1984).

26. This analysis and the following discussion of the industry are from B. R. Kalisch, "Shoe Manufacturing," in *The Improvement of Productivity*, ed. J. E. Ullmann (New York: Praeger, 1980), 146–56.

27. P. Brodeur, *The Asbestos Hazard* (New York: New York Academy of Sciences, 1980). A chronology of control efforts to date is in W. J. Nicholson, "Regulatory Actions and Experiences in Controlling Exposure to Asbestos in the United States," in *Public Control of Environmental Health Hazards*, ed. E. C. Hammond and I. J. Selikoff, *Annals of New York Academy of Sciences*, vol. 329 (1979), 293–303.

28. Ullmann, *American Industrial Recovery*, 149–50.

29. The troubles of the machine tool industry are discussed extensively in S. Melman, *Profits without Production* (New York: Knopf, 1984), 3–14, 167–68, 251; see also Ullmann, *American Industrial Recovery*, 160–71.

30. "Annual Industry Outlook," *Business Week*, January 14, 1985, 82.

31. "New Bedford Tool Plant in New Battle over Jobs," *New York Times*, May 31, 1987.

32. "Stirrings in the U.S.," *New York Times*, June 14, 1987.

33. C. F. Sabel and G. B. Herrigel, "Losing a Market to a High-Wage Nation," *New York Times*, June 14, 1987.

34. U.S. Bureau of Labor Statistics, Productivity Statistics for Selected Industries, Special computer run, November 1, 1985.

35. *U.S. Industrial Outlook 1985*, 26.1, 26.2.

36. For an account of this change, see Ullmann, "Criteria of Change in Machinery Design," 136–89.

37. The earliest major work dealing with this subject was another report in the Hofstra thesis series: J. E. Ullmann, ed., *Conversion Prospects of the Defense Electronics Industry* (Hempstead, N.Y.: Hofstra Yearbooks of Business, 1964).

38. Ullmann, *American Industrial Recovery*, 21–24, 107–9.

39. For a useful account of the differences in approach by U.S. and Japanese industry, including the preemption of the former by military work, see Y. Tsurumi "The U.S. Trade Deficit with Japan," *World Policy Journal*, Spring 1987, 207, 215–18.

40. "IBM: Big Changes at Big Blue," *Business Week*, February 15, 1988, 92.

41. "Detroit Has Little Choice but to Downshift," *Business Week*, December 7, 1987, 62.

42. J. E. Ullmann, "See What You Made Me Do," in *Private Management and Public Policy*, ed. L. R. Benton (Lexington, Mass.: Heath, 1980), 198.

43. "Detroit has Little Choice," *Business Week*, 62.

44. Consumers Union of the U.S., *Passenger Car Design and Highway Safety* (Mount Vernon, N.Y.: Consumers Union, 1962).

45. "What Ended VW's American Dream," *Business Week*, December 7, 1987, 63.

46. Tsurumi, "U.S. Trade Deficit," 218-22.

47. These problems have been extensively reported in congressional investigations and news articles. For a summary, see Melman, *Profits*, 213, 217-19.

48. A. E. Fitzgerald, *The High Priests of Waste* (New York: W. W. Norton, 1972).

49. Ullmann, *American Industrial Recovery*, 192-95.

50. J. E. Ullmann, "Managerial and Quality Constraints in SDI," *IEEE Science and Technology*, March 1987, 15.

51. Cited in "Stopping the Incredible Rise in Weapons Costs," *Business Week*, February 19, 1972, 60-61.

52. Cited in A. T. Marlin, "Dragging Down the Economy," *Washington Star*, January 21, 1981.

CAPITAL INPUT

3

DEFINITIONS AND MEASUREMENT

The problems of quantifying capital input are at least as daunting as those concerning output of products. In this volume, capital input is considered in relation to labor productivity, that is, the basic measure considered is spending for plant and equipment (capital spending) per employee, measured in constant dollars (CDSC/E). This is based on the rather self-evident fact that in a factory system the output depends on the tools that are being provided for the workers. Especially because strictly worker-paced operations are diminishing as automation becomes more comprehensive, capital spending is an important indication of managerial concern over, or commitment to, the industry at issue. The nature and trends of capital spending are thus clearly crucial.

Capital spending in a given year is not the same as capital input, as it is defined in the literature. In a standard work on the subject, Bela Gold defines capital input (CI) of an enterprise or industry as a quasi-inventory relationship:

CI = (invested capital at beginning of year) + (additions, i.e., new investments in the year) - (depreciation for the year)

Ideally, such a measure, divided into output, should provide an indicator of capital productivity—the quantity of output per dollar of invested capital. This, however, is so difficult to derive that some writers have proposed simply using the comventional monetary return on investment instead.[1]

The problem stems from the fact that meaningful numbers for the three terms in the formula for CI are difficult to get; the first and third term, especially, are so manipulable that their meaning in terms of actual operations is very unclear. A general problem is simply that they reflect management actions and policies over many years and that therefore, in their totals, they combine amounts that are subject to great variation in the effects of inflation. Especially in capital equipment, this has been a major factor, and therefore long-term phenomena that consist of combining dollars of ever shrinking size are not useful for operational analysis, as distinct from bookkeeping purposes.

The third term presents even more far-reaching problems. Depreciation is determined by the depreciation methods used (e.g., straight line or sum of the years' digits) and the time over which the asset is written off. Investment credits also affect the total. All these have changed drastically over the years. Multiple methods may be used in the same enterprise because of grandfather clauses in tax laws and flexibility in the laws themselves. And the depreciation periods themselves went from short periods to longer ones, then were shortened again, and most recently lengthened once more.

During World War II, factories being built for wartime purposes were granted certificates of necessity, allowing them to be written off over five years. Later, depreciation periods were greatly extended, as set forth in Bulletin F of the Internal Revenue Service. This, as amended, was the rule at the beginning of the study period of this volume. Then, in 1981, the laws were changed again, substantially cutting write-off periods and, indeed, allowing some assets to be expensed (i.e., charged to the current year), where previously they had been subject to write-off over a longer time. The Tax Reform Act of 1986 repealed several of these concessions.

In addition, the capital-intensive industries particularly have long argued in favor of letting depreciation allowances be charged up to replacement cost, rather than to recovery of original costs. The reason is that a basic assumption in depreciation does not hold when a firm cannot, so to speak, replace or perpetuate itself through charging off its equipment as it uses it up. Opponents have taken the view that, especially given technological changes and the long actual (as opposed to accounting) life of industrial equipment, it would be next to impossible to define what constitutes replacement rather than a new and improved plant. In practical terms, there is little industrial equipment that is ever replaced exactly in kind. Although replacement-cost accounting has often been put forward as a desirable option for business—by, among others, such prestigious professional bodies as the Financial Accounting Standards Board (FASB)—it is not allowed in accounting for tax purposes, and the latter are usually what determine accounting practice.

It is, in fact, important to recognize that depreciation is a creature of the tax laws and, specifically, of the income tax laws. The Tax Reform Act of 1986 again tightened standards somewhat, but because it also cut the marginal tax rate, these probably had, in the main, a minor effect. In any case, these changes came after the period of the present study.

The effect of all the above changes was to turn depreciation (i.e., the third term in the expression for CI) from what is still sometimes called a fixed expense into a regulated one. Firms can and do follow policies that will fulfill certain objectives in profit and loss statements, tax liability, etc. Moreover, the first term in the formula for CI is the invested capital at the beginning of the year, and that, in turn, is the direct result of years of such accounting and thus subject to the same kinds of adjustments.

From the viewpoint of capital investment analysis, however, there is a still more serious issue: whatever money valuation is placed on a firm's fixed assets says little or nothing as to their operational quality. Put simply, some assets are being depreciated in their regular way but are really obsolete, even though still used. Writing them off before time may make sense technically and economically, but not financially. Other equipment, having been subjected under the law to quick depreciation, is, in effect, carried at zero in the balance sheet but is a real and valuable piece of property. Especially given the lagging pace of investment in new plant in many industries, there must be a great deal of this "zero capital" about.

In the face of these problems of valuation versus reality, it seems most appropriate to measure investment in a given industry by annual spending on plant and equipment. True, these expenses show sharp fluctuations in many industries; in some, a major expansion by a large firm skews the record badly for the year in which the firm chooses to pay for the new items, because that is the year to which they are charged. Such problems may, however, be substantially reduced by working with long-term trends; these have the effect of damping sharp fluctuations from year to year. This has been done here, and the later discussion of individual industries focuses on constant dollar capital spending per employee (CDCS/E), specifically on its trend over time, rather than on absolute value.

There is an even more important reason for choosing this measure. The interest of managements in sustaining, improving, or expanding their operations in a given industry is determined by many factors of policy and corporate objectives, but surely a central "bottom line" measure is what they are willing to invest, how much money they are willing to funnel into a particular kind of production system year by year. Fixed investments are necessarily acts of faith with long-term implications, and there is no clearer indication of such faith than in what is being invested.

It is an even more significant mark of confidence when the *rate of change* of capital investment in constant dollars (CDCS) shows a rising or positive trend. The reported expenditures for plant and equipment in each industry were deflated by a price index as closely related as possible to the equipment used by the industry. If not available, the ones for producers' durable goods were used instead.

Obtaining a measure of the capital resources available to the employees of the industry then suggests a focus on the rate of change in capital spending in constant dollars *per employee* (CDCS/E). The rates of change of CDCS/E for each industry are thus the principal result of the quantitative analyses that underlie this chapter and are presented later, in the discussion of the individual industry groups. A falling rate suggests a lesser commitment than does one that has been rising. The measure makes sense from another viewpoint as well: Throughout much of industrial development, human labor has been automated out of existence at ever increasing rates. It is thus logical that, in the long run, the remaining employees should be furnished with capital equipment at a rising *rate*.

This is not to say that such a measure is fully reliable when reviewed on an industry-wide basis. There are still two problems. The first is simply that where firms have gone through an intensive period of investment, new construction, and equipment, they can probably and very properly coast along for a while; certainly, in such a case, there would be little reason for insisting on a rising trend in the following years as an indication of commitment. In the present study, this is most important because intensive new development took place before the study period. Unfortunately, this is true of a number of industries; by 1967, as the result of the financial stringency imposed by the needs of the Vietnam War, industrial investment was down compared with the activity in the 1950s, when such industries as petrochemicals, primary metals, petroleum refining, and many other capital-intensive industries saw a great deal of new development. Such changes are reflected in what may well be lower rates during the study period. Wherever possible, this is considered in the comments on the results for the individual industry groups.

A second caveat concerns the *nature* of investment, that is, the kinds of plant and equipment on which manufacturing industries have spent their money. For example, in recent years firms have concentrated on putting in computer systems which, in turn, may not have had much of an impact on manufacturing operations as such. Rather, they served to expedite clerical work in the offices and, to the extent that they were successful, may well have reduced total costs. Note that it is the *kind* of computer system that would have to be at issue here, so that a measure such as, for example, the share of computer sales in total machinery sales would not, of itself, shed much light on the effects on productivity in manufacturing as such. The construction of elaborate corporate headquarters also enjoyed a boom during the study period; how much that contributed to productivity in a given case is perhaps an even more debatable point.

Finally, one must note the alternative of using energy input as a surrogate for some measure of capital equipment utilization. For a long time, growth in the use of energy, especially electric power, was considered the hallmark of progress in production systems. As labor costs rose more rapidly than power costs, which were actually declining in real terms until the end of the 1960s, substitution of kilowatts for labor-hours was an obvious and rational strategy for managements. When energy costs began to soar, this substitution became much more questionable; in fact, there were concerns that human labor would have to be brought back, as its costs declined relative to power.

However, this did not happen, mainly because when it came down to cases, the issue was not one of having workers instead of machines doing the actual jobs where most of the power was used. Those cases also were usually the ones where no conceivable human labor could do the job. Rather, the advantages of automation were at the *control stages* of industrial processes, and these increasingly computerized systems did not themselves use significant quantities of electric power in comparison with the "business end" of the process.

There was, in any case, so much opportunity to redesign plants in order to save energy that such attempts to bring on "more hard work for our sins" were limited and short-lived. Energy saving, however, created other burdens on capital spending, as did the need to cope with often badly overdue environmental regulations. Such expenditures began to be called "defensive," with the word taking on an ever more pejorative tone. Yet it should have been a source of satisfaction to managements rather than a burden that they were able to overcome these difficulties, using methods that, especially in energy conservation, often paid for themselves quickly.

THE STRUCTURE OF MANUFACTURING

The kind of investment that must be made in manufacturing operations depends on whether an industry turns out bulk products or piece parts. The former group includes basic metals, textiles, paper, cement, chemicals, and petroleum products; the latter includes clothing, automobiles, machines and machine parts, appliances, books, and many other items. Some bulk products are eventually sold to the public as packages carrying brand names and then become more like piece parts, but the distinction turns in part on the kind of plant in which they are made.

There are two basic ways of organizing a manufacturing system: mass-production systems and job shops, also known as product layouts and process layouts. Most bulk products are made in highly specialized mass-production systems that usually turn out a narrowly defined product line, although, as in the case of textiles, the system may make possible a considerable variation in design details. Piece parts are also often mass produced, as in automobiles and appliances, but also make wide use of job shops. These are facilities that usually group unit operations by type, as appropriate for the industry, with a wide variety of products shuttling between the different operations as they are required in the particular case. Thus machine shops may have all lathes together in one department, all grinders together, all heat treatment, and so on.

These different ways of organizing production also have implications for productivity. Mass-production systems tend to be relatively much more capitalized than job shops. The industries that are usually regarded as capital intensive are nearly always mass-production industries as well. Mass-production systems sacrifice flexibility for efficiency in that the product flows right through the system, using most or all of the stages of manufacturing built into it, thus reducing idle time and internal transport of material beyond the minimum necessary. For the most part, one is therefore able to offer a technically meaningful estimate of system capacity, such as x tons a day for a steel works or a paper or cement mill. Capacity utilization (i.e., the amount actually turned out as a proportion of the feasible) is then also definable.

In a job shop, on the other hand, what is turned out depends on the operations required for a particular product, and this varies greatly. There is thus some built-in idleness in the system in that some operations may not be required for a particular job and others may have to wait because one particular machine or unit in the plant is overloaded with work. Clearly, that puts a drag on labor productivity, but this is simply unavoidable as long as the job shop remains reasonably busy. The capacity of job shops is therefore hard to define.

Economy of scale is another issue here, especially in the mass production of bulk products. It is not only that equipment as such often has economy of scale, in that a larger unit has a lower first cost per unit of capacity or output than a smaller one, but also that the cost is the same whether a worker pushes a start button on a large system, which controls itself thereafter, or on a small one. Obviously, however, there are limits here. The mathematical relationship found most appropriate to describe economy of scale has the characteristic that a given cut in unit costs of a certain percentage can be attained only by doubling the size of the production unit.[2] If this cannot be justified by the market for the product, then economy of scale comes to an end as a way of improving productivity.

THE RESULTS

In the discussion of individual industries that follows, their needs are closely related to these categories, distinctions and resulting needs. The numerical results for the rate of change of CDCS/E are given in the right-hand column of the Appendix. Together with the results for CDVAM/E in the left column, the table will also serve as a basis for discussing the relationships between these two measures at the end of this chapter.

Food and Kindred Products (SIC 20)

The forty-four industries in this major group have experienced wide variation in rates of change of CDCS/E. As the Appendix shows, there are six industries (13.6 percent) with negative rates and another six with rates below 1 percent. On the other hand, twenty-two, or one-half, of the industries had rates of increase greater than that of constant dollar GNP (2.8 percent).

The two highest rates are to be found in the malt industry (SIC 2083) (13.9 percent) and in wet corn milling (SIC 2046). Other high rates of between 9 and 9.5 percent appear in macaroni and spaghetti (SIC 2098), rice milling (SIC 2044), and vegetable oil mills, n.e.c. (SIC 2076).

The variation in these results reflects the diversity of this industry. Since much of its investment in capital equipment has been related to automation, the degree to which the industry has been able to resort to it has likewise varied greatly among its constituents. Some parts, especially those making highly processed foods and food specialties, are still labor intensive. Others, like cereal products or fats and oils, resemble chemical processing operations, with highly automated, specialized production systems having a low labor content; such industries might be expected to have a relatively high rate of capital spending, but there is substantial variation even within that group, depending no doubt on its market fortunes.

By the nature of their product, many food industries turn out a bulk product, but very few manufactured foods, outside of service counters, are sold in bulk form. They are packaged either by manufacturers themselves or by retailers, in order to facilitate checkouts at the supermarket. This gives them the characteristics of piece parts, the decisive element in materials handling design for manufacturers as well as in distribution.

The industry also covers a wide range along the classification of job shop and mass production. Obviously, much of it is the latter, but job shops or other small operations are frequently found in the manufacture of private label brands, in baked goods, and in other areas where small businesses are still common.

Given this diversity in production systems and products, it is not surprising to note that some food industries have seen high rates of investment, especially shortly before the period of the current study, and that this has continued, to a degree. One example is the poultry industry (SIC 2015), which has extensively automated and was thus able to sustain the boom in the consumption of chicken products that has drastically changed the entire meat industries. Its expansion sustained the economies of many once distressed farm areas where the poultry business had been on a much more modest scale.

The meatpacking industry (SIC 2011) also saw intensive automation, beginning in the late 1950s and continuing intermittently since then. However, the effects have not been especially salubrious. The industry has long had a bad reputation for safety and for working conditions in general. In 1905, in his novel *The Jungle*, Upton Sinclair stirred the public with his graphic descriptions of the abuses and filth prevalent in meatpacking. As often happens in industries that provide a miserable environment for their workers, the product itself came to share in the misery and squalor of the factories.

The new machines have their troubles too. As a news report in the summer of 1987 put it, workers were still being "sliced and crushed by machines that were not even invented" in Sinclair's time.[3] Losses of fingers and other bad accidents were common, especially as a result of excessive fatigue on assembly lines which, as in earlier times of poor working conditions, were periodically speeded up. Worst of all, simple safety devices for keeping workers' hands away from moving parts, such as had long been familiar in other kinds of equipment like metal presses, had not been provided. All this, together with poor labor relations resulting in protracted strikes, made the industry a highly troubled one. Certainly, it had the highest accident rate in manufacturing.

Another factor is the wave of mergers, consolidations, and takeovers to which the whole food industry has been subjected during the past twenty years. As it happens, meatpacking was a conspicuous example, as the erstwhile Big Four—Armour, Swift, Wilson, and Cudahy—were merged and shuttled about and rearranged into other groupings. Such changes also came to other parts of the food industry, as in the constant shufflings, purchases, and sales of the divisions of such firms as General Foods and Beatrice Foods, and the dismantling and liquidation of the latter, very much to the profit of the investors who had bought it four years previously.

From this viewpoint of capital investment, this often resulted in the diversion of funds from potential modernizations of plants, to financial maneuverings. In addition, mergers in some industries, such as breweries, have resulted in a consolidation of production facilities. The new owners typically had several plants, some old and some new. It was then often possible to concentrate production in the new plants and close the old ones. The new ones were then able to operate at higher capacity. This is a very significant cost saving in highly capitalized industries, where the variable costs of production are often very low relative to the fixed costs.

Tobacco Products (SIC 21)

The well-known market troubles of the tobacco industries, notably cigarettes (SIC 2111), have been reflected in the typical changes that occur when a highly automated industry is faced with trends that cut the degree of capacity utilization. Diseconomy of scale then quickly produces higher costs that must be passed along in higher prices if profit margins are to be maintained. As noted in chapter 2, prices have in fact doubled, in part because of a doubling of the federal excise tax, but for operating reasons as well.

Still, the cigarette industry shows a relatively high annual growth rate in CDCS/E (10.81 percent) over the study period. The industry is highly capitalized, and cigarette-making machines have long been among the most sophisticated high-speed mechanisms. By 1987, the industry was considering changing to even higher speed machines, and automation had, for some time, been steadily coming to cutting, drying, and blending, which used to be done by hand.

However, the limits of economy of scale were eventually clear. Except for the industry leaders, Philip Morris and R. J. Reynolds, which have about 70 percent of the market between them, the firms are down to single plants where really major economies are no longer feasible.[4] The high rate of investment thus represents large programs, notably by the industry leaders, which, even for them, appear to have reached their practical limits.

Textile Mill Products (SIC 22)

The textile industries are, as noted in chapter 2, a particularly beleaguered group in their markets. The industry has nevertheless had periods of intensive capital investment, especially in the late 1960s and early 1970s. One problem was, however, that the textile machine industry (SIC 3552), which is discussed in more detail in its major group, lost the technical superiority that it had enjoyed for a long time. The result was that the textile industry has come to rely almost exclusively on foreign suppliers for introducing such modern equipment as shuttleless looms and ringless spindles. But these, as well as computer aids in controls and manufacturing in general, have given it a modest, though by no means decisive, advantage over its international competitors. The industry's capital investments have been so extensive that in many product lines it is competitive, especially given the anemic dollar. Textiles retain a large domestic market that benefits from the extremely high speeds of modern equipment. That, in turn, reduces labor time per unit of output and thus diminishes the key advantage of the foreign competitors.

Nevertheless, as the Appendix indicates, the *rate* of change of CDCS/E in 1967–81 slowed down and turned negative for eighteen out of the twenty-seven industries in this group for which consistent data are available (66.7 percent). Three industries (11.1 percent), broad-woven fabrics of cotton (SIC 2211), knit underwear mills (SIC 2254), and felt goods except hats (SIC 2291), increased more than 2.8 percent. Of the remaining six industries, five had rates between 0 and 1 percent. This industry group clearly slowed down very much in its rate of investment. In two of its constituent industries, carpets and rugs, n.e.c. (SIC 2279), a small industry, and in the larger tire cord and fabric industry (SIC 2296), investment appears to have come to a virtual halt. Volume declined in the latter after the mid-1970s as longer-lasting steel-belted radial tires took an ever larger share of the market.

Apparel and Fabricated Textile Products (SIC 23)

This is the largest industry group in which individual operators working on individual machines are still the rule in the majority of constituent industries. As a result, capital spending tends to be low. A further element here is the rapid turnover of firms, as a result of which there is a large market in second-hand equipment available at reasonable cost to firms that enter the industry. Some sewing operations done on a very large scale, such as underwear manufacture or standardized pockets, have been automated to some extent. However, fabrics are not rigid and therefore cannot be oriented and presented to the work heads of sewing machines with the kinds of feeds possible, say, in metalworking. This has put a severe limitation on automation and thus on the prospect of using machinery to replace labor. Thus the industry must still be considered very sensitive to labor cost and to the pressures to seek ever cheaper labor, as discussed in the last chapter.

The trends in capital spending, as given by CDCS/E in the Appendix, show a very wide range. It has been increasing sharply in some industries, with seven out of the thirty (23.3 percent) for which complete data were available having rates of increase of 4 percent or more. However, twelve (40.0 percent) had negative rates and a further six had rates between 0 and 1 percent. Therefore, though there are more positive readings than in the textile group, the results for the apparel industry show a very mixed picture.

Lumber and Wood Products (SIC 24)

The technology underlying this industry has not changed much for a long time and changed very little in the study period. One noteworthy change is that the number of establishments has been declining for a long time, whereas output has increased, thus reflecting an increase in scale of enterprises and an attempt to realize the economies presented as a result.[5] However, the equipment that can be used in removing felled trees is determined by the tree diameters. Huge skid-grapples are pointless when the trees have small diameters, as often happens, especially in forests whose output is destined for pulp and particle board manufacture. This is because the trees are grown in "tree farms" where a rapid harvest cycle is the usual practice. This natural characteristic of the industry's raw material thus determines the nature and ultimately the extent of its capital investments.

Another issue of interest is the fact that, for this industry, production facilities must follow the raw material supply. Saw mills and similar facilities are thus, to some extent, not expected to remain permanently on one site, falling into disuse once the supply is exhausted. The high costs of modern facilities, however, with their heavy equipment, have made this practice uneconomical and have for some time made imperative the systematic reforesting of cut-over lands. Even so, small operations especially do not look that far ahead, and deeply distressed or abandoned communities in lumber-producing regions are still often found. Typically, such perils depress worker morale, as the central anxiety of the workers must necessarily be the rate at which they literally work themselves out of their jobs.

Unfortunately, the extensive redefinitions in the SIC in 1972 considerably reduced the available rates for this industry group. Still, it is possible to note that the softwood processing industries—like logging camps and contractors (whose volume is mainly in softwoods) (SIC 2411), softwood sawmills (SIC 2421), and softwood veneer and plywood (SIC 2436)—had relatively high rates of increase. Wood preserving (SIC 2491), which likewise deals mainly with softwoods, also had a high rate; it had to be reequipped to use new preservatives that largely replaced the time-honored creosote. By contrast, hardwood dimension and flooring mills (SIC 2426) and hardwood veneer and plywood (SIC 2435) had negative rates.

This no doubt reflects the not very encouraging experience of the industry with hardwoods. There is a great deal of hardwood in the forests of the United States, but much of it is of poor quality since the original, high-quality trees were not properly replaced. In the 1950s, there was much interest in using this resource, especially the large tracts in the South, for various purposes, especially for pulp and particle board. However, as discussed further in the next section, this proved to be an expensive proposition, and thus the utilization of hardwoods did not come up to earlier expectations.

Furniture and Fixtures (SIC 25)

The equipment for this group varies greatly, from hand tools and small portable woodworking machines that differ little, if at all, from those used by do-it-yourselfers, to job shops and mass production plants that use heavy machinery. This variation is dictated by the nature of the products and the markets they serve. In several constituents of this major group, there are large numbers of small workshops that primarily do custom work; they are typical, for example, of wood and metal partitions, shelving, lockers, and office and store fixtures (SIC 2541 and 2542). Even in such large industries as wood furniture (SIC 2511, 2512, and 2521), custom shops or other small batch production units coexist with large plants. Sometimes the products are made on large machines and standardized assembly rigs that form the centerpiece of a factory, but economy of scale is limited so that one or two units can assure an adequate output. This too allows wide variation in plant size; mattresses (SIC 2515) are an example.

In other industries, there may be relatively small production establishments, but their products are standardized and made in large quantities. Drapery hardware, which is part of SIC 2591, would be an example. The rest of this industry, which makes window blinds and shades, does a lot of custom work, but even this consists mainly of cutting standard components to special sizes.

The equipment itself has benefited from the redesign of electric motors that made them smaller and more compact for given power output; this was described in the discussion of electrical machinery in the previous chapter. Since the 1950s, moreover, the industry has made use of so-called high-cycle motors for which the periodicity of AC is changed from 60 to 400 cycles, i.e., to the standard used in aircraft. For woodworking this has the great advantage that the maximum speed of the cutting heads is increased from slightly below

3,600 revolutions per minute to close to 24,000. This uses less power, works more quickly, and produces a better finish. The change from rotating machinery to electronic means of making this frequency change has also been beneficial, but so far the method has been confined to larger machines or to factories that could justify a separate 400-cycle distribution system.

Like many other industries, furniture making also uses a lot more plastic products, though these tend to be bought as supplies rather than made in the establishments themselves. The industry has also changed—some would say downgraded—its products by replacing plywood plus veneer with particle board covered by adhesive coated vinyl made to look like wood. From the viewpoint of equipment, however, there is little difference; conventional veneer presses can be replaced by simple benches with roller-dispenser equipment, and as to particle board, it owes its success to the fact that it can be worked easily with existing woodworking machinery.

The results in the Appendix show the two industries that make office furniture (SIC 2521 and 2522) with particularly high rates of increase in CDCS/E, reflecting the market growth in those industries. The rest of the eleven industries for which complete data could be obtained show more modest changes, with two negative entries (mattresses and wood partitions) and two more, upholstered furniture (SIC 2512) and metal partitions, with rates between 0 and 1 percent.

Paper and Allied Products (SIC 26)

The main point of interest concerning capital spending in this industry is that the paper manufacturing end of it is an almost classical case of the use of economy of scale. The basic process of the Fourdrinier machines has changed little since the machines were invented. A pulp-water mixture is poured onto a screen belt where it drains and is then taken off into an elaborate set of drying rolls. There have been some improvements in the form of electronic controls of web alignment and moisture and temperature, but these are by no means universal.[6] For many years it was taken for granted that the total number of Fourdrinier machines would not increase much and that instead the machines would only grow bigger. Indeed, the "going rate" of output of Fourdrinier machines went from twenty to fifty tons a day in the late 1940s to three hundred to five hundred tons a day at present. Small units still survive here and there for making specialty papers; as noted, this is feasible because the overall technology has changed so little.

This trend in the paper industry is quite similar to what used to hold true for electric power plants where it was observed that the size of the units being installed used to double about every ten years, reflecting an increase in consumption of about 7.5 percent a year. The overall number of power plants and generating units hardly increased at all.

A second area of at least attempted change was the industry's perennial desire to use hardwood pulp more extensively. Where this has been successfully implemented, the industry is able to use relatively low grade woods, like Southern post oak, which took over some of the forests after the primeval growth had been cut down and quality replantings neglected. The problem is primarily that making hardwood pulp requires more intensive chemical treatment and thus increases the potential for pollution, which is already a major problem for pulp and paper makers.

This industry has also long been struggling with a little noted, but important industrial problem. Wood consists of cellulosic fibers held together by a natural plastic material called lignin. This has traditionally been disposed of or burned during the manufacture of pulp, which is essentially the cellulosic material. It would be very useful if a more productive use could be found for this material. At least it now serves more extensively as plant fuel, rather than being burned off unproductively as in times before energy prices soared. Being able to use lignin as a base for new kinds of plastics that do not depend on petroleum feed stocks would be a welcome opportunity for this industry.

The results for the rate of change of CDCS/E for this major group show particularly high rates of increase for the two most capital-intensive constituents, paper mills (SIC 2621) and paperboard mills (SIC 2631). A sharp decline is recorded for pressed and molded pulp goods (SIC 2646), a relatively small industry much beset by competition from plastic foam. The remaining rates range from slightly negative to slightly positive.

Printing, Publishing, and Allied Industries (SIC 27)

As noted in chapter 2, this industry saw drastic changes in its equipment during the study period as long-established mechanical methods were replaced by electro-mechanical or electronic ones.

Also as noted in chapter 2, this resulted in discontinuities in productivity statistics. In capital spending, however, the industry has experienced both positive and negative trends which, in the main, give it relatively low rates of CDCS/E. On the one hand, some intensively capitalized industries like newspapers were consolidating, which often meant shutdowns of plants and more intensive usage of those remaining. Although the changes were most conspicuous in typesetting and pre-press operations generally, presses gained improved speeds with less weight, thus saving energy as well as worker time. This helped justify investment at a rising rate even at times of consolidations. There was also more automation in binding, handling, and mailing, so that these aspects of the industry have also had advantages from the new equipment.[7]

In general, the new equipment, though costly, benefited greatly from the decline in the prices of electronic equipment generally and computers in particular. Such operations as photocomposition, electronic scanning of color film, electronic pagination of page layouts, and laser plate making were all affected by these trends. Photoengraving (SIC 2793) and especially electrotyping and stereotyping (SIC 2794), which has the highest rate of increase of CDCS/E in this major group, were strong beneficiaries of these trends. So was miscellaneous publishing (SIC 2741) which, at an accelerating rate, is making use of computerized desktop publishing, for which ever more versatile software has been developed. Prices for this kind of equipment have been falling, however, so that a sizeable but still relatively modest rate of increase in CDCS/E (4.2 percent) buys a great deal of new equipment.

These positive changes were not universal, however. As the appendix shows, of the thirteen industries for which consistent data could be obtained, four (30.8 percent) have negative rates of change of CDCS/E, and two more are between 0 and 1 percent.

Chemicals and Allied Products, Except Plastics
(SIC 28, Except 282)

This industry is capital-intensive and has been so from its beginnings; much of the industrial instrumentation having to do with measurement and control of temperature, pressure, and flow of materials originated with the suppliers of capital equipment to this industry. The integration of such measurements in complex control systems for entire plants or processing units likewise originated here.

In particular, integrated computer controls for whole processes were first developed for the chemical industry and similar operations for petroleum refining.

A second important element is that for much of this industry, economy of scale is decisive. This was noted in chapter 2 in connection with labor productivity, but it holds equally true in equipment purchases. This has the effect that the statistics on capital spending are especially volatile. In many parts of this industry group, large firms dominate output shares anyway, so that decisions taken by a very few enterprises, or by a single major participant, can affect statistics drastically, in both directions.

The industry is affected not merely by decisions to expand, but also by decisions to contract. Major production facilities have been consolidated in response to market needs. These are often still serviceable and would be viable were it not for corporate decisions made for reasons other than operational efficiency of the affected plants. These need not be arbitrary on the part of the managements; as in so many other industries, competition from imports or from alternative products may dictate contraction, just as the opposite may prompt expansion. The experiences of this industry, especially in a time of general industrial decline, illustrate the point made at the outset of this chapter that financial valuations of fixed assets often have little to do with their practical usefulness.

Several parts of this major group have been at the forefront of technical progress and have required constant infusions of new capital equipment. Indeed, some industries—like alkalies and chlorine (SIC 2812), which turned in a lackluster performance during the study period—saw much better times in the 1940s and 1950s when substantial new capacity was built. New processes and materials replaced the time-honored Solvay process; thus, soda ash began to be made more simply and cheaply from trona ore (sodium sesquicarbonate), which is found in huge deposits in California and Wyoming. In this and similar cases, the very size of the production units, both old and new, resulted in the assurance that any changes would necessarily be very substantial and come in large doses.

One of the most noteworthy new technologies came about in the pharmaceutical industry, where the mass production of antibiotics called for entirely new ways of manufacture. Indeed, the mass production of complex drugs is the most conspicuous example of scientific and technical innovation in this major group, as it has been defined here. At the same time, the industry also has the task of producing drugs for the treatment of relatively rare diseases, that is, drugs that will never have a true mass market, as do tranquilizers or major antibiotics. In such work, the industry often claims to be acting in a sort of *pro bono* capacity, but whatever the merits of this claim, the small-scale production of such items introduces something of a job shop characteristic into what otherwise tends to be a mass-production industry.

The industry is actually rather adept at making its production systems flexible within the possible scientific limits. In part this is because the manufacture of nonprescription drugs, especially, often only involves buying the active or other ingredients from specialized manufacturers, with the remaining operations consisting mainly of such operations as blending, pill pressing, and packaging. In that area, the industry suffered a severe setback in the rash of cases in which capsules were poisoned; caplets, which are essentially sealed capsules, have largely replaced capsules in the nonprescription drug field.

Packaging is also a major part of the job to be done in some other instances, as in the manufacturing processes of industries like soap and toiletries (SIC 284) and other household products. In general, when a bulk product is put up in packages, significant piece parts characteristics are introduced to an industry that otherwise concentrates on bulk products.

Turning to the recorded changes in CDCS/E in the Appendix, the results range from a negative reading for adhesives and gelatin (SIC 2891), which had seen rapid expansion in the 1950s and early 1960s, to substantial rates of investment in industries like fertilizer mixing (SIC 2875) (9.8 percent) and surface active agents (SIC 2843) (8.8 percent). It is noteworthy that these industries also rank second and first, respectively, in CDVAM/E of chemicals and allied products except plastics.

Petroleum Refining and Related Industries (SIC 29)

This is a highly capital-intensive industry whose profits, because of this, are also very vulnerable to diminished capacity utilization. The great disturbances in the raw material supply of this industry have also been reflected in its capital investments. The industry had long enjoyed favorable treatment in its import quotas and tax, depreciation, and depletion laws, at least until the oil shock in 1973. Still, responding to the new conditions it quickly embarked on a major expansion of refinery capacity. The number of operable refineries increased from 277 in 1973 to 324 in 1981 and capacity increased by 36 percent.[8] However, when the surplus developed and prices fell, so did the number of refineries; over 100 of them were closed, but since these were often smaller or older plants, capacity fell by only 13 percent. Such shutdowns are costly, but refinery output can only be varied within a limited range. Below that it is a matter of essentially deciding either to run at what may be too high a rate for the market or to shut down altogether. In closing these units, the industry sought to preserve economies of scale for those refineries remaining, even though keeping these going at what appears to be a break-even point of about 75 percent of capacity proved difficult in some areas.[9]

The CDCS/E trends are thus quite low, though they do show an increase. They reflect not a single trend, however, but rather an increase followed by a decline. An exception is the high rate for petroleum and coal products, n.e.c. (SIC 2999), but this is a small industry where a major expansion by one sector can easily appear large in otherwise limited activity.

Much of the technology of refining is well known; the last main process innovations mostly had to do with the production and formulation of gasoline. They were put forth in World War II and the late 1940s and were quickly incorporated in the many new plants that were built in the 1950s.

In the more difficult times of the energy shortage, however, there was one conspicuous failure related to capital facilities and process development. It was the Synthetic Fuels Corporation, a government entity that was supposed to develop a process for producing liquid fuel from coal. It was to offer only loan guarantees but was eventually forced to give price supports. Yet its synthetic fuel cost about $67 a barrel whereas oil was below $30. Major private firms refused to participate, and the large amounts of money earmarked were wasted on studies and on a few contracts that quickly became mired in cost overruns, product failures, general mismanagement, and allegations of conflicts of interest that were more reminiscent of weapons contracts than of industrial projects.[10] The project expired in 1985.

This project attracted much adverse attention, but meanwhile the industry had another major problem related to its capital equipment. It was one of the industry groups most seriously affected by environmental concerns, as well as by the need to save energy in its own operations. By and large, the industry had been laggard in both, in spite of constant public relations efforts to show the contrary. Oil refining and allied operations can generate a multitude of toxins, including carcinogens, and the industry was long a major culprit in causing the smogs that beset major metropolitan areas; Los Angeles was, perhaps, the clearest case. Much of the capital investment in the latter part of the study period, therefore, had to do with environmental protection and energy conservation.

As noted in chapter 1, this is sometimes criticized as "defensive" expenditure, but many conservation projects, particularly, paid for themselves in operating savings and thus helped to increase value added by manufacture. Moreover, since much of this equipment called for little or no added labor input, CDVAM/E was increased as well. Of course, as noted in chapter 2, the overall trends were negative in most of this industry group, but without the response to the changed operating and cost conditions they might have been even worse.

Rubber and Plastics Products (SIC 282 and 30)

As noted earlier, these are capital-intensive industries essentially in the category of chemical processes. Like others similarly situated, part of this industry group's obligations in capital investment consisted of meeting environmental regulations and implementing energy conservation. In some respects, their environmental problems are even worse than those of petroleum refining. Many of the firms are relatively small and thus, judging from news reports, are often involved in the illegal dumping of wastes or of surplus product. The environmental problems of some of these industries often involve odors, as well as other air or water pollution; the rubber tire industries are perhaps the best examples.

These industries, moreover, tend to deal with solids rather than liquids, as is the case with petroleum refining and its allied industries. Because much of the work consists of mass-produced items like tires, plastic bottles, and many other large-volume items, these are industries that support, or try to benefit from, much research in materials handling (meaning the transportation of piece parts between work stations) and in the integration of materials handling with actual production processes. Capital intensity is thus often combined with the use of rather sophisticated automatic machinery. Major work had to be done during the period of this study in order to make feasible the mass production of steel-belted radial tires and to further refine and speed up the production of plastic products.

The industry is therefore much given to seeking advantage from economy of scale. Major machines, like those making tires or plastic moldings, have steadily increased their working speeds and cycling times. One measure of this shows a rapid rise in pounds of raw materials used per establishment in the plastics fabricating industry (SIC 3079); from 1958 to 1972, it had been increasing at a rate of 10.3 percent a year, reaching a level of 1,390,000 pounds per establishment in the latter year.[11]

This is a high tonnage, especially in an industry that, as noted before, has quite a few small establishments. These tend to make small runs and specialty products, but tooling in the form of dies and molds is expensive, so that even small runs tend to have substantial setup costs.

In the CDCS/E statistics, the available data show a declining rate from 1967 to 1982 for tires and inner tubes (SIC 3011) and reclaimed rubber (SIC 3031). Rates also declined in the period 1972–82, except for rubber and plastic hose and belting (SIC 3041), where CDCS/E rose. In the SIC 282 group, the makers of materials, CDCS/E decreased as well.

In some respects, these results may reflect the huge capital expansion that some of these industries experienced in the 1950s and early 1960s. Later expenditures clearly were at a more modest level.

Leather and Leather Products (SIC 31)

The extensive troubles of this industry group are also reflected in its capital equipment. First, much of it is heavily dependent on labor and thus not readily amenable to automation beyond a certain stage; in this it resembles the apparel industry. Like cloth, leather is not dimensionally stable; thus even where machines do such operations as stitching or other assembly, as is usually the case, the material has to be manually loaded and oriented in the machine.

The largest constituent industries are those making footwear, and so its equipment problems merit special attention. The shoe industry is unusual among manufacturing industries in that most of the principal machines used for making a pair of shoes are leased and not owned by manufacturers. USM Corporation, formerly United Shoe Machinery Corporation, dominated the development of these machines from the early 1900s to 1955, when its exclusive leasing practices and the agreements that went with them were ruled illegal in an antitrust suit.[12]

One feature was restrictions on output and machine speed. Also required were tie-in sales of other equipment, some of which was also leased. Shoe machinery is very specialized and represents a very sophisticated kind of mechanical design which has most recently been augmented by electronic controls as well as by hydraulic power assists. By careful patent protection and international agreements, USM managed to maintain its monopoly for decades. That monopoly and its leasing practices, however, also discouraged USM from any major or drastic changes in its machines.

The innovations in equipment thus largely came from abroad, and so, as is usual for industries that rely on imported equipment, foreign manufacturers had been able to acquire the new machines earlier. For example, a cement sole attaching machine and a cement side laster both came from Europe. Another change was from the arithmetic to the geometric last, which helped decrease the number of sizes that had to be made and which made the machines easier to adjust. However, the traditional arithmetic lasts had to be discarded, a major cost that proved difficult for an industry already in severe trouble. There was also considerable resistance from powerful customers, such as department stores that were concerned over customer acceptance. As noted in chapter 2, that seems to be a growing problem, especially with women's shoes.

In all the footwear industries, including those of rubber and plastic shoes, conveyors and mechanized materials handling have long been major factors in innovation, having displaced the former tote-boxes and handcarts. Such equipment requires certain minimum volumes and thus calls for the ability to utilize at least some economy of scale. As in apparel, that is somewhat limited; even though shoe making machines are far more complex than sewing machines, they are still, in the main, paced by individual operators who, as noted above, must load and orient the work.

Rates of investment are seen in the Appendix to be limited, if not negative, except for leather tanning and finishing (SIC 3111). As to men's and women's shoes (SIC 3143 and 3144), data were only available from 1972 on; they indicate a rise of CDCS/E until about 1977, followed by a decline.

Stone, Clay, and Glass Products (SIC 32)

The industries in this major group vary greatly in capital intensity. Some constituents, notably cement (SIC 3241), are among those with the highest capital intensity in manufacturing, whereas others are small, local enterprises with modest capital investments that are often built around some principal machine or processing unit. Many processing steps in these industries share chemical industry technology and unit operations, notably in such items as furnaces, mixing and blending equipment, and materials handling both for bulk commodities and piece parts. Chemical research is of course crucial in the formulation of many products themselves, as for instance in ceramics, glazes, and glass.

The capital input of these industries has also been affected by the need to satisfy environmental restrictions. These became considerably more rigorous throughout the study period. It is true that many of the industries have long had environmental problems, even aside from the principal problem area of asbestos. In such early industrial regions as the English Potteries, as the Northern Midlands came to be called, air pollution from the furnaces making earthenware and china became notorious from the beginning of the Industrial Revolution onward. The valleys of Pennsylvania, where much of the American industry started, were similarly afflicted. Thus in trying to cope with what is clearly a perennial problem, a large proportion of capital expenditures during the study period reflects the need to reduce air pollution, and most of this increase was mandated by the Environmental Protection Agency.[13]

A second area of concern was energy conservation. Several major parts of this group are users of furnaces, so their thermal efficiency and possibilities of heat recovery become important considerations in plant design. Some industries, like cement, have problems both in air pollution and energy use; cement also has a dust problem that primarily affects its workers but also bothers people in the surrounding communities. A badly designed and operated cement mill can wreak extensive environmental damage. By 1980, this industry group's expenditures for environmental protection were rising at a rate of 33 percent a year, as opposed to 8 percent for all manufacturing.[14]

The annual rates of change of CDCS/E in the Appendix thus show substantial increases for a number of major industries in the group. Five of them had rates of increases for 1967–81 of 4 percent or more; they were cement (SIC 3241), brick (SIC 3251), vitreous chinaware (SIC 3262), gypsum (SIC 3275), non-metallic mineral products, n.e.c. (SIC 3299) which are mainly items made of plaster and papier mache, and asbestos (SIC 3292)—the latter being something in the nature of a last stand.

Primary Metal Industries (SIC 33)

Of all the major industry groups, this is perhaps the one that has had the most trouble with the nature of its capital input. Some industries within it, notably those in the fabrication and aluminum industries, have tried to keep up with technology changes and have been able to maintain themselves in this way. Still, the Appendix shows the trends in CDCS/E to be either negative or very low.

The largest single member of this group is the steel industry, which has had some of the worst problems. Specifically, it has failed to respond to the technical challenges posed by innovations; moreover, it has done so deliberately. According to a report by the congressional Office of Technology Assessment, the industry prefers to buy any new technology from outsiders, if at all, and believes, as the report puts it, "that the costs and risks of innovation outweigh its benefits and that it is cheaper in the long run to buy proven technology than to create it."[15]

However, such a strategy, if it can be called that, has several flaws that have cost the industry dearly. First of all, the U.S. industry has little to say on how the processes are developed, as a result of which they may appear unattractive when offered for sale. For instance, the processes may not be geared to the resource mix available to U.S. producers or to environmental and other regulatory constraints. They may thus require elaborate reworking before they can be used in the United States, but whether or not this is the case, foreign producers have installed them first and are reaping their benefits long before the American industry has bestirred itself. The U.S. industry has always claimed to know what is good and how to get it, but the OTA report puts it differently, "A uniquely domestic steelmaking knowledge cannot exist without domestic innovation based on research (basic and applied), development and demonstration that are shaped by the current needs and opportunities of domestic steelmakers."[16] Meanwhile its research spending remains among the lowest of any major industry; by contrast, its foreign competitors spend large amounts themselves and often sponsor highly successful research institutes.

One would, in short, be hard put to find another industry that neglects its future to such an extent. One could perhaps understand if the steel industry were an essentially antiquated one, but within the past forty years or so, the industry has been completely transformed technologically. The way these innovations were and are handled by the American industry makes for melancholy reading.

There were three major technological changes: the basic oxygen process, continuous casting, and direct reduction. The first two changes were badly misunderstood and tardily introduced, and the third is almost ignored by the American industry, as far as installations are concerned.

The basic oxygen process eliminated the slow and expensive open hearth furnace. Continuous casting eliminated the soaking pits and reheating operations, cut out several other steps in steel processing, and used the raw materials far more efficiently. In an industry much beset by high capital intensity, both processes also had huge savings in capital cost. The third process, direct reduction, cuts out the blast furnace and the pig iron stage and goes directly from ore to steel.

The first two processes were developed in Switzerland and Austria during World War II and were fully known to Allied industrial investigators after the war. Nevertheless, when the American industry had its biggest postwar expansion in the 1950s, these essential new methods were largely ignored, and it was a long time before they were slowly introduced. Thus, in 1983, the steel industry reported that from 26 to 30 percent of American steel was made in continuous casters and that "close to half" would be made that way by the end of the decade. But Japan was at over 50 percent in 1978 and at almost 100 percent by the mid-1980s, and the Europeans were at about the two-thirds level.[17]

Direct reduction is almost nonexistent in the United States, yet Westinghouse developed the Plasma-melt process, which is one of the best systems under development. It is also highly energy efficient; units in Europe, notably Sweden, furnish enough by-product steam and gas for district heating and cooking fuel in their communities in order to help to pay their electric bills.[18]

There are many other issues in energy use as well as in environmental protection. The American steel industry, for instance, used sulfuric acid for pickling long after others had switched to hydrochloric acid, which can be recycled and does less damage to rivers; that too had long been a standard practice in competing industries overseas. Environmental problems, in fact, have required much investment, even though the industry had long ago been forced to take steps to curb the worst air pollution. In the Pittsburgh area, for instance, serious attempts at cleanup date back to the 1940s.

Finally, the industry has rendered what is perhaps the most drastic judgment on its own capital input. In the course of reducing its capacity, it began blowing up surplus plants, even where, as in Youngstown, Ohio, there were sustained local attempts to save a large plant. One major steel complex is now protected from a similar fate only by a court injunction. In short, this is an industry *in extremis.*

Fabricated Metal Products (SIC 34)

The production facilities of this group are as diverse as its product, ranging from small custom workshops to larger job shops and to mass-production facilities that turn out items like screws and fittings of various sorts in very large quantities, indeed almost like bulk products. Several are, in essence, service activities for other branches of metalworking and are carried out in plants that center on a single set of specialized production units. Electroplating (SIC 3471) would be an example.

The troubles of its client industries, as well as import problems for some of its constituent industries, have tended to reduce interest in process innovation for this group. Nevertheless, the Appendix indicates some industries that have spent increasing amounts on capital equipment, thus giving them quite substantial rates of increase in relation to employment. Four industries—handsaws and saw blades (SIC 3425), enameled iron and metal sanitary ware (SIC 3431), iron and steel forgings (SIC 3462), and automotive stampings (SIC 3465)— had rates of increase of CDCS/E in excess of 6 percent a year. The reason was response to competitive pressures, mainly from imports in the first of these industries and, in the other three, from substitute products such as special castings or plastic parts or coatings. On the other hand, five industries had negative rates of change of CDCS/E, and another six had rates between 0 and 1 percent. These eleven industries are 31.4 percent of the thirty-five industries for which data were available.

Machinery, Except Electrical (SIC 35, Except 357)

This major group is unique in that its own metalworking section (SIC 354) provides a large share of the group's capital equipment, so that its troubles are quickly and directly transferred to its customers. Though the industry continues to spend money for capital equipment, it was noted earlier that the stock of machinery keeps getting older. New features, such as numerical controls of machine tools, are being introduced very slowly; in 1983, only 5.4 percent of all metal cutting machines and 1.8 percent of metal forming machines had numerical controls.[19]

Although some of its products are made in substantial quantities and more could be, if the product lines were rationalized effectively, the job shop is the principal mode of layout and organization of this group's production systems. The less business there is, the more its dysfunctions manifest themselves. The numerical controls, however, were supposed to reduce the high setup and tooling costs and thus bring new life to the industry.

Even higher hopes were raised by the prospect of robots, but they turned out to have what can only be called a particularly star-crossed product introduction. Robots are based on electronic controls and therefore tend to be thought of as electronic equipment. However, their "business ends"—the holding mechanisms and work stations that do the actual work—are mechanical, and it is precisely in the capability of manufacturing the fine mechanisms required that the decline of the U.S. machine tool industry has had the most severe impact. The case of robots is thus instructive not only as a market problem for the machine industry but also as an illustration of the difficulty in providing a substantial improvement of the capital stock of this entire major group.

Robots were long touted as the sort of universal new machine, incorporating new electronic sophistication—high tech—that would provide new life to the manufacture of machinery, electronic equipment, and related goods. Unfortunately, this did not happen. Robots have important niches to fill but only as parts of other major automation systems. The automobile industry turned out to be the biggest customer, especially for painting and welding, but once it had equipped itself, the market was saturated. There was little more to be done, especially given the troubled market situation of the American automobile industry. General Motors and Fanuc, the principal Japanese maker, established GMF as a joint venture. It was to supply, among other things, a very ambitious automation program for GM itself, but that had to be abandoned in 1987.

Robots were not significant quantitatively during the period of this study and only became so afterwards. By the end of 1987, however, the market almost appeared to have run its course. Unimation, a major manufacturer and part of Westinghouse, closed and turned over to Prab, a relatively small independent company, the servicing and apparently extensive reworking required to make its units in the field work properly. Westinghouse meanwhile was trying to become a sales agent for Japanese makers.

General Electric had entered the business by supplying the vision apparatus and electronic controls for Japanese units but in the fall of 1987 abandoned this business and became a sales agent for Fanuc instead. The problem with such arrangements, of course, is that foreign firms can readily set up their own distribution networks and may not need American partners at all to sell their wares. Other U.S. makers like Cincinnati Milacron or Prab are hanging on, attempting to break even.[20] For this major group, it seemed that there was no simple answer to its production problems and its increasingly antiquated stock of machinery.

Within the period of this study, the major group's own rates of spending increased slowly. As the Appendix shows, CDCS/E grew at rates that were largely negative or between 0 and 1 percent, except for SIC 357, which is discussed below. For industries in decline, this is not an unexpected result.

Electrical Machinery, Except Electronics (SIC 361–364)

As noted before, this group comprises electric transmission and distribution equipment (SIC 361), electrical industrial apparatus (SIC 362), household appliances (SIC 363), and electric lighting and wiring equipment (SIC 364). These products vary greatly in size and complexity. The group's production systems thus encompass job shops of all sizes but more particularly mass production of both complex items, like major appliances, and smaller items requiring a certain sophistication, like light bulbs, or simpler ones, like wiring devices and other electrical hardware. Such mass-production facilities are highly capital intensive and thus are vulnerable to declines in capacity utilization. This has happened both to industrial equipment, like transformers, and to major and small domestic appliances.

In chapter 2, the reasons for the relatively stagnant performance of this industry were outlined. Its capital spending, as indicated by the CDCS/E statistics, largely shows a slow or negative rate of change.

Electronic Products (SIC 357, 365–369)

The above industries make use of a considerable variety of production technology which changed more completely during the period of this study than that in almost any other group of industries. Furthermore, redefinitions of product—fully understandable under the circumstances—make consistent trends difficult to obtain.

The industry has of course invested extensively, but as the discussion in chapter 2 showed, many of the products are not made in the United States, nor were they ever. In this connection, therefore, capital requirements are often little more than what is needed for the assembly of imported subunits or major components.

At the beginning of the study period, much of manufacture still consisted of wiring discrete components together. The early machine aids to assembly, which were developed in the late 1950s, consisted of what were essentially stapling machines that attached the components to their circuit boards. By 1967, printed circuitry was much advanced, but the computer on a chip was still some time in the future. Electronic calculators with primitive one-button memories still cost about one hundred dollars in 1974. By 1981, much of the presently used technology was in place, with the first successful PC's entering the market.

It is in tooling up for chips and ever more elaborate circuitry that, as described in chapter 1, Japanese competitors have the advantage. The manufacture of chips requires extremely tight controls not only over materials but also over the printing of the circuits. Extremely fine tolerances are essential if the manufacturer is to avoid the conditions of earlier years, where it was not a matter of worrying about fractions defective of the product but of trying to increase the very small fraction of product that worked properly. In a real sense, therefore, the effective survival of the electronics component industry would depend on more favorable conditions in machine manufacturing generally. This is an important point in view of the fact that it was long considered feasible to separate the technology of making the new, high-technology products from that of making the more traditional, high-precision parts. Clearly, however, the technologies are linked much more closely than had been expected.

Motor Vehicles (SIC 371, 3751, 379)

The makers of motor vehicles generally employ the most elaborate mass-production production systems anywhere; especially with their many added features, automobiles are probably the most complex mass-produced products. Their complexity has, in fact, been steadily increasing as features have been added; some of these were mandated during the study period in the interest of fuel efficiency and, above all, pollution abatement. A glance at the engine compartments of, say, 1967 and 1982 models clearly shows the much more elaborate arrangements that evolved during the time and that put substantially greater burdens on the designers of assembly lines and on production workers and managers generally. The industry has therefore constantly attempted to develop its production systems to ever greater levels of complexity and automation, and this trend continued during the study period.

Beginning in the 1950s, automatic inspection was first instituted. There were systems for shutting down the transfer machines and other processing units when tools wore out and when other problems arose. The next stage was to exchange certain tools automatically when there was trouble. For example, drill bits were exchanged as one wore out.

Beginning about 1980, major attempts were made to introduce robots; in the United States, the automobile industry is by far their largest user. Robots were mainly used to do welding and painting, two operations with health problems that received much new attention in the 1970s. On the one hand, many jobs were eliminated, but on the other, one cannot mourn the end of often very unhealthy work environments due to toxic fumes and aerosols as well as high temperatures and welding sparks.

The automobile makers made enormous investments towards the end of the study period and subsequently. During 1978–84, the domestic industry invested $69 billion worldwide in plant, equipment, and special tooling.[21] This followed a long sales slump, compounded by import competition and a perceived decline in the quality of American products. The strategy worked for a while because the worst of the recession of 1982–83 ended and gasoline prices stabilized and declined somewhat. However, beginning in 1985, more trouble arrived in the form of potent new entries in imports both at the cheap and expensive end of the market, as noted in the last chapter, and in what promises to be enormous global overcapacity in automobile manufacture.

It is also noteworthy that the makers of automobile parts (SIC 3714) have followed quite similar strategies of investment and modernization but have, in part, tried to detach themselves from the vagaries of the new auto market and to expand instead into replacement parts and various specialties. The dependence on auto makers cannot, of course, be reduced much, but some flexibility had to be created. This has, in some instances, taken the form of independent innovation, in the form of lighter components and the use of new materials, notably of plastics. Throughout much of the study period, plastics have steadily increased their share of the materials going into cars, and the trend accelerated after the fuel crisis. The auto makers themselves have, of course, also participated, but to parts producers, notable redesigns are an important competitive tool.

The same trend toward lighter designs was to be noted in the builders of truck trailers (SIC 3715). Such changes often call for the capability of handling new materials, requiring new plant investment instead of getting by with older facilities geared to sheet steel and other metalforming and metalworking.

Finally, tank production (SIC 3795), which had also been a mass-production operation in World War II, became more of a job shop or small batch operation. Constant design changes and above all gross overcomplication of design took their toll in terms of efficiency.

For the industries for which data are available, the Appendix shows modest rates of increase overall. It should be noted, however, that these longer term trends, extending back to 1967, cannot take into account the sharp acceleration that took place toward the end of the study period and that continued beyond it, as noted above.

Other Transportation Equipment (SIC 372, 373, 374, 376)

In various ways, these industries have had to cope with a decline in the number of units produced, coupled with considerable elaboration of their designs. As a result, what had once been large batch production, with many elements of mass-production systems, gradually became much more of a job shop operation.

In military aircraft, for instance, their complexity, as well as the constant design changes, is a far cry from the simple mass production of aircraft in World War II. The lower number of planes needed by airlines makes the production of passenger aircraft also less of a quantity operation than it had been. As to rail equipment, General Motors had brought about the dieselization of American railroads in the 1940s by essentially making standard models. Traditionally, locomotive builders had customized their steam engines for the individual railroads, and some of them had done the same when they very tentatively moved into diesel production as well. Meanwhile, General Motors, in a well-known marketing end run around the competition, offered its standard models with modifications only for climatic variations and, echoing car marketing, would paint them any color the railroad wanted, with the warranty "run it for six months. At the end send us either a check or the engine."

It is worth recalling those days, because that business too has become a small batch operation. During the study period, only General Motors and General Electric, which reentered the business in a major way during that time, were producing diesel engines. Their market, however, became highly irregular as railroads cut back and consolidated and as the whole network shrank to about three-quarters of what it had been after World War II. As noted in chapter 2, moreover, the industry has largely given up on passenger equipment for rapid transit or other rail travel, as well as on electric traction, which is a major market for its international competitors.

Finally, though missiles could be thought of as a kind of ammunition of the sort that has long been mass produced, their technical complication also makes them candidates only for what is at best batch production. For the larger ones, job shop methods are the rule. Indeed, to an observer of their production operations, it appears that there is an amount of waiting around, delay, and trouble with products and equipment that no well-run job shop would countenance.

The rates of investment in these industries have grown, by and large, at low positive rates. Missiles show a higher one, mainly because the technical complications require a constant influx of new equipment.

Instruments and Related Products (SIC 38)

This industry group also combines quantity production with highly specialized job shop operations. Many standard instruments are of the kind that can be bought off the shelf by way of laboratory equipment catalogs or from wholesalers. The units are then integrated into systems that meet the particular needs of customers. The specific operations are thus largely those associated with high-quality mechanical manufacture, with a rising electronic component. Much of the latter is probably imported, given the realities of the electronics industry.

As noted, the photo industry (SIC 3861) has been forced to concentrate on quasi-chemical operations as its camera manufacture has virtually ceased. Those too, however, are mass-production operations on a very large scale.

The rate of increase in investment, as shown by the CDCS/E statistics, has been low. Of the eleven industries for which data are available, five have negative rates of change, whereas another two have rates between 0 and 1 percent a year.

Miscellaneous Manufactures (SIC 39)

This industry grouping extends over the whole spectrum of manufacturing technology, from small operations with highly skilled craftsmanship, as in jewelry (SIC 391), to large-scale low-skill assembly, as in toy manufacture (SIC 3944), to mass production of piece parts in specialized systems at very high rates, as in the various industries making writing instruments (SIC 395), to quasi-chemical processing, as in linoleum (SIC 3996), and to job shops, as in signs and advertising displays (SIC 3993).

The record of capital investment is correspondingly varied, ranging from rates of change of an increase of 7.2 percent a year in dolls (SIC 3942) to a negative 5 percent in jewelry, silverware, and plated ware (SIC 3914), an industry especially hard hit by imports.

INVESTMENT AND LABOR PRODUCTIVITY

In this section, the relationships of productivity, as given by CDVAM/E, to capital spending per employee (CDCS/E) will be examined. In the development of a method to demonstrate a relationship, year-to-year variations in capital spending particularly were so considerable that a general measure of each, extending over the study period, is more meaningful. This was put forth earlier in this chapter as a justification for focusing on the rate of change in constant dollar capital spending per employee (CDCS/E) and on the rate of change in constant dollar value added by manufacture per employee (CDVAM/E).

It was first decided to conduct a simple test on the data which considers only whether the rates are positive or negative. It was found that each of the following four cases was represented by the number of four-digit industries shown:

	CDCS/E	CDVAM/E	Number of industries
1.	positive	positive	200
2.	positive	negative	71
3.	negative	positive	72
4.	negative	negative	35

It is not surprising that each case is represented because it is readily possible to develop scenarios that would make each group appropriate:

1. The industry is showing an increase in CDVAM/E which is driven by a rising trend in capital investment as well. This would be an industry trying at least to maintain itself, with its managements trying to keep a rate of progress going, whatever its magnitude.

2. The industry is investing in plant at a rising rate, but not enough to prevent a fall in CDVAM/E. This can happen when firms try to hang on, but their means for physical improvement are limited. It may also be a situation where investments in plant have long been neglected so that some catching up is in order. In some cases, there may even be a threshold below which capital spending does not produce much improvement, but above which there is a stepwise improvement that does express itself in better results and that moves the industry (or company) concerned into group 1 above.

3. The industry's value of CDVAM/E is rising, perhaps because its profits, which are also contained in value added by manufacture, have been rising, but because of such favorable conditions the industry can get away with less investment. At least equally likely would be that the industry had just finished a major reequipment program at the beginning of the study period and, not unreasonably, feels that it can coast along on that effort for a while.

4. Finally, both capital spending and value added per employee falling is clearly an industry where productivity has been falling as its capital spending has lagged. One can assume that this is a group in trouble.

This classification of the data in the Appendix into the above four categories may be interpreted as a 2 × 2 array; a chi-square analysis then yields a calculated value of 1.61 as against a table value for a significance level of 0.05 of 3.84. Thus the null hypothesis cannot be rejected, and the test does not yield a significant result, i.e., it does not demonstrate a simple, unidirectional relationship between productivity and investment.

More precise tests were then conducted. The first was a simple correlation between CDVAM/E and CDCS/E, with the latter as independent variable. This yielded a value of the correlation coefficient r of 0.1214, which leads to a calculated t-value (equivalent to the normal variate z for $n = 378$) of 2.40, that is, a significance level slightly less than 0.02. Thus, taking the data set as a whole, there is a direct and significant relationship between CDVAM/E and CDCS/E.

It is noteworthy, however, that the coefficient of determination r^2 is only 0.01474, so that only a little less than 1.5 percent of the variation of CDVAM/E is accounted for by CDCS/E.

To isolate the effects of particular industries, this simple correlation was then repeated within each major group as defined or redefined for this study, with CDCS/E as the independent variable. As shown in the first results column in Table 1, there were only six major groups within which a significant relationship at the 5 percent level could be found, that is, where it could be shown that an increas-

Table 1
Summary of Results of Correlations of Rates of Change
of CDVAM/E and CDCS/E

SIC	NAME	WITHIN GROUPS	LEVELS	INTER-ATIONS
20	Food and kindred products	+		
21	Tobacco manufactures			
22	Textile mill products	+	+	
23	Apparel and related products		+	
24	Lumber and related products			
25	Furniture and fixtures			
26	Paper and allied products	+		
27	Printing and publishing			−
(a)	Chemicals exc. plastics	+		
29	Petroleum and coal products		−	
(b)	Rubber and plastics products			−
31	Leather and leather products			
32	Stone, clay, and glass products			−
33	Primary metal products			
34	Fabricated metal products			
(c)	Machinery, exc. electrical		+	
(d)	Electric power equipment	+	+	
(e)	Electronics		+	
(f)	Motor vehicles		+	−
(g)	Other transportation equipment			
38	Instruments and related products			
39	Miscellaneous manufacturing	+	benchmark	

Legend:
+ significant at 0.05 level: positive r
− significant at 0.05 level; negative r
a. 28, exc. 282
b. 282, 30
c. 35, exc. 357
d. 361 − 364
e. 357, 365 − 369
f. 371, 3751, 379
g. 372 − 374, 376

Source: From Appendix.

ing trend in investment per employee had a directly favorable effect on productivity as measured by CDVAM/E.

Finally; a multiple regression and analysis of covariance was conducted on the data set, using a matrix of dummy variables to denote the individual industry groups. For this purpose, miscellaneous manufacturers (SIC 39) was taken as benchmark, but it is important to note that the results for significance are not affected by this choice. There are two sets of significance levels. The first is that of differences in CDVAM/E across different industry groups, after controlling for capital spending. These are differences in overall levels (i.e., in the intercepts). As shown in the middle column of results in Table 1, there are seven industries that differ significantly from the benchmark. These differences are inherent in the industries and may be visualized as built-in initial advantages where shown as positive and as disadvantages where shown as negative.

The second set of results is that of interactions; these are the differences in the slopes of individual variables relating to CDVAM/E. Here there are four industries with significant results, which may be considered as measures of the rate of response in CDVAM/E to a rising trend in CDCS/E. Since all four industries shown in the right-hand column of Table 1 have significance in a negative direction, it must be concluded that they are likely to respond more slowly than the others. It is noteworthy that they are all relatively capital intensive, but if that were the main criterion there could have been many other candidates.

Based on reviewing Table 1 as a whole, the analysis does not produce any clear or strong pattern. There is only one industry with significant differences in both levels and interactions. It is motor vehicles, an industry group which, in many respects, is at the extreme in capital requirements in piece parts manufacture and which has also been required to come up with very substantial productivity improvement in the course of trying to assure a viable future for itself. As shown in the table, the result for levels indicates positive significance, whereas that for interactions is negative. This may indicate that high capital investment rates give the industry a high level of CDVAM/E to start with but that the industry otherwise responds significantly more slowly than others to further rising infusions of capital.

The multiple regression also shows a multiple coefficient of determination (r^2) of 0.3723, with a calculated F value of 4.606 and a significance level of 0.0001. Viewed as part of the multiple correlation process, the significance level of CDCS/E is approximately 3 percent. The sensitivity of the analysis is thus markedly improved by the multiple correlation model.

Nevertheless, it seems legitimate to conclude that for the most part the effects of investment in a given industry are sui generis and have to be examined qualitatively and individually, rather than by generalized quantitative rules. One would probably prefer a simple relationship where virtue in the form of high and rising rates of capital investment invariably brings its own reward in the form of higher productivity. However, this is true only in very general terms and is much less applicable once the major industry groups are examined separately. The results should therefore help direct managerial attention to the nature and quality of what is behind output figures per employee and amounts of capital investment and to an understanding that the related problems are technical and scientific at least as much as financial and economic.

NOTES

1. S. Eilon, B. Gold, and J. Soesan, *Applied Productivity Analysis for Industry* (Oxford: Pergamon Press, 1976), 22–23.

2. J. E. Ullmann, *The Prospects of American Industrial Recovery* (Westport, Conn.: Quorum Books, 1985), 87.

3. W. Glaberson, "Misery on the Meatpacking Line," *New York Times*, June 14, 1987.

4. "Big Tobacco's Fortunes Are Withering in the Heat," *Business Week*, July 27, 1987, 47.

5. G. Horvath, "Lumber, Pulp and Paper," in *The Improvement of Productivity*, ed. J. E. Ullmann (New York: Praeger, 1980), 170.

6. Ibid.

7. U.S. Department of Commerce, *U.S. Industrial Outlook 1985* (Washington, D.C.: Government Printing Office, 1986), 27.1.

8. "Petroleum Refining," in *U.S. Industrial Outlook 1985*, 10.1.

9. Ibid.

10. Ullmann, *American Industrial Recovery*, 189.

11. C. M. Hazel, "The Plastics-Fabricating Industry," in *The Improvement of Productivity*, 209–27.

12. B. R. Kalisch, "Shoe Manufacturing," in *The Improvement of Productivity*, 150–53.

13. "Stone, Clay and Glass Companies Expend for Government Required Pollution Control," *Annual Survey of Pollution Control*, 1980, 7.

14. "Leaner Years, Fatter Outlays," *Chemical Week*, January 2, 1980, 11; "Antipollution Capital Spending Stays Moderate," *Chemical & Engineering News*, May 19, 1980, 8.

15. Office of Technology Assessment, *Technology and Steel Industry Competitiveness* (Washington, D.C.: Government Printing Office, 1980), 269–81.

16. Ibid., 271.

17. Ibid.

18. Ullmann, *American Industrial Recovery*, 144–48.

19. Ibid., 163.

20. H. Brody, "U.S. Robot Makers Try to Bounce Back," *High Technology Business*, October 1987, 18.

21. *U.S. Industrial Outlook 1985*, 36.1.

LOCATION

4

Sunset in the Sunbelt

PRINCIPLES AND PRACTICE

This chapter attempts to define the significance of changes in the location of manufacturing within the United States. Specifically, it asks whether the much discussed shift of population and resources toward what came to be called the Sunbelt changed the lineup of industrial states significantly. If it were found that significantly more Sunbelt states are now among those in which the various industries are concentrated, one would have to conclude that a major shift in industrial resources has taken place.

It is appropriate to consider, first of all, some of the specific problems and policies that prompted the migration to the Sunbelt and, specifically, the problems in industrial location. The location of economic activity and of industrial plants in particular has long been recognized in works on industrial development as a function both of technical and scientific analysis and of sociopolitical trends. This combination of determinants is not always recognized. As texts in plant location or business logistics note, the basic principle is that in choosing a location, a firm can make its decision with regard to advantage in three areas: markets, labor, and materials.[1]

If the markets are the principal criterion, the firm locates itself so that it can be near its customers, or at least a majority of them. The objective is to minimize transportation costs of finished product and also to keep in close touch with customer needs. Although it is true that modern methods of communication reduce the importance of the latter factor, there is still a great deal to be said for interaction between customers and suppliers when this can readily involve people other than the sales departments; this is especially true of technically oriented firms, where engineers should be able to interact without extensive travel.

The important point here is that any firm making a location decision under the guidelines of market orientation must necessarily follow location decisions taken previously by its customers. For consumer products, the decision is based primarily on what areas have developed most, on where population has been growing. The primary objective in market-based location decisions is in fact a reduction in transportation costs for finished product. Otherwise the competitors of a firm that did locate near its markets would have a cost advantage; the company not nearby would either have to absorb the extra transportation costs or accept that the competitors had created a so-called exclusion zone, that is, a part of the market that the firm cannot serve.

For firms that locate near their materials, which include energy inputs as well, nature makes the decision for those using primary materials directly or those using exceptionally large amounts of electric power. Otherwise, it is again a matter of somebody else's previous decision, in this case, of suppliers of other inputs. Finally, as to a labor orientation in plant location, it is a matter of finding a labor force with skills that can be adapted to the needs of the industry, at costs that allow the enterprise to stay competitive.

The three choices defined above are not necessarily mutually exclusive. Rather, it is often possible to combine at least two sets of the above advantages; labor and markets are probably most often found in combination because large concentrations of population improve the chances of finding workers for factories as well.

Once these basic orientations have been decided, it is possible to narrow the search for industrial real estate more exactly and to focus on issues of access, transportation, building needs, local taxes, and general amenities and on how the advantages of a region with respect to labor, materials, and markets manifest themselves in a specific locality. To aid in this analysis, writers in the field have provided extensive checklists that attempt to include some sort of weighting system or rating scale for the many variables that cannot be readily quantified.

It is here that the process begins to lose some of what might at first appear to be commendable precision and impartiality. The plain fact is that in a large country like the United States there are multiple choices that can be made in almost all location decisions. These choices are not and cannot be made without regard to value judgments of one kind or another. There is no known method for making such judgments on a purely quantitative basis, except by assigning values to intangibles, a process that obviously allows any desired bias in the outcome.

It is also logical that such qualitative factors often should primarily reflect the preferences of the executives of the firm. Thus, for example, a study of plant location practices on Long Island, done at a time of rapid industrial growth in the early 1960s, found that the final choice was closely related to where the chief executives lived.[2] The influx of corporate headquarters to Westchester County, New York, and to the northern part of Fairfield County, near Danbury, Connecticut, was likewise determined by where most of the senior executives lived, with Connecticut also offering the advantage of much lower personal income taxes.

The practical effect of these flexibilities is to make possible a range of decisions that have had a profound effect on the redistribution not only of businesses but also of population and of the political power that stems from it. There were two such trends—the move to the suburbs and the move to what came to be called the Sunbelt.

THE MOVE TO THE SUBURBS

The eclipse of manufacturing in the central cities and the comparatively much more rapid, albeit highly selective, development of the suburbs have brought about a major part of the decline of manufacturing, on the one hand, and of the economic base of the central cities, on the other. New York, Chicago, Cleveland, and many other cities were, for a long time, world-famous centers of manufacturing, including heavy manufacturing.

There were a number of reasons for their decline, but buildings thought to be unsuitable for modern manufacturing, and lack of land for expansion, were among the most serious. The industrial property available was often in multi-story loft-type structures that depended on elevators which, by their nature, were fixed, discontinuous in operation, and generally slow. This made them unsuitable for integration in manufacturing processes with continuous flow characteristics.

When a firm or department was small enough to be housed on one floor, the problem was less acute, since only finished products and raw materials had to go out or come in by elevator, and this did not generally happen too often in a day. However, when firms were spread over more than one floor, the fixed floor size became a serious impediment to good plant layout. This was because the elevators had to be used for transportation within departments as well, and in job shops especially, the materials often had to be shuttled back and forth. Moreover, in some cases extra supervision had to be provided for each floor of a department. At any rate, though there are designs that could have alleviated some of these problems, these were never implemented on a significant scale.[3]

The result was that there has been a sustained exodus from inner cities to their own suburbs. Many of the older firms in the New York suburbs, for example, were once in the inner city. By 1963, the process had been going on for some time and was reflected in much higher rates of increase in value added by manufacture in the suburbs than in the inner cities.

It is a trend that has continued steadily. The bedroom suburb was the dominant mode of development until the late 1950s. As noted, business migration to the suburbs was already significant in the early 1960s. It was the time not only when many shopping malls were built (overbuilt in some areas) but also when the first suburban industrial parks and office centers were constructed.

The structures in the industrial park were mainly single-story open buildings that permitted a wide range of customizing for the production systems of individual firms. However, in many of these industrial parks there were few conventional factories, in the sense of taking in large volumes of raw material and making finished products. Rather, the buildings were often the district or regional centers for national corporations that made the product elsewhere, with the new plants offering only sales and servicing. Furthermore, to an ever increasing extent the products were imported. They thus reflected the decline of American manufacturing.

Industries located in the new industrial parks of the suburbs generally were of the most decorous kind, meaning they were high-tech producers rather than, say, foundries or garment factories. In fact, as the move to the suburbs has continued up to the present, most of the new suburban jobs have not been in manufacturing at all, but in clerical work related to banking and other business services and, above all, in retailing.[4]

From the overall viewpoint of job creation, a principal result was that the work had moved away from the inner cities where the unemployed were concentrated. Whatever educational and training problems their employment in the suburbs would have entailed, they never had much of a chance to participate. Meanwhile, in shopping centers in the more affluent parts of the nation, help-wanted signs have blossomed in almost every store or fast-food restaurant.

Suburbs, being relatively low-density settlements, cannot usually support much of a public transportation system, and thus there is little chance of anybody being able to commute to jobs. That too has been a problem for a long time. Beginning in the 1970s, some metropolitan areas have expensively built or painfully reconstructed rail transit systems, amid the growing technical incompetence in this field that was discussed in chapter 2. Yet major existing systems, such as the Pacific Electric lines of the Los Angeles area and the Key System in the San Francisco Bay area, were only eliminated in the 1960s. Watts, California, had been a major junction of the Pacific Electric, and its shops were located there. Pictures of the 1964 riots showed children playing on the weed-grown tracks of what had once been the world's longest (over thirteen hundred route miles) transit system, whereas one of their elders' main complaints was that they could not get to jobs even if they could find them; when the old cars, which they had to use instead, smoked too much, the drivers fell afoul of the police.[5]

The pressures on the inner cities from these changes will not soon abate and must be considered a major reason why urban economic problems have remained so intractable. Some answers might have been found had the attempts at socioeconomic betterment, which first came about in a serious way in the Johnson Administration, not been short-circuited by the Vietnam War. In a few places, industrial urban renewal was attempted, but in the main the results were limited.

THE MOVE TO THE SUNBELT

The problems of manufacturing decline linked to urban decay were greatly exacerbated by a second migration which is the focus of the major analysis of locational trends in this chapter. This was the relocation of manufacturing out of the metropolitan areas altogether, specifically towards the rural areas of what came to be known as the Sunbelt, especially the Southeast. This move accompanied a comparable shift of population to those regions as well. The Sunbelt states are essentially on the southern rim of the continental United States and are taken to comprise Alabama, Arkansas, Arizona, California,

Florida, Georgia, Louisiana, Mississippi, North and South Carolina, New Mexico, Nevada, Oklahoma, Tennessee, Texas, and Virginia.

It was a portentous trend not only from an industrial viewpoint but also from a political one. One of the first to note the political implications of the change was Kirkpatrick Sale.[6] The move had been into a region of generally prevailing political conservatism, which had led to the right-to-work laws and, not infrequently, to extralegal attacks on unions and their organizing efforts and, where federal law did not provide otherwise, to less protective legislation for workers and the environment. These characteristics were touted as part of an agreeable "business climate" and expected to serve as major attractions for business.

In the promotional efforts of the industrial real estate industry and in the economic development commissions of the states, another way of attracting new industry was to assert that higher worker productivity would emanate from a presumably properly grateful new work force. It would also be possible to introduce new machinery, without such restrictions as those in union contracts of some industries. It was noted by some, of course, that a poorly educated, novice work force would also pose problems of training or retraining. Still, others supported the move, for example, Leonard D. Yaseen, a prominent consultant in New York who became one of the earliest to argue strongly in favor of the new migration, especially to the rural South. Unfortunately, some of the new homes that he had found for his clients and that illustrate his book were soon to see major civil rights turmoil.[7] Moving was considered a major forward step, even though it is a traumatic experience for most businesses, and there is evidence that many firms do not long survive their geographic transplantations.[8]

The change was soon regarded as an essentially irreversible and inevitable historic trend, which had the advantage of absolving political leaders at least in part from dealing with the resulting dislocations. A President's Commission for a National Agenda for the Eighties was appointed by President Carter in 1979; in its recommendations published in December 1980, it proposed that the struggle to revitalize the older industrial areas be abandoned and that migration to the Sunbelt be encouraged.[9] The Reagan Administration, much of whose political base was in the Sunbelt, favored this proposal, advising people to "vote with their feet"; this, to say the least, was a curious use of a phrase that had originated as a way of describing the migration from Eastern to Western Europe by people fleeing Communism.

The reasons for the move were not purely political, however. Much of the Southeast was indeed industrially underdeveloped. In the 1930s, the Tennessee Valley Authority had given the South a good supply of electric power and had broken new ground in regional planning. However, the main impetus came with the war industries and military bases of World War II, which were often located in the South to please one of the many senior members of Congress who, in disproportionately large numbers, were southerners. Once these industrial nuclei were established, they continued, kept going in large part by similar political pressures and by the needs of the arms industries of later wars and the Cold War.

Another reason, which became especially important in the early 1970s, was the energy boom in Texas and the other oil-producing areas of the Sunbelt. It was the engine that propelled the deals, the booms, and the growth.

The clear distress of the Northeast and Midwest over the prospect of being written off as the Frost Belt and having to contend with what came to be called "runaway plants" was not, however, balanced by unanimous enthusiasm on the part of the Sunbelt states. They were pleased by their enhanced political influence, which translated itself into more federal aid, as well as more seats in the House of Representatives, once the Census of Population began to reflect the big change. But there were expressions of concern over the dislocations and environmental problems that ever more intensive development would bring. The water supply, precarious over most of the region, was an obvious major problem.

The move into a new area of cheaper labor costs and other advantages was constantly stressed in descriptions of industrial change. In 1976, *Business Week* reported on the change in an article titled "The Second War between the States: A Bitter Struggle for Jobs, Capital and People."[10] The question was, however, how much of this really affected manufacturing, rather than the service occupations, white-collar work, or extractive industries that were clearly involved, as were the retirees who took to the Sunbelt in ever larger numbers.

There is no question that there was a substantial shift in industrial employment to the Sunbelt. As Table 2 indicates, the share of manufacturing employment in the Sunbelt states increased from 29.1 percent of the national total in 1967 to 34.4 percent in the 1977 Census of Manufactures and to 41.0 percent in 1985. The totals indicate that between 1967 and 1985 manufacturing employment in the Sun-

Table 2
**Numbers (in Millions) and Proportion of Manufacturing Employees
in the Sunbelt and Other Areas, 1967, 1977, 1985**

	1967		1977		1985	
	Number	Percent	Number	Percent	Number	Percent
Sunbelt	5.6	29.1	6.8	34.4	7.9	41.0
Other areas	13.7	70.9	12.9	65.6	11.4	59.0
Total	19.3	100.0	19.7	100.0	19.3	100.0

Source: U.S. Department of Commerce, *1987 Statistical Abstract of the United States* (Washington, D.C.: Government Printing Office, 1987), 634.

belt increased by 40.7 percent, whereas it declined in the other areas by 16.7 percent, or by about one job in six.

These totals, however, require further explanation. It is certainly true that many traditional industries have declined, but the reason is not that the jobs have gone to the Sunbelt but rather that they are gone altogether from the United States. New plants in the Sunbelt were often built to make new and more promising products, but in such very important areas as consumer electronics, the jobs went to foreign parts. The analysis in chapter 5, following, clearly bears this out.

One must first note that, as the pilot study discussed in chapter 1 showed, manufacturing was concentrated in remarkably few states. Taking the twenty major SIC groups and then identifying those states that were the first six in value added within each major group makes it possible to show how often each state was listed in the first six. The result, based on the *1977 U.S. Census of Manufactures*, appears in Table 3. Since there are twenty major industry groups, a reading that, say, Pennsylvania was mentioned seventeen times means that it ranked in the first six in seventeen out of the twenty major groups. With the first six states in each group being considered, there are 6 × 20, or 120, possible "slots" or mentions; the table shows that five states—Pennsylvania, California, Illinois, New York, and Ohio—occupy seventy of them, or 58.3 percent. Michigan and Texas account for a further thirteen mentions between them, or 10.8 percent. Fully half of the states, as shown, are not listed at all. Among the most prominent states in manufacturing, therefore, only one out of the first five and one out of the next two—California and Texas, respectively—are Sunbelt states. Of greatest interest for the present study,

Table 3
Distribution of States among the First Six, by Value Added
in Each Major Industry Group, 1977

No. of Times Listed	States[a]	No. of States
17	PA	1
15	CA	1
13	IL, NY	2
12	OH	1
7	MI	1
6	TX	1
4	MA, NC	2
3	GA, IN, NJ, WY	4
2	LA, MO, TN, VA, WI	5
1	FL, KY, ME, OR, RI, SC, WA	7

[a] Not represented: AK, AL, AR, AZ, CO, CT, DE, HI, IA, ID, KS, MD, MN, MS, MT, ND, NE, NH, NM, NV, OK, SD, UT, VT, WV

Source: Computed from *1977 U.S. Census of Manufactures* (Washington, D.C.: Government Printing Office, 1977).

the proportion of Sunbelt states in the 120 "slots" defined above did not show any statistically significant change in the decade 1967–77, a time when the Sunbelt boom was clearly going strong.[11]

The present study brings the relationship up to date and expands it to the individual (four-digit) industries. Furthermore, it was decided to expand the study from using only the first six states to all states in all industries in which there are more than five hundred workers in a given state. The proportion of Sunbelt states in each industry was then compared for 1967 and 1982, using a *t*-test for comparison of the two proportions.

The second part of this phase of the study attempts to determine whether there is a significant difference in productivity, as expressed by CDVAM/E, between Sunbelt states and the others. To determine this in the individual industries was not easy, since much data on a state basis is withheld by the Census in order to avoid disclosure of information on individual establishments. The analysis thus could not be done for all industries. Still, orders of magnitude were given in some cases; rather than working only with limited numerical data, therefore, it was decided to use the Mann-Whitney-Wilcoxon rank sum test, that is, to rank the CDVAM/E's for all states and then see whether a statistically significant proportion of the high ranks were to be found in the Sunbelt column or among the other states.[12] As before, the results are presented below for the major industry groups, as modified for this study.

Finally, a similar comparative study is made of constant dollar capital spending per employee (CDCS/E), because if a significant difference in favor of the Sunbelt is found, it might indicate a greater commitment on the part of management to their new plants as well as perhaps to newer technology.

There is another aspect of this analysis that may affect some of the results. Ideally, one should have an output measure and price index for each region. That would eliminate the problem of having, say, the cheapest items made in the Sunbelt and the higher priced ones elsewhere, or vice versa. On a per employee basis, that might not make much difference, because presumably cheaper items may also require less labor time. It is possible that gross differences between the regions in the grades of product made may distort certain results somewhat, but the overall effect is negligible.

THE RESULTS

Food and Kindred Products (SIC 20)

The food industries are widely dispersed, with many enterprises serving local markets and with the large national firms having branch plants in the major markets. A few, like cottonseed oil mills (SIC 2074), are concentrated near their raw materials which, in this case, means predominantly Sunbelt locations. California is, of course, the premier state, and many of its food industries located there to be near their raw materials. However, California's large population (which has, in fact, encroached severely on its agricultural land in some areas) also constitutes a nearby market, so that an unequivocal choice between raw material and market location was not required. The t-tests showed that there was no significant movement of any industry to the Sunbelt.

As to differences in CDVAM/E between the Sunbelt and other locations, there were three industries, among the thirty for which the analysis could be completed, where the Sunbelt firms had significantly lower readings. In 1967, they were ice cream (SIC 2024), canned fruits and vegetables (SIC 2033), and bottled and canned soft drinks (SIC 2086). In 1977, meatpacking (SIC 2011), sausages (SIC 2013), and pet foods and prepared feeds (SIC 2047/2048) had lower readings. There is thus no systematic pattern.

For CDCS/E in 1967, canned fruits and vegetables again had lower levels for its Sunbelt establishments; sausages were lower in 1977. It is instructive to note that these two also had lower CDVAM/E readings in those years. The reasons cannot be pinpointed without much more detailed study; it may have something to do with the particular products, but ice cream is similar or identical all over. Perhaps the premium brands, which charge multiples of the cheap ones, are found less often in the Sunbelt.

Tobacco Products (SIC 21)

Among all the major industry groups, this is the one that, for obvious reasons, is most strongly concentrated in the Sunbelt. Two-thirds of the establishments in its bellwether industry of cigarette manufacture (SIC 2111) are in the Southeast, where much of the tobacco is grown as well. The proportions of Sunbelt locations did not change significantly between 1967 and 1982, nor were there any significant differences among Sunbelt and other locations with respect to CDVAM/E and CDCS/E.

Textile Mill Products (SIC 22)

In this group, it is clear that there has been no additional movement to the Sunbelt in the period of this study. Much of the migration from New England to the Piedmont region of the Carolinas was accomplished long ago, and much of whatever was left migrated south in the 1950s and early 1960s, this time it was to destinations such as Anniston, Alabama, and to other parts of the Deep South.[13]

The analysis of locational change within the United States thus shows no significant movement, as shown by the t-test on the proportions of Sunbelt establishments in 1967 and 1977. As to CDVAM/E, cotton fabric mills (SIC 2211) in the Sunbelt were ahead of the others in 1977, as were non–wool yarn spinning mills (SIC 2281). Thus two out of twenty-three industries showed a significant difference. Coated fabrics (SIC 2295) were ahead in non-Sunbelt locations in 1967, the only significant result among nineteen industries analyzed.

In CDCS/E, the results of nineteen industries in 1977 show cotton and other non-wool broad-woven fabric mills (SIC 2211 and 2221) and tufted carpets and rugs (SIC 2272) as ahead in the Sunbelt, and wool mills (SIC 2231) ahead in the other areas. In 1967, the narrow fabrics industry (SIC 2241) was ahead in the Sunbelt, whereas coated fabrics were ahead in the other regions. Note that again there is a correspondence with the CDVAM/E rankings—that was a time of major research activity in the industry and thus of new product introduction.

Apparel and Related Products (SIC 23)

The apparel industry is widely dispersed; among its thirty-three constituents, there were ten industries in 1977 and seven in 1967 that employed more than five hundred people in twenty states or more. A further nine industries had more than twelve high-employment states in 1967, and a further seven were so situated in 1977.

The industry has always tended to search out low-cost labor. In the present situation, this translates itself into a preference for locations where relatively low income or underprivileged people can furnish low-cost workers. This industry therefore has expanded considerably in the Sunbelt, especially in areas near the Mexican border, where even sweatshops are not likely to be questioned too frequently.

It does not follow from this, however, that significant numbers of enterprises moved to the Sunbelt from their traditional homes in the Northeast and Midwest. Rather, although the industries' expansions tended to happen in the Sunbelt, the contractions were more likely to occur outside the area.

This shows itself in the fact that for the more troubled parts of the industry there were greater declines in the number of non-Sunbelt states with over five hundred employees than in the Sunbelt states, but the latter did not increase. In other words, there were no industries in which a decline in the non-Sunbelt states was offset by an increase in the Sunbelt. For example, in 1967 in men's and boys' neckwear (SIC 2323), there were three each of states with five hundred or more employees in the Sunbelt and the other states. The Sunbelt states remained at three in 1977, but the non-Sunbelt states fell to only one. In women's dresses (SIC 2335), non-Sunbelt states fell from eighteen to ten, whereas Sunbelt states remained at eleven. For these industries, the *t*-test was statistically significant.

As to the Mann-Whitney-Wilcoxon analysis of the CDVAM/E, in 1967 there were five industries—men's suits (SIC 2311), women's outerwear, n.e.c. (SIC 2339), robes (SIC 2384), rainwear (SIC 2385), and house furnishings, n.e.c. (SIC 2392)—that ranked significantly lower in the Sunbelt. In 1977, there were only two such industries: men's clothing, n.e.c. (SIC 2329) and fabricated textile products, n.e.c. (SIC 2399). Again, for an explanation one would probably have to consider the different qualities and grades of garments made. If the better items are still made predominantly in the traditional centers of the industry, that might account for lower CDVAM/E in the Sunbelt. There were no significant differences in CDCS/E in this group which, it may be recalled, is one of the least capital intensive.

Lumber and Related Products (SIC 24)

The location policies of this industry are essentially to be near its raw materials; it is one of the most clear-cut cases of this among all manufacturing industries. There is therefore no significant change in the locations of the constituents of this major group. This, to some degree, is a noteworthy finding, because the more intensive use of southern forests was a major part of development efforts in some Sunbelt regions in the 1950s. Evidently this had largely reached its term by the beginning of the present study. To expand, southern forests would have to be managed better than they were after the original woods were logged. Yet the kind of softwood monoculture to which they have been subjected in some areas in order to supply the local paper and pulp mills creates its own ecological problems. Managing the local state of nature better than has been the case could be a major source of industrial and related agricultural growth.

As to significant differences in CDVAM/E and CDCS/E among Sunbelt and non-Sunbelt states, these favor the former as well as the latter. Data are limited, but logging camps and logging contractors (SIC 2411) had higher rates of CDVAM/E outside the Sunbelt in 1967 and 1977, and of CDCS/E in 1967. Sawmills (SIC 2421) had higher rates outside the Sunbelt in 1967 and higher rates of CDCS/E in the Sunbelt in 1977. Otherwise, within the limitations of the data, no significant differences were found.

Furniture and Fixtures (SIC 25)

This major group is more dispersed geographically than lumber, but it too has shown no significant movement to the Sunbelt. It is noteworthy, however, that there has long been a distinguished furniture manufacturing industry in the South, centered in North Carolina, which was established to utilize the local hardwoods. Some of its materials must now be drawn from much farther away, and some, such as particle board, owe more to the chemical industry than to lumber, but the industry is one of the few relatively successful combinations of modern equipment and traditional craftsmanship. At any rate, some of the most prestigious American makers of furniture do most or all of their manufacturing in the region, and, in addition, there are many smaller enterprises doing high-quality custom work of all kinds.

The analysis of differences in CDVAM/E shows Sunbelt establishments in upholstered furniture (SIC 2512) ahead in 1967, and wood partitions (SIC 2541) outside the Sunbelt ahead for 1977. That industry was also ahead of the Sunbelt in CDCS/E in 1967. In addition, wood furniture (SIC 2511) had higher rates of CDCS/E outside the Sunbelt in 1967 and 1977, as did wood partitions in 1967 only. Sunbelt establishments making mattresses and bedsprings (SIC 2515) had higher CDCS/E in 1977.

Paper and Allied Products (SIC 26)

For reasons of material availability, especially following the extensive development of southern softwoods, major parts of this industry are located in the Southeast, (i.e., in the Sunbelt). For example, for pulp mills (SIC 2611), 70 percent of states with over five hundred employees are in the Sunbelt. Paper mills (SIC 2621) and paperboard mills (SIC 2631) likewise have a relatively high concentration there, with 43 and 44 percent respectively. However, as for migration to the Sunbelt, there has been no statistically significant shift.

Some industries have declined overall, as measured in the numbers of states with over five hundred employees in successive years. Thus, pressed and molded pulp goods (SIC 2646), which as noted before has been losing most of its markets to plastic foams, went from five states in 1967 to one in 1982. Set-up paper boxes (SIC 2652) went from eleven to seven states. An industry primarily located in the Sunbelt, in part because it was much involved in the use of hardwood pulp for such products as Masonite, is building paper and paper board (SIC 2661). Sharing the vicissitudes of the building industry, it went from four states in 1967 to eight in 1972 and fell to only one state in 1982.

Turning to regional differences among industries with respect to CDVAM/E in 1967, we find three industries—paperboard mills (SIC 2631), bags, except textile bags (SIC 2643), and fiber cans, tubes, etc. (SIC 2655)—whose Sunbelt establishments had significantly lower readings than those elsewhere. Yet in 1963, paperboard mills had significantly higher CDCS/E. In 1977, they still showed lower CDVAM/E than non-Sunbelt locations, whereas paper coating and glazing (SIC 2641) and corrugated and solid fiber boxes (SIC 2653) had higher ones.

Printing and Publishing (SIC 27)

The t-tests on this industry group disclose that there were no major shifts to the Sunbelt. The largest industry, newspaper publishing (SIC 2711), had more than five hundred employees in all states in both 1967 and 1982. Periodical publishing (SIC 2721) went from three to eight Sunbelt states in that time, but this was a general time of growth in the industry, including startups of major regional publications. In order to save costs, some publishers located subscriber service operations away from their metropolitan headquarters. Again, there was one noticeable decline: photoengraving and stereotyping (SIC 2793 and 2794) went from eight states with over five hundred employees in 1967 to only one in 1982, due to the technological changes that created widespread obsolescence in these industries.

Periodical publishing had higher CDVAM/E for Sunbelt locations in both 1967 and 1977 and higher CDCS/E in the latter year. In 1967, manifold business forms (SIC 2761) also scored higher in both CDVAM/E and CDCS/E, whereas bookbinding (SIC 2789) scored lower in CDCS/E. In 1977, book publishing and printing (SIC 2731) and miscellaneous publishing (SIC 2741) had higher CDVAM/E values in the Sunbelt locations than elsewhere. The rest of this major group showed no significant differences.

Chemicals and Allied Products, Except Plastics (SIC 28, Except 282)

Developments in major parts of this industry group were related to petrochemicals, and this in turn prompted a tendency to locate in the oil-producing regions of the Sunbelt. Major new petrochemical complexes were built near such areas as Beaumont, Texas, and Baton Rouge, Louisiana, and as appendages to oil refineries in the region. Much of this kind of development took place in the 1950s and was over by the early 1960s.

For this reason, the changes observed between 1967 and 1977 for which data were available reveal only very limited movement. In 1967, there were two industries having a majority of the states with over five hundred employees in the Sunbelt: industrial gases (SIC 2813) and fertilizer mixing (SIC 2875). In 1977, nitrogenous fertilizers (SIC 2873) and agricultural chemicals (SIC 2879) also showed such a majority of states. However, the lineup did not change significantly for most of the industries. Only the producers of surface active agents (SIC 2843) showed significant movement to the Sunbelt, as shown by the t-tests.

A comparison of CDVAM/E and CDCS/E also shows little difference in 1967. Only pharmaceuticals (SIC 2834) showed significantly higher CDVAM/E in the Sunbelt, and there were no significant differences in CDCS/E. In 1977, however, five out of the thirteen industries for which adequate data were available showed higher CDVAM/E in the Sunbelt. These were industrial inorganic chemicals (SIC 2819), soap and other detergents (SIC 2841), toilet preparations (SIC 2844), agricultural chemicals, and adhesives and gelatin (SIC 2891). Again, there were no significant differences for CDCS/E. These differences may be accounted for by differences in products and by the facts that most of these industries are capital intensive and that many of the new plants built not long before the study period were located in the Sunbelt.

Petroleum Refining and Related Industries (SIC 29)

The location of petroleum refining (SIC 2911) did not change significantly between 1967 and 1977, as between Sunbelt and other areas. There was a gain of five states with over five hundred employees in the period. By contrast, two other industries in the group (SIC 2951 and 2952) lost ground. There was also no significant difference in the rankings of CDVAM/E and CDCS/E for the two areas in 1967 or 1977.

Rubber and Plastics Products (SIC 282 and 30)

The data available for these industry groups were too limited to indicate either a significant shift to the Sunbelt or any significant variation between Sunbelt and other locations in CDVAM/E and CDCS/E. The most rapidly growing sector turned out to be miscellaneous plastics products (SIC 3079), which added four states with over five hundred employees between 1967 and 1977. One of them was a Sunbelt state; the others were not. Much of plastics fabrication ties in with other manufactures that use the moldings as components; therefore, this industry frequently locates near its users. On the other hand, the troubles of the rubber tire industry (SIC 3011) caused a loss of no less than thirteen states among those with over five hundred employees. Four of them were in the Sunbelt.

Leather and Leather Products (SIC 31)

Employment in these industries has steadily decreased and so has the number of states with over five hundred employees. Employment decreased in the shoe industries (SIC 3111, 3131, and 314) by some 31 percent from 1972 to 1982. Industries making other leather goods saw a decline of about 17 percent; in 1982, these industries had about 23.8 percent of total employment in this major group.

The declines of the shoe industries hit the states outside the Sunbelt most severely; between 1967 and 1982, there were thirteen states outside the Sunbelt and only one Sunbelt state that fell below the limit of five hundred employees. The change in this lineup, therefore, does not indicate any sort of migration to the Sunbelt but rather a tendency to keep open any factories already there and to shut down the others.

Stone, Clay, and Glass Products (SIC 32)

This group is for the most part constrained to locate near its sources of raw materials because many of the materials are heavy, bulky, and of low specific value, so that they cannot be economically transported for long distances. At the same time, however, so are many of its products, which would argue for a location near the markets. Fortunately, its raw materials are fairly widespread, except for some specialty minerals. As a result, a location near the market is feasible. The construction industry, in particular, needs suppliers offering reliability and quick delivery.

There has, therefore, been some expansion of building materials suppliers among the industries in this group in the Sunbelt, because of the population increase and building activities in those regions. The differences, however, are not statistically significant. There were also few significant differences in CDVAM/E between Sunbelt and other states. In 1967, SIC 327 (essentially concrete products, lime, and gypsum) did better outside the Sunbelt; CDCS/E was higher in the Sunbelt for SIC 329. In 1977, cement (SIC 3241) and brick (SIC 3251) scored higher in CDVAM/E in the Sunbelt, whereas cut stone and stone products (SIC 3281) did worse. In 1977, cement also had a higher CDCS/E in the Sunbelt, no doubt reflecting, among other developments, the substantial expansion that took place in Texas.

Primary Metal Industries (SIC 33)

These, as noted in earlier discussions, are for the most part deeply troubled industries that have contracted a great deal. Their locations had traditionally been determined by the presence of raw materials, or at least by some of them. When the materials could be obtained by cheap and ready means of transportation, however, the industry could locate near markets as well.

This was always true of fabricators like foundries, which always had to be near their customers, but even smelters and basic processors could locate near ports, make use of imported ores or concentrates, and thus be near their customers as well. Such, for instance, was the case with the establishment of nonferrous metal smelters in New Jersey and even one in Maspeth in New York City. New steel complexes established in the 1950s in Fontana, California, Morrisville, Pennsylvania (near Trenton, New Jersey), and Sparrows Point, Maryland, were to use imported ores and coal brought from the nearby mines of Pennsylvania and serve the user industries of their regions.

It is also true that these are not industries whose plants can be moved. Rather, whatever development in the Sunbelt took place, it was originally planned as additional to whatever was present elsewhere and not as replacement. Analysis of the data shows that there was no significant change in the lineup between the Sunbelt states and the others and that there were no significant differences in CDVAM/E and CDCS/E. Rather, cutbacks affected the entire industry; thus the Fontana plant of Kaiser Steel Corporation was closed, just as were midwestern and northeastern plants, including several of the new East Coast facilities.

Fabricated Metal Products (SIC 34)

This industry group has generally been shrinking or stagnant, and so there have not been many opportunities to establish new facilities anywhere. Rather, markets have been lost to imports. For this reason, there has been little change in the industrial lineup between 1967 and 1982. Several industries had declines in the number of states with over five hundred employees, but in general the percentages of Sunbelt states did not change significantly. The exception was hand tools (SIC 3423), where the number of Sunbelt states with over five hundred employees went from one in 1967 to seven in 1982, whereas other states increased only from thirteen to fifteen in that time.

There also were few significant differences shown by the Mann-Whitney-Wilcoxon tests on CDVAM/E and CDCS/E. For 1967, fabricated structural metal (SIC 3441) and metal doors, etc. (SIC 3442)—two construction-related industries—were lower in CDVAM/E in the Sunbelt, but fabricated pipe and fittings (SIC 3498) ranked higher. In 1977, sheet metalwork (SIC 3444) and automotive stampings (SIC 3465) ranked lower, but iron and steel forgings (SIC 3462) were higher.

As to capital spending per employee (CDCS/E), there were no significant differences in 1967; in 1977, heating equipment (SIC 3433) and wire springs (SIC 3495) ranked lower, and iron and steel forgings and valve and pipe fittings (SIC 3494) ranked higher.

Machinery, Except Electrical (SIC 35, Except 357)

As with any major group in difficulty, the issue is not primarily who moved where but rather whether the various enterprises survived and whether they survived as American manufacturers rather than as agents for foreign makers of the equipment, as is now common. Only one industry, the relatively minor one of machine tool accessories (SIC 3545), showed a statistically significant move to Sunbelt locations. The rest of the group saw the eclipse of many of its erstwhile centers of activity in other parts of the country; it was only partially offset by the industrial boom generated in the oil industry after 1973. Yet that, as noted before, has also come to a halt.

By contrast, the Mann-Whitney-Wilcoxon tests showed almost no significant results between Sunbelt and other locations. In 1967, industrial trucks and tractors (SIC 3537) scored lower on CDVAM/E in the Sunbelt, and special industry machinery (SIC 3559) scored higher. In 1977, conveyors (SIC 3535), machine tool accessories (SIC 3545), and general industrial machinery (SIC 3569) scored higher in the Sunbelt. As to CDCS/E, there were no significant differences in 1967; in 1977, blowers and fans (SIC 3564) scored higher in the Sunbelt.

Electrical Machinery, Except Electronics (SIC 361–364)

The migration of this industry is again not borne out by any of the data. As in other essentially stagnant groups, the only statistically significant change is that in one industry, carbon and graphite products (SIC 3624), three out of seven states with more than five hundred employees in 1967 were in the Sunbelt. By 1982, there were only four states altogether, none of them in the Sunbelt. There also was virtually no difference in the CDVAM/E and CDCS/E statistics for Sunbelt and other states.

Electronic Products (SIC 357, 365–369)

The location policies of the domestic makers of electronic products, including office machines, have resulted in a combination of traditional locations, such as the plants of IBM in Endicott and Poughkeepsie, New York, and at least two new clusters of activity that have attracted national attention. Both of these developed during the study period. They are Silicon Valley between Palo Alto and San Jose, California, and the Route 128 area near Boston.

In both cases, these were locations near major centers of scientific activity—Stanford University and the Massachusetts Institute of Technology, respectively—and several of the major firms in the areas had been founded by people affiliated with those institutions. This is a somewhat unusual location criterion not generally found in any of the other industries. It can be put in more general terms by describing the location as one with a large pool of specially qualified scientists, engineers, and technicians. It is thus a location near well-trained labor, albeit of a very special kind.

Even though the industries in this grouping were the principal new ones that came about during the study period, their existence in these new locations and elsewhere was overshadowed by the threat of imports. In the 1980s, the Japanese success in the "chip wars" had a severe impact in Silicon Valley, where there were major producers of chip circuitry who had once been able to serve domestic computer producers as well as military customers. There were outright shutdowns, layoffs, and reliance on imported components, instead of integrated domestic manufacture. In Silicon Valley and near Route 128, such events proved quite traumatic. This was simply unexpected for a group of industries that had been considered the wave of the future and quite immune against such troubles. Many affected individuals were subjected to grave personal financial troubles. The price of houses particularly had been bid up during the glory days, which made them hard to support in leaner times.

In Silicon Valley, Apple Computer went through a particularly turbulent time but managed to recover somewhat. One feature of that recovery was the ability of its newest machines to use at least some software developed for IBM; before then, the programs were mutually incompatible. The present convergence seems likely to prove helpful to both rivals.

Since Silicon Valley is in a Sunbelt state and Route 128 is not, the net effect of locational changes and especially of where the new enterprises decided to locate does not lead to much in the way of significant differences as between Sunbelt and other locations. Only electromedical and electrotherapeutic apparatus (SIC 3693) showed a significant change towards the Sunbelt. That was a rapidly growing industry; in 1967 there were only six states with over five hundred employees, none of them in the Sunbelt. In 1982, there were nineteen, with four in the Sunbelt. This produced a statistically significant difference, but clearly there has not been a "migration" as such. Rather, four out of the thirteen new states in the lineup turned out to be in the Sunbelt.

As to significant differences in CDVAM/E and CDCS/E, data for 1967 are quite inadequate. In 1977, electronic coils, etc. (SIC 3677) had a significant difference in CDVAM/E, favoring the Sunbelt. No differences were found for capital spending per employee (CDCS/E).

Motor Vehicles (SIC 371, 3751, 379)

During the study period, these industries were mainly affected by widespread plant shutdowns in the auto industry and by corresponding cutbacks elsewhere. In addition, during that time (in 1974),

Volkswagen became the first of what was to become a major influx of foreign car manufacturers who established branch plants in the United States. These were designed in part to offset protectionist sentiment at a time when the domestic content of cars made by the major American makers was dropping. After a great deal of bidding by many areas and localities, Volkswagen finally settled in Westmoreland County, Pennsylvania, just east of Pittsburgh. For reasons having to do with the lack of market success of its post-Beetle designs, it announced in November 1987 that the plant would be closed and that by the end of 1988 all Volkswagen cars sold in the United States would again be imports.[14]

By contrast, Honda had a highly successful American production facility in Detroit and in November 1987 announced that it would build a second automobile manufacturing plant and would become a self-reliant U.S. manufacturer.[15] The joint venture of Toyota and General Motors in Fremont, California, is also successful and so are facilities of Nissan in Smyrna, Tennessee. The trend was expected to accelerate because of the fallen dollar. Meanwhile Hyundai announced that it would build a plant in Canada, which would also have implications for the United States because of the special North American trade relationships in this industry.

As to locational changes in the study period, the arrivals and departures balanced themselves sufficiently to result in no significant shift to the Sunbelt. Nor were there any significant differences in CDVAM/E or CDCS/E, except for truck trailers (SIC 3715), which had a lower reading of CDVAM/E in its Sunbelt locations.

Other Transportation Equipment (SIC 372, 373, 374, 376)

The location of the aircraft industry has long been a matter of happenstance related to the residences of its founders and to politics, in which it was decided to locate a plant in the district or state of some powerful congressional figure. This latter policy often favored the Sunbelt, especially for locations in the southeastern United States. California was also favored by climate, but evidently the sunny Southwest did not offer a competitively decisive advantage over the rainy Northwest, where Boeing of Seattle is located, nor over such other major locations as St. Louis or Wichita, Kansas.

The remains of the railroad equipment industries have stayed in their traditional locations in the Northeast and Middle West. For a time during the study period, Rohr Industries of San Diego made transit equipment for the Bay Area Rapid Transit system (BART), but that venture ended in failure.

What is left of shipbuilding has also remained in its accustomed areas, and there have been major cutbacks rather than new ventures.

In general, there was no statistically significant movement to the Sunbelt, or away from it, in any of the nine constituent industries of this grouping. For the five for which data were available, there also was no significant difference in CDVAM/E and CDCS/E.

Instruments and Related Products (SIC 38)

In this industry group, there is a mix of old and new firms, but again there was no significant movement to the Sunbelt. This is an industry in which many parts depend on a highly skilled and committed work force, and that is not easy to re-create in a new location. Accordingly, there is little incentive to move anywhere else as long as the business is viable otherwise. The data for 1977, however, showed significantly higher rates of capital spending for Sunbelt locations in three out of the thirteen industries in this group. They were process control instruments (SIC 3823), instruments to measure electricity (SIC 3825), and measuring and controlling devices, n.e.c. (SIC 3829). Some of these industries were associated especially with the electronic versions of their products. There were no significant differences in CDVAM/E.

Miscellaneous Manufactures (SIC 39)

For the diverse members of this industry group, imports are a far more serious issue than internal migration. The industry is widely dispersed geographically. There were ten new states in the Sunbelt with over five hundred employees in the whole group, and a decline of four non-Sunbelt states, but viewed one industry at a time, the difference did not turn out to be statistically significant. The ten new Sunbelt states were spread over seven individual industries. There were no significant differences between the two sets of locations with respect to CDVAM/E and CDCS/E.

GENERAL CONCLUSIONS

The finding that the progress made by the Sunbelt region in securing a larger share of manufacturing is not impressive should not be regarded as a source of satisfaction for other regions. As this volume has shown, there is widespread decay elsewhere, and the industrial picture as a whole is quite dismal. In judging the progress of the Sunbelt regions, moreover, we should make a distinction between California and the Southwest on the one hand and the Old South on the other. The former includes California, which has long been a powerful industrial state that needed little in the way of outside stimulation but that worried instead about overdevelopment. Florida likewise had other forces driving its development forward, such as the influx of Cubans, and there overdevelopment is also in evidence in several major areas. Overdevelopment, in fact, is often synonymous with water problems, if not actual shortages.

As to the rest of the region, no one would wish to suggest that it should be left stuck in underdevelopment. When he was chairman of the Tennessee Valley Authority, David Lilienthal used to illustrate this condition by his account of a Tennessee funeral. The shroud had been made in New York from cloth woven in New England; the coffin came from Pennsylvania. The grave was dug with shovels made in Chicago. Tennessee furnished only the corpse and the hole in the ground.

There has been appreciable industrial development, even though it did not change the lineup materially. Still, the troubles of much of the region in the middle 1980s were almost classic examples of those mineral booms and busts that have beset economies that depend mainly on natural resources and a few associated primary industries. While the oil fields of Texas created boom conditions at one time, there were exceedingly painful contractions and collapses as the price of oil fell. The collapse took with it not only industrial enterprises but also banks, retailers, and real estate ventures of all kinds. Worst of all was the human cost in terms of ruined lives and stranded populations.

Nevertheless, it is useful to recall the early high expectations and to recognize that the reasoning behind the earlier plans had certain built-in contradictions. In 1955, the principal author of this volume was asked by the state development commission of one of the states in the region to undertake a study of the potential for the chemical process industries in the state. There were raw material sources there, both mineral and agricultural, enough water for all but the most water-intensive chemical industries, land at low cost, and enough labor for what are usually not labor-intensive operations.

The executive director of the commission noted at the outset that the people of the state would "give a fair day's work for a fair day's pay." It was pointed out to him that industrial engineers had vainly tried to define a fair day's work ever since their profession was founded and that if it became plain that paying people as little as possible for as much work as possible was a major attraction of the state, the newcomers would include many unstable and marginal businesses, including outright sweat shops. He replied: "Oh no, we wouldn't want anybody to come down here and exploit our people!"

The objectives of securing quality employment and of using the locally prevailing low wages as an incentive were clearly in conflict. Yet the desirability of locating in small communities with just such conditions was powerfully advocated at the time, as noted at the outset of this chapter. The difficulties of creating a viable industrial region and of development generally were brought out in a report by the 1986 Commission on the Future of the South. It takes its title, *Halfway Home and a Long Way to Go*, from a description of the South by Governor Bill Clinton of Arkansas and says of earlier and more euphoric days:

During the 1970's, the fabled "New South" seemed to become at long last really *new*, not just the Old South painted over. After 100 years as a prodigal region, the New South appeared to be coming home to the national family. There were glowing economic reports from the country's Sunbelt; blacks and whites were experiencing brotherhood there; and a Southern state had supplied a homegrown President of the United States. But now it is 1986, and that prodigal South is still on the road. . . . The sunshine on the Sunbelt has proved to be a narrow beam of light, brightening futures along the Atlantic Seaboard, and in large cities, but skipping over many small towns and rural areas. The decade's widely publicized jobs at higher pay have been largely claimed by educated, urban, middle-class Southerners. Although their economic progress has lifted per capita income to 88 percent of the national average, millions of us—approximately the same number as in 1965—still struggle in poverty.[16]

In searching for reasons, the report notes that the South has had to contend with both external and internal factors. The external one is, of course, the challenge of imports, but this takes on special significance because even in the earlier days, in the 1950s, there already was competition from locations such as Puerto Rico where costs were even lower, provided employers were willing to train people.

It was exactly that problem that ultimately short-circuited southern progress. At a time when the skill and especially the literacy requirements of employment were rapidly rising, the report notes that the South, despite recent improvements, still spends below the national average per pupil, has higher rates of adult functional illiteracy, reports lower scores on college entrance exams, graduates fewer high school students and sends fewer to college, and has a population in which one-fourth of white adults and 37 percent of black adults dropped out of school by grade eight. Facing the 1990's, the South must decide how to rescue those Southerners left behind.[17]

To undertake such a task at a time when proposals for social improvement face what are, in the near term at least, probably insurmountable fiscal obstacles, is clearly formidable. Worse, current efforts to improve educational and cultural resources in the region all too often call forth ideological and religious obscurantism that rules ever larger areas of the sciences and humanities out of bounds. Thus, improvements that focus on improving the education and skills of the population become very difficult indeed. The report stresses these shortcomings and rightly regards their elimination as the key to progress.

That, however, is a national challenge as well. In the rest of the country, the mismatch of skills and opportunities and what has been termed a growing underclass call for quite similar remedies. If these can be implemented, the entire nation will benefit. Meanwhile, as this chapter shows, the industrial lineup has not changed much; with an eye to the national industrial decline one could, in fact, conclude that not even the deck chairs aboard the R.M.S. *Titanic* have been significantly rearranged.

NOTES

1. W. R. Latham III, *Locational Behavior in Manufacturing Industries* (Boston: Nijhoff, 1976), 35; for a more extended treatment, see R. H. Ballou, *Business Logistics Management* (Englewood Cliffs, N.J.: Prentice-Hall, 1973), 224–77.

2. C. Stonier, ed., *Industrial Location Principles and Their Role in Site Selection on Long Island* (Hempstead, N.Y.: Hofstra University Yearbooks of Business, 1964).

3. J. E. Ullmann, "Cut-and-burn Industrialization or Boosterism Revisited," *Hofstra Review*, Winter 1966, 25.

4. T. A. Hartshorn and P. O. Muller, *Suburban Business Centers: Implications for Employment*, Report to U.S. Department of Commerce (Washington, D.C.: Government Printing Office, 1987).

5. J. E. Ullmann, "Transportation: A Missed Opportunity," in *The Suburban Economic Network: Economic Activity, Resource Use and the Great Sprawl*, ed. J. E. Ullmann (New York: Praeger, 1977).

6. K. Sale, *Power Shift: The Rise of the Southern Rim and Its Challenge to the Eastern Establishment* (New York: Random House, 1975).

7. L. D. Yaseen, *Plant Location* (New York: American Research Council, 1956).

8. The New York City Planning Commission 1969 survey on firms that had moved away from New York found that a large proportion of them had gone out of business. Others had ceased manufacturing and had become importers. See New York City Planning Commission, *Planning for Jobs* (New York: New York City Planning Commission, 1971). The principal author of this volume was a consultant to the Commission for this report.

9. "Perspectives on Urban America and Key Policy Issues for the Eighties," *President's Commission for a National Agenda for the Eighties* (Washington, D.C.: Government Printing Office, 1979), 99, 101.

10. "The Second War between the States: A Bitter Struggle for Jobs, Capital and People," *Business Week*, May 17, 1976, 92-98.

11. J. Wenzel, "Regional Changes in Manufacturing Productivity" (M.B.A. thesis, Hofstra University, 1980).

12. The procedure and tables of critical values are given in many statistics texts. See, for example, J. L. Kenkel, *Introductory Statistics for Management and Economics* (Boston: PWS/Duxbury, 1981), 726.

13. For a study of the consequences to one of the communities that lost out, see C. Rapkin et al., *Industrial Renewal in the Utica Urban Area* (Albany, N.Y.: New York State Division of Housing and Community Renewal, 1963). The principal author of this volume participated in this study.

14. "What Ended VW's American Dream," *Business Week*, December 7, 1987, 63.

15. L. M. Fisher, "Building Plants in U.S. Adds Up for Foreigners," *New York Times*, November 27, 1987; "The Americanization of Honda," *Business Week*, April 25, 1988, 93-96.

16. Commission on the Future of the South, *Halfway Home and Far to Go*, (Chapel Hill, N.C.: Southern Growth Policies Board, 1986), 7.

17. Ibid.

INDUSTRIAL DECLINE   5
AND THE TRADE GAP

THE ORIGINS OF DECLINE

In 1987 the United States had an adverse trade balance of about
$160 billion, much of which represented a deficit in the merchandise
account, that is, an excess of imports over exports. It was a growing
problem, because it was essentially a way of assuring levels of current
consumption, yet it could only be sustained by selling off American
assets to foreigners. It was this that made the United States a net
international debtor by 1985 for the first time since the earliest years
of the century. The difference then, however, was that the net in-
debtedness came from real investments, from foreign-owned income-
producing property. It was not intended to finance, year by year, a
level of consumption that could not be justified otherwise.

The problem first arose in the early 1960s, just before the beginning of the period of this study. It did not, however, involve a
merchandise deficit then but rather was due to overseas military expenditures by the United States, especially in West Germany. There
was a twofold response then, neither of which deserves the term
remedy. The first was to get the West German government to buy
U.S. government bonds; this, of course, not only failed to give budget-
ary relief for the costs of the troops but also required American tax-
payers to pay interest on their cost. The other scheme was that of
the Eurodollars, which essentially meant dollar instruments that
would never be presented for payment but that could be used to
generate further credit. It was an arrangement that many individuals

would no doubt appreciate; however, if indulged in, the practice is called check-kiting and is quite illegal.

Whatever fiscal legerdemain has been used since the beginning to gloss over the problem, it has been made infinitely worse by the concomitant industrial decline described earlier in this volume. What is involved is nothing less than a gross deterioration in the level of technical, industrial, and managerial competence in the United States.

The level of a country's industrial skills and development must be measured against the achievements—past, present, and in prospect—of its international competitors. It consists of a combination of abilities, resources, and activities in commercial development, scientific and technical innovation, and the organization of production. That the United States has lost a great deal of ground in these fields is no longer in dispute; beginning with a few identifiable trouble spots in the early 1960s, the decline has continued without letup ever since, accelerating after the early 1970s. The fact that it was long ignored is itself a study in national self-deception; for many years one had to make a considerable effort to persuade one's readers or audiences that the decline existed at all. Now the miseries it has engendered are so plain and so general that such persuasion is no longer needed.

There are two major issues that must be addressed in judging the extent of the decline. The first is the course of the trade balance of the various industries over time. The second is the impact of international trade on the volume of a given industry. Here it is not particularly meaningful to chart the falling export sales of particular industries by themselves. Global needs and markets change, and therefore not all such declines have to do with a loss of industrial skill and competence.

The deteriorating trade balance within industries is conveniently measured by the changing relationships between imports and exports of selected products and commodities. When an erstwhile major export product shows a net import balance or an adverse shift in proportion, then it is legitimate to infer a significant decline in that industry. Its products still have a domestic market, but now relatively more of the market must be satisfied by imports.

Table 4 gives the ratios of exports to imports (EIR) in 1967, 1980, and 1985 for selected key categories of products and commodities that pertain especially to the more technically oriented industries. The three columns on the right then give the ratios of the EIR's for the periods 1967–80, 1980–85, and 1967–85. When such ratios are greater than unity, they denote a relative improvement in the export/

Table 4
Export-Import Ratios for Selected Items, 1967, 1980, 1985

Item	Ratio of Exports To Imports (EIR)			Ratio		
	1967	1980	1985	$\dfrac{\text{EIR (80)}}{\text{EIR (67)}}$	$\dfrac{\text{EIR (85)}}{\text{EIR (80)}}$	$\dfrac{\text{EIR (85)}}{\text{EIR (67)}}$
Chemicals, total	2.91	2.42	1.49	0.83	0.62	0.51
Organics	3.42	2.24		0.65		
Inorganics	1.51	1.27		0.84		
Dyes, Etc.	2.10	1.73		0.82		
Medical, pharmaceutical	4.00	3.80	2.50	0.95	0.66	0.63
Essential oils	2.04	2.16		1.06		
Fertilizers	1.63	2.05	2.23	1.26	1.09	1.37
Explosives	0.44	1.47		3.34		
Synthetic resins, etc.	7.88	6.01		0.76		
Other chemicals	6.21	3.48		0.56		
Food (inc. beverages, tobacco, animal and vegetable oils and fats)	1.05	1.70	1.40	1.62	0.82	1.33

Table 4 (continued)

Item	Ratio of Exports To Imports (EIR)			Ratio		
	1967	1980	1985	$\frac{\text{EIR (80)}}{\text{EIR (67)}}$	$\frac{\text{EIR (85)}}{\text{EIR (80)}}$	$\frac{\text{EIR (85)}}{\text{EIR (67)}}$
Machinery and transport equipment	2.17	1.40	0.69	0.65	0.49	0.32
Power generation	2.74	2.20	1.43	0.80	0.65	0.52
Special machinery	1.67	0.97		0.58		
Metalworking machinery	1.67	0.97	0.45	0.58	0.46	0.27
General industrial machinery	3.21	2.64		0.82		
Office machines, computers	3.14	2.97	1.12	0.95	0.38	0.36
Telecommunications	0.89	0.51	0.22	0.57	0.43	0.25
Electrical machinery	1.84	1.30		0.71		
Road vehicles	1.12	0.57	0.43	0.51	0.75	0.38
Other transport	5.69	5.56	3.70	0.98	0.67	0.65
Steel mill products	0.49	0.45	0.11	0.92	0.24	0.22
Crude materials, exc. fuels	1.10	2.27	1.63	2.06	0.72	1.48
Fuels	0.49	0.10	0.18	0.20	1.85	0.37
Total raw materials	0.84	0.35	0.42	0.42	1.20	0.50
Textiles, exc. clothing	0.61	1.45	0.48	2.20	0.33	0.79
Clothing	0.19	0.19	0.05	0.72	0.26	0.26
Total, textiles & clothing	0.41	0.54	0.16	1.08	0.30	0.39

Source: J. E. Ullmann, *The Prospects of American Industrial Recovery* (Westport, Conn.: Quorum, 1985), 9; U.S. Department of Commerce, *1987 Statistical Abstract of the United States* (Washington, D.C.: Government Printing Office, 1987), 796–99.

import balance, that is, a relatively greater share of exports. When they are less than one, it means that imports have been gaining.

The first EIR ratio thus corresponds approximately to the study period (1967–80), whereas 1980–85 was a time when, in spite of talk about industrial recovery—reindustrialization, to cite the buzzword current at its beginning—things were left to the free market without much in the way of government action to remedy what was clearly becoming one of the central problems of the economy.

The results are discouraging in the extreme. In 1967–80, only food (which includes beverages and tobacco, animal and vegetable oils and fats), crude materials other than fuels, textiles among major categories, and a few chemical products, notably fertilizers, show values greater than one.

The record for 1980–85, however, is worse still. Except for fuels—where the decline in oil prices is obviously responsible—and fertilizer, all the EIR ratios are less than one, in several cases very much less. It is particularly unfortunate to note that by 1985 the entire sector of machinery and transport equipment was in deficit, whereas it enjoyed substantial export surpluses in both 1967 and 1980. The available tabulations do not permit direct comparisons for all items listed, but for those that could be computed, a comparison between the EIR ratios for 1967–80 and those for 1980–85 reveals that the latter were smaller than the former in all but three out of the fifteen listed. This means that the disadvantage accelerated in 1980–85, producing a sharper decline in five years than what was experienced in the previous thirteen.

It was also possible to obtain a tabulation of imports and exports classified by SIC groups, in accordance with the scheme followed throughout this volume. The underlying tabulation of imports and exports was available only from 1977 to 1985. The results are given in Table 5. With the exception of tobacco (SIC 21)—hardly a salubrious product—and petroleum products (SIC 29)—where, again, lower crude prices created an advantage for an industry rather depressed at the beginning of the period—the EIR ratios are uniformly less than one. Indeed, seven out of the twenty major groups have EIR ratios less than 0.5, meaning that relative import dependency, as meaured by the value of the goods involved, has more than doubled.

As to the EIR's of specific industries, there were seven major groups with an export surplus in 1977 (i.e., an EIR greater than one). They were food and kindred products (SIC 20), tobacco manufactures (SIC 21), printing and publishing (SIC 27), chemicals and allied

Table 5

Export-Import Ratios by SIC Major Group, 1977, 1984, 1985

SIC	NAME	EIR 1977	EIR 1985	$\dfrac{EIR(85)}{EIR(77)}$	$\dfrac{EIR(84)}{EIR(77)}$
20	Food and kindred products	1.06	0.80	0.75	0.86
21	Tobacco manufactures	13.85	16.20	1.17	0.98
22	Textile mill products	0.94	0.40	0.42	0.46
23	Apparel and related products	0.21	0.06	0.29	0.38
24	Lumber and related products	0.65	0.52	0.80	0.86
25	Furniture and fixtures	0.36	0.15	0.42	0.56
26	Paper and allied products	0.68	0.52	0.76	0.85
27	Printing and publishing	1.86	1.04	0.56	0.69
28	Chemicals and allied products	2.41	1.70	0.70	0.77
29	Petroleum and coal products	0.15	0.30	2.00	1.60
30	Rubber and plastics products	0.71	0.59	0.83	0.94
31	Leather and leather products	0.13	0.06	0.46	0.61
32	Stone, clay, and glass products	0.84	0.42	0.50	0.59
33	Primary metal products	0.29	0.23	0.79	0.83
34	Fabricated metal products	1.66	0.74	0.45	0.58
35	Machinery, exc. electrical	3.00	1.20	0.40	0.45
36	Electric and electronic equipment	0.92	0.50	0.54	0.62
37	Transportation equipment	0.98	0.58	0.59	0.60
38	Instruments and related products	1.63	0.98	0.60	0.69
39	Miscellaneous manufacturing	0.47	0.16	0.34	0.40
	All manufacturing	1.01	0.63	0.62	0.66
	All products	0.81	0.60	0.74	0.66

Source: U.S. Department of Commerce, *1987 Statistical Abstract of the United States* (Washington, D.C.: Government Printing Office, 1987), 800.

products (SIC 28), fabricated metal products (SIC 34), machinery except electrical (SIC 35), with an impressive ratio of 3.00, and instruments (SIC 38). By 1985, only eight years later, there were only four such industries. Fabricated metal products and instruments had gone into the net import column, the latter only by a small margin. Printing and publishing went from substantial export surplus to little more than balance. Most incredibly, considering the importance of food exports to the American economy, the manufacture of food products lost its export edge. The EIR ratios of these industry groups further illustrate these patterns of decline, as noted above.

In addition, Table 5 shows EIR ratios for 1984, in the column headed EIR(84)/EIR(77). These will be required for the next step in the analysis. It is useful, nevertheless, to contrast the EIR ratios for 1985/1977 with those for 1984/1977. In all but two cases—again, tobacco and petroleum products—they declined from 1984 to 1985. The deterioration in the EIR's is thus observable even in this year-to-year comparison.

The significance of these statistics further depends on the second set of measures, which tries to quantify the impact of international trade on different industries. Here, one can conveniently use the concept of *apparent consumption*, which is well familiar from the way mineral statistics are compiled. Apparent consumption (A) is simply domestic production or volume of shipments (S) plus imports (I) minus exports (E). Therefore $A = S + I - E$. Dividing through by S gives $A/S = 1 + (I/S) - (E/S)$, where I/S and E/S are the import and export proportions respectively. A/S is then the ratio of apparent consumption to domestic shipments. If it is less than 1 or 100 percent, then the country produces more than it uses domestically; if greater than 1 or 100 percent, it has a net dependence on outside sources. This measure, therefore, gives an indication of the significance of international trade and puts the above EIR statistics in perspective. One could argue, after all, that no matter how badly exports and imports are in adverse balance, they do not matter much because international trade is not significant in the overall situation of the particular industry group.

The results for 1984 (the latest year available) appear in Table 6, which includes an average value for all manufacturing. The results show that nine out of twenty major groups have above average readings for A/S. Four of them show particularly high readings. They are apparel (SIC 23), leather goods (SIC 31), primary metal products (SIC 33), and miscellaneous manufactures (SIC 39). In these indus-

Table 6
Apparent Consumption as a Percentage of Volume of Shipments, by
SIC Major Group, 1977, 1984

SIC	NAME	I/S	E/S	A/S
			percent	
20	Food and kindred products	4.0	3.7	100.3
21	Tobacco manufactures	0.5	6.8	93.7
22	Textile mill products	6.3	2.7	103.6
23	Apparel and related products	24.1	1.8	122.3
24	Lumber and related products	8.8	4.9	103.9
25	Furniture and fixtures	8.2	1.8	106.4
26	Paper and allied products	7.8	4.5	103.3
27	Printing and publishing	1.0	1.3	99.7
28	Chemicals and allied products	6.0	11.2	94.8
29	Petroleum and coal products	11.2	2.7	108.5
30	Rubber and plastics products	6.2	4.2	102.0
31	Leather and leather products	73.0	5.7	167.3
32	Stone, clay, and glass products	7.1	3.6	103.5
33	Primary metal products	18.6	4.5	114.1
34	Fabricated metal products	5.0	4.7	100.3
35	Machinery, exc. electrical	31.1	17.7	95.4
36	Electric and electronic equipment	18.1	10.7	108.1
37	Transportation equipment	19.4	11.5	107.9
38	Instruments and related products	13.0	14.6	98.4
39	Miscellaneous manufacturing	34.9	6.8	128.1
	All manufacturing	11.4	7.7	103.7

Legend: I = Volume of imports
          E = Volume of exports
          S = Volume of shipments
          A = Apparent consumption = S + I - E
          A/S = 1 + (I/S) - (E/S)

Source: U.S. Department of Commerce, *1987 Statistical Abstract of the United States* (Washington, D.C.: Government Printing Office, 1987), 724–28.

tries, therefore, the effects of net imports must be considered high. Other industries are much more favorably situated, but again, a result such as the approximate balance in food (SIC 20) is alarming because a substantial surplus was long taken for granted in this sector.

If one considers the average values for all manufacturing as the breakpoint between satisfactory and unsatisfactory situations, then a juxtaposition of the *A/S* results with the EIR ratios for 1984 (i.e., EIR(84)/EIR(77) in Table 5) must be examined. The industries in the most serious trouble then are those with an EIR ratio *below* the average value for all manufactures; just as in the *A/S* ratios, those with readings *above* the average must be regarded as most seriously deficient. A summary of the joint effects of these results shows the following:

1. *High* A/S, *low EIR*. This is the most seriously damaged group; it consists of apparel, furniture and fixtures, leather goods, electrical and electronic equipment, transportation equipment, and miscellaneous manufacturing.

2. *High* A/S, *above-average EIR*. This group consists of lumber, petroleum and coal products, and primary metals. The total consumption of their products is thus well beyond domestic production, but the ratio of exports to imports has been falling at a less serious rate than in other groups.

3. *Low* A/S, *low EIR*. In this group, the EIR's have been deteriorating, but the relative importance of imports in the groups as a whole has been more limited. This group consists of textile products, stone, clay and glass products, fabricated metal products, and machinery, except electrical. This is not to say, of course, that certain constituent industries of these groups have not been seriously affected.

4. *Low* A/S, *above-average EIR*. This group was least affected, as of 1984. It comprises the remaining groups: food, tobacco, paper, printing and publishing, chemicals and allied products, rubber and plastics, and instruments. Still, the outlook is poor even for them.

Before the last group is counted among the blessed, however, it is well to recall that even between 1984 and 1985 the EIR ratios of this group became worse. Specifically, by 1985 printing and publishing and instruments had slipped into below average readings of the EIR ratio. If data allowing a computation of the A/S ratio for 1985 had been available, they would no doubt also have reflected a further adverse change.

Using above- and below-average levels as criteria for a satisfactory or unsatisfactory situation is, in any event, an extremely if not excessively generous standard. An industrialized country should normally have a *surplus* in its trade in manufactured goods. The A/S ratio should be less than 100 percent and the EIR's greater than 1. Those were exactly the conditions that obtained in earlier, more ample times.

It should finally be noted that in 1985 the dollar still was at what was considered a high level and did not begin its protracted decline until the end of that year. However, the trade gap has not materially changed since then, and it has, in fact, increased, in spite of a decline in the dollar amounting to a huge subsidy by foreign currencies. Thus it is highly likely that when it becomes possible to do this analysis for 1986 and 1987, there will be no significant improvements, if any at all.

Following the prior practice in this volume, the situation in the different major industry groups will now be reviewed. Their individual problems vary greatly and involve many considerations of public policy, both domestic and foreign, but there is a common thread of growing difficulties, first shown in the EIR and A/S analysis above.

PROBLEMS OF SPECIFIC INDUSTRIES

Food and Kindred Products (SIC 20)

Food had long been a crucial area of U.S. export surplus. As Table 5 shows, however, the EIR moved from a rough balance in 1977 to a net import balance in 1985 and an EIR ratio of 0.75. That is still above the current average, but the margin is shrinking rapidly. Table 4 includes in its food entry agricultural commodities as well as the manufactured foods of SIC 20, but it too shows an unfavorable EIR ratio for 1967–85 and 1980–85. Most recently, the United States has become a net food importer in total; the A/S ratio for 1984 still shows a virtual balance.

Certainly, one's observations of food labels or even crates in fruit and vegetable stores show increasingly international sources beyond the traditional import specialties. Vegetables of all kinds now come from Mexico, and Brazilian orange juice concentrates are combined with Florida juices in many brands of orange juice sold on the East Coast, where Florida juices by themselves long had an effective monopoly.

Indeed, American food businesses have engaged in much foreign sourcing for their products, in some cases very much to the detriment of the supplier countries. Thus, the beef for some of the fast-food chains now comes from Central America. When such trade practices are followed, export crops often displace others in much of the available agricultural land of the supplier countries. This has happened in Costa Rica, Brazil, and elsewhere in South American countries, as well as in parts of Africa for the European market; it has happened especially where, as for instance in El Salvador, land ownership is concentrated in a few hands. As a result, the food supply for the local people has deteriorated, and it requires no elaborate analysis to conclude that this is a factor in the current struggles in Central America.

The protectionist issues in food industries have always been difficult, and the United States has had its share of problems in exports as well as imports. Thus there have long been attempts to get the Japanese to buy more American food products, such as rice, beef, fruit (including orange juice), and grains. However, the Japanese farm lobby is powerful, and a political map gerrymandered in favor of farm districts is what keeps the ruling Liberal Democratic party in power. Any alternative would be from the left and would produce a government far less willing to share U.S. geopolitical interests. The United States has also tried to increase its food exports to the European Economic Community, but its member states have quite determined and sometimes conflicting farm lobbies of their own. In fact, probably the most serious quarrels within the EEC have been over farm policies. In such an atmosphere, American export expansion is clearly difficult.

There have also been problems with particular imports, like Danish cookies and Italian pasta. In general, however, the main issues concern overall commodities rather than manufactured products and are then related to a multitude of international commodity agreements and subsidies, a detailed examination of which is beyond the scope of this volume. One matter should be mentioned, however. The United States has lost considerable ground as a supplier of wheat in the international markets. One reason is that there are now some major new players in the industry, for instance India. Another, however, is the political use of food sales. When, in response to the invasion of Afghanistan, the United States embargoed wheat to the Soviet Union, the latter turned to less fastidious suppliers and now uses American wheat only after its main import orders have been placed elsewhere. In short, the issue is not just one of price (wheat is, of course, subsidized) but also one of political reliability.

Tobacco Products (SIC 21)

Tobacco products are only one of two major groups that have actually seen an improvement in the EIR ratio; Table 5 shows it to be 1.17 for 1977–85. Although its export percentage is a creditable 6.8, foreign trade does not bulk large in relation to this industry; its A/S ratio is the lowest of all the major groups.

The United States still subsidizes tobacco growing; so far, Congress has not acted on the rather obvious contradiction between subsidies for these crops and the great damage to public health caused by their end uses. American cigarettes are being promoted with particular fervor; they enjoy a high international reputation even though their use some forty years ago as a virtual reserve currency has passed. The industry also takes advantage of the facts that in many countries smoking still is more universal (among men) than in the United States and that the decline in the socioeconomic status of smokers, which was discussed in chapter 2, has not yet become significant.

Textile Mill Products (SIC 22)

Textiles have extensive international trade problems, though not in the same measure as apparel. The two industries are, however, closely linked, so that the following discussion really applies to both. As Tables 4 and 5 show, the EIR ratios are poor indeed; note also that as late as 1980, there was an export surplus, mainly because many textiles were exported to be shipped back as clothing for the American market.

The A/S ratio for textiles is, as shown in Table 6, about equal to the national average for manufacturing. However, there appears to be a deterioration here also in the years since 1984. In 1986, imports accounted for some 10 percent of domestic consumption, but the industry is operating at close to capacity after its long efforts at modernization and consolidation.[1]

The problems of this industry, though severe, are still not as bad as those of the apparel industry, yet there are few major industry groups other than these two whose troubles from import problems are more extensively addressed in public policy and international trade regulations. Basically, the issues are quotas on imports, mainly from the Asian producers, but their ranks there and elsewhere are constantly being added to. Where Hong Kong, Taiwan, and South Korea were once the principal suppliers, now China, India, Sri Lanka, Bangladesh, Malaysia, Singapore, and Thailand have been added. Latin American countries, including Mexico, Brazil, and Costa Rica, also participate. There is also substantial competition, much of it on the high end of the product range, from other industrial countries, notably from Japan and Italy whose designers are among the best in the world.

Whenever competition from a new supplier becomes significant, quota negotiations must be started. Here, in many cases, the United States is torn between protecting a domestic industry with powerful congressional backing and safeguarding the foreign policy relationships with the countries involved, which in such cases as South Korea and especially Taiwan have their own congressional backers.

The American textile industry has been successful to some extent in preventing further inroads of imports, by stressing high-design fabrics and avoiding mass markets where the importers typically have the greatest advantage. Political pressures for further quotas, however, have only increased.

Yet quotas have the same effects as tariffs. It has been estimated that, as a result, clothing and textile prices have been raised by about $20 billion a year. Therefore, for every job protected thereby, there is a cost of about $86,000. Yet apparel and textile wages are less than $7 per hour, or at least $2 less than the average for the private sector. These are, therefore, not the kind of jobs whose preservation should receive this high a priority.[2] Rather, if job training is to be done, the resources would be better expended elsewhere.

That, however, is a viewpoint that has proved hard to sell. The main reason is the neglect of social legislation and programs in recent years. Free trade is a commendable concept, but it becomes domestically infeasible when it is coupled with official indifferences to the economic displacements it causes in some industries. Moreover, it often affects states whose stock in trade in attracting business (see chapter 4) had been the poor protection and services afforded to workers.

Apparel and Related Products (SIC 23)

Apparel is in an even worse situation than the textile industry. Its export trade has declined to the point where, as Table 5 shows, it ties with leather and leather products (SIC 31) for the lowest EIR. As the EIR ratio shows, moreover, the situation has worsened. Furthermore, at about 18 percent above the national average, the apparel industry's A/S ratio is the third highest among the industry groups, so that on both counts it must qualify as one of the most severely stressed.

Apparel is subject to quota arrangements with importers, and thus the comments in the last section on the textile industry apply here as well. They apply particularly to the fact that this is a low-wage industry, with many abuses such as sweat shops in immigrant communities, and that therefore it is arguable whether major costs to the public by way of quotas or tariffs should be incurred to save what are often poor jobs. The better levels of the American apparel industry are in very much better shape in withstanding competition from imports.

Lumber and Related Products (SIC 24)

As noted in other chapters, this industry group is highly sensitive to the ups and downs of home construction. This fact dwarfs all other major problems. Yet this industry too has seen encroachments from imports; even though U.S. exports of wood products are still substantial, the country is a net importer, with an A/S ratio only very slightly above the national average (Table 6). Meanwhile its EIR ratio for 1977–85 also shows a decline (Table 5), even though it is better than the average for all groups.

The principal foreign supplier is Canada, and the disputes over the imports of wood products and pulp are among the most contentious between the two countries. Quotas and penalties have been exacted at various times. In the fall of 1987, a comprehensive free trade treaty was signed by the United States and by the Canadian government of Prime Minister Brian Mulroney. However, its future must be rated highly doubtful, even though it is one of the most comprehensive agreements of this sort ever signed. It has not been submitted to the United States Senate for ratification, and as for Canada, the government there, according to public opinion polls, appears to have fallen out of grace with the electorate. The treaty seems to have contributed to this, and the Liberal and New Democratic opposition parties both promise to scrap it or prevent its ratification, on the grounds that it would make Canada even more dependent on the United States than it already is.

Furniture and Fixtures (SIC 25)

This industry too has its share of import troubles, as the EIR statistics, especially the EIR ratios, indicate. Furthermore, the A/S ratio is also above average. However, much of the problem comes from specialty items, such as wicker furniture from the Far East. The European designers, particularly those of Italy and Scandinavia, have had considerable success at the upper range of the scale. Because many products of this group are heavy and bulky in relation to value, and because some must be tailored exactly to their sites, they generally do not easily lend themselves to imports. Although in 1985 imports exceeded exports by a margin of almost 7 to 1, they are not a problem on the scale found in other industries.

Paper and Allied Products (SIC 26)

The United States is a net importer of paper products, and just as in the case of lumber, the main foreign source is Canada. As the EIR and A/S ratios indicate, however, the former is above and the latter below the national averages, so that this must be considered one of the less afflicted industries.

Nevertheless, the controversies that lumber imports have generated apply to much of the paper import problem as well and promise to be one of the more controversial parts of the trade negotiations with Canada. Basically, apart from some specialty papers used in graphic arts, imports are concentrated in some of the major bulk products like newsprint, paperboard, and corrugated cardboard. Still, these all have substantial domestic production as well. Southern newsprint development especially has for a long time been among the major industries of the region.

Printing and Publishing (SIC 27)

Although this industry shows export surpluses, between 1977 and 1985 the EIR ratio shows a sharp decline in the trade balance. This is particularly noteworthy because most of the constituent industries must necessarily be homegrown, as its A/S ratio of about 1 indicates. One cannot readily visualize newspapers, nor the several commercial printing services that make up this industry, being imported. To be sure, imported paper may be used, but that is a raw material, and considered in SIC 26.

Where imports are getting more prominent is in book publishing, where fine printing, as in color printing for art books, is often done abroad. Italy, Britain, West Germany, Japan, and Hong Kong all are important factors. Typesetting too has been done abroad in some cases, in low-cost English-speaking countries such as the Republic of Ireland and the Caribbean islands.

Chemicals and Allied Products, Except Plastics (SIC 28, Except 282)

This industry group in its entirety (i.e., including plastics) has long enjoyed a substantial export surplus, but as shown by the EIR ratio in Table 5, that has diminished sharply in recent years. Still, its A/S ratio is the second best of all groups and only a little worse than tobacco products. Some chemical products have, from time to time, presented import problems, including accusations of dumping, although this industry group as a whole has not been among those most seriously affected.

The export-import problems of the pharmaceutical industry also deserve comment. American products have a high world reputation, and the industry does much research. However, several of its principal firms are multinational, and their research activities—and, at times, production operations—are shared among domestic and foreign facilities. Furthermore, though not many drugs are imported, the U.S. firms have been beset by some generic drugs in third-country markets, mainly because pharmaceutical patents are unenforceable in certain countries.

Also at issue are the particularly rigorous drug approval procedures required for drugs used in the United States. The U.S. industry has long objected to this situation, and in the 1980s the issue became entangled in the broader political campaign for deregulation, with the argument being that the industry was at an international disadvantage because of these requirements. Still, in the early 1960s, the thalidomide tragedy struck in several countries where the drug had been freely used. Only the procedures established by the Food and Drug Administration prevented a similar tragedy in the United States. While those needing drugs not yet licensed are sometimes forced to secure them from abroad, the safeguards built into the current system no doubt command wide public support.

Petroleum Refining and Related Industries (SIC 29)

As noted earlier, this industry has been buffeted by the turmoil in the oil markets. Before 1973, the domestic industry was protected by quotas and favorable tax treatment, but after the oil price shock it was obviously easy for it to produce at its maximum capacity. Still, not all potential could be realized, because many of the refineries had been built on the Atlantic and Pacific coasts and relied heavily on imported raw materials.

As the EIR statistics indicate, the industry was able to better itself in 1977–85 because of the great price reductions. However, it is clearly heavily import-dependent, as shown by an A/S ratio that is the fourth highest among the major groups (Table 6) and would no doubt be much higher if another price explosion were to take place.

One trend to be considered is that, for some time, purchases of fuel have increasingly been in the form of gasoline and heating oil from the refineries of the producing countries, like Venezuela, Saudi Arabia, Kuwait, and other Gulf states. This is so, even though overall U.S. dependence on oil from the Gulf has sharply diminished. Though much traffic is still in the form of crude oil, which for one thing is safer to transport than gasoline or jet fuel, the OPEC countries have spent great sums on new refineries, granting them direct and indirect subsidies paid out of profits from crude oil.[3] Some of these new re- fineries, several of which were completed only very recently, have American partners, thus clouding the import picture considerably.[4]

The biggest issue in international trade relating to this industry group, of course, remains the huge dependence of the United States on imported fuel. It declined for an extended period after the oil shock but started to rise again once oil prices fell. As noted above, the Reagan Administration conspicuously delayed filling the National Petroleum Reserve and, as one of its first acts, cut out most support for energy conservation. Refineries themselves are only part of the overall problem of oil supply, but clearly that cannot be left to the kinds of ups and downs in relation to price that the industry has been experiencing.

Rubber and Plastics Products (SIC 282 and 30)

This group is best discussed in two parts, the first dealing with its raw material supply (SIC 282) and the second with fabrication (SIC 30). The former is essentially related to petrochemical production and was therefore subjected to the price shocks of petroleum pro- ducts during much of the study period. The petrochemical industry of the United States had long been regarded, with justification, as highly innovative and competent. Certainly its expansion in the 1950s and early 1960s—taking place mostly along the Gulf Coast between Corpus Christi, Texas, and Baton Rouge, Louisiana—was by far the largest aggregation of its kind in the world.

When the price of oil soared, the industry's prospects dimmed, and as late as the early 1980s, it could be called depressed. It was thought likely, moreover, that petrochemical facilities put in place by such primary producers as Saudi Arabia and Venezuela would soon be important enough to preclude any significant revival of the American industry, even though the use of plastics continued its expansion at a significant pace.

This, however, did not happen. First, the American plants were both very large to benefit from economies of scale, and were kept in a reasonably modern state. They were thus well able to take advantage of the lower prices for the oil fractions they needed as their own feedstocks, as well as of the declining dollar, which made their output more competitively priced internationally.

Second, petrochemical plants can often use refinery intermediates that would otherwise be hard to sell as such, and oil refineries can price them very competitively, especially when the petrochemical plants are part of the same integrated oil company. Petrochemical output such as monomers for plastic resins can then sometimes simply be pumped over the back fence to a resin fabricator. These combined advantages took some time to make themselves evident, but by the beginning of 1988 the industry was doing well internationally, with a $10 billion export surplus and substantial plans for expansion.[5]

The fabricating end of the plastics industry in SIC 30 also had considerable export advantages, but as Table 5 shows, the EIRs of the whole industry group have been going down steadily. In the matter of the ratio of apparent consumption to volume of shipment (A/S), the fabricating sector (SIC 30) of this industry group is now slightly below the average for all industry, but at 102.0 percent, it means that the country now uses more of the product than it produces. Considering the extent to which the basic discoveries were made in the United States and, above all, successfully developed commercially, this is a sad record indeed.

The problems, however, are concentrated in a few industries that have been hard hit by imports, notably tires. The American industry was tardy in pushing steel-belted radials, which had been invented by Michelin in France, and so imports grew steadily, attaining a market share of about 20 percent in 1984. One element in this is the growing practice of American producers to have the tires they sell in the United States made by their foreign subsidiaries.[6] The importation of plastic products in general, on the other hand, is to a large extent a result of their being built into imported manufactured items of all kinds, rather than imported as components.

Leather and Leather Products (SIC 31)

As noted in prior discussion, this industry is by far the most seriously affected by competition from imports. It is thus necessary mainly to review its quantitative measures of foreign trade performance that were developed in this chapter. As shown in Table 6, the A/S ratio of this major group is 167.3. This means that about two-thirds more was consumed in the United States than was produced. This is by far the worst score of any major group. Furthermore, as Table 5 shows, in 1977 the ratio of exports to imports was the lowest of any major group, and in 1985 it was tied with apparel for the lowest score. Meanwhile the EIR ratio showed further deterioration in the balance.

The remedies tried, whether tariffs or quotas, have so far done nothing to stem the decline. The problem is that the competition from imports extends over the whole spectrum of products. Cheap shoes may come in from Korea, the Philippines, or Brazil, but expensive shoes are, if anything, subjected to even worse competition from Italy, Switzerland, Britain, and other countries. The same is true of other leather products, where Mexico, Italy, Brazil, Uruguay, and others are potent competitors both on price and on style.

The frequent rationalization for import damage, to the effect that the American industry will still be able to hang on to the high end of the product line, is thus completely unacceptable. The United States will never be able to eliminate competition from countries with fashion and design experience that carries with it ancient artistic traditions as well as industrial skills. Nor should it try to do so. What seems to be indicated here is the need to strive for coexistence as a way of extending the choices offered to consumers and meanwhile to reexamine this industry and to see what reequipment and new production methods can do. As noted at the beginning of the discussion of this industry in chapter 2, this has been the most conspicuous failure of the adjustment legislation now on the books.

Stone, Clay, and Glass Products (SIC 32)

In view of the fact that much of the product of this industry group is heavy, bulky, not easily transported, and closely linked to local markets, it might be thought that import pressures would not be among this industry's leading problems. The statistics, however, belie this. The A/S ratio is slightly below the average for all manufacturing (Table 6), but this, by rights, should be an industry that does considerably better. As it is, apparent consumption is slightly ahead of production. In the EIR ratios, however, this industry group has one of the lowest, meaning that imports have been exceeding exports at an ever increasing rate. As Table 5 shows, the EIR ratio for 1985 in relation to 1977 is only 0.50, meaning that relative import dependence has doubled in that time.

The explanation is that this is a highly diverse group and that it includes industries that have been particularly hard hit. They are, essentially, the makers of glassware, china, and earthenware. The import competition, moreover bears some resemblance to the one for shoes, as described in the last section. It affects all parts of the product line and comes from countries where the manufacture of these products may go back centuries or even millenia and was once powerfully supported by the royal courts and other rulers. The manufacturing skills and artistic traditions developed as a result present formidable challenges. Japan is a case in point. Years ago, Japan produced attractive but cheap chinaware and earthenware. Japanese designs and quality, however, improved to the extent that its products are now among the most sought after, even though they are no longer cheap.

Yet the United States has its own tradition of high-quality goods. In one type of glassware, for instance that of pressed glass, the United States originated the process, and many of the early items particularly are prized by museums and collectors. The current import competition, however, extends from the finest products to many of the simplest ones, where cheap labor, mostly in Asia and Latin America, is the main determinant.

There is here, however, a second element for which there is far less excuse than there is for the greater experience or artistic talents of others. It is that the industries now most seriously hurt have long neglected research on both products and processes. It started with the new methods of making flat glass of high optical quality, developed mainly by Pilkington's in England and only later introduced in the United States in the 1960s, (i.e., about the start of this study).

A second missed opportunity was the development of tempered glassware by St. Gobain and Crystal d'Arques in France. This soon became popular for drinking glasses and glass plates and provided formidable competition to such traditional American makers as Owens-Illinois and Anchor-Hocking. During the 1970s, however, following some years of relatively poor business, the American makers of all these products cut back severely on research.[7] As is frequently the case, this turned out to be an invitation to disaster.

Primary Metal Industries (SIC 33)

The central difficulties presented by imports in this field are reflected in very poor EIR ratios as well as the fourth highest A/S ratio.

The United States, according to the latter, uses about 14 percent more primary metals than it produces. Considering that the United States was once by far the world's largest producer and a substantial net exporter as well, the change is a drastic one. It also reflects the increasing amount of primary processing done in the producing countries. It is no longer economic in many cases to import the ores and refine them here.

It is sometimes possible to present the question as a chicken-and-egg issue: whether imports of an industry's product caused its decay or whether the decay caused the customers to buy more from abroad. This is not tenable in several of the industries in this group, notably in steel. The neglect of its research and its failure to make use of highly advantageous innovations have led directly to its commercial troubles. The American industry is now so distressed that its productivity in tons per worker is lower than that of Japan by a large margin. Thus traditional arguments about cheap labor are no longer valid. Thanks to the inflated value of the yen and Western European currencies, that gap has been virtually closed. The issue is then simply physical; the plants are more modern in Japan and also in part have larger production units. Thus the advantage is both one of technical superiority and economy of scale.

Much has been made of the fact that the Japanese industry is itself beset by competition from others, most notably South Korea, whose steel capacity has been growing apace. For political reasons, the United States has not pressured South Korea to revalue its currency significantly against the dollar. Thus Japan is at a particular disadvantage against South Korea, with which its relations are in any case troubled by historical memories. It is thus noteworthy that Japanese steel mills have also been cut back, but unlike U.S. steel areas where such opportunities generally disappeared at the same time the steel mills closed, the workers could be absorbed in other heavy industry.

Most ominously for what remains of the American steel industry, however, its Japanese competitors are going into direct reduction, that is, they are eliminating their blast furnaces. This, as noted in chapter 3, has so far been mostly ignored by American makers, even though some of the basic processes were developed in the United States.

Meanwhile, global overcapacity is a fact of life; predictions are sometimes made of a coming steel shortage, but these appear to have little foundation except as whistlings past the cemetery. At any rate, the conditions of technology as well as of markets are such that the American industry must remain endangered, even in its reduced state.

Fabricated Metal Products (SIC 34)

As of 1984, this industry group was in approximate balance, the apparent consumption of its products roughly matching domestic output. However, its EIR's were low and the EIR ratios showed a decline. The industry thus appeared to be headed for an import surplus.

Much of the product of this industry is bulky or heavy or of low specific value and cannot, therefore, absorb much in the nature of transportation costs. Still the group has several import problems in some of its constituent industries as, for instance, in cutlery (SIC 3421), saws and hand tools (SIC 3423 and 3425), and general hardware (SIC 3429).

In the latter two areas, price appears to have been the major incentive. These items are almost universally mass produced by automatic machinery that for many products runs at such high speeds that labor costs per unit are measured in seconds or less. Thus labor cost per se is not the crucial variable. Rather, if an overseas supplier has modern machinery that runs faster than the old-fashioned equipment still used by the American industry, a severe competitive disadvantage is created for the domestic suppliers. Though much of the industry's product has designs of what can only be called ancient lineage, there is innovation; the problem is that even American innovators or inventors may well consider having their product manufactured for them abroad, with themselves only as distributors.

The import problems of cutlery are quite similar to those discussed earlier for tableware. The importing countries of Europe have high traditions of craftsmanship and design and have, in fact, been at the forefront of innovation; the work done in the Scandinavian countries is particularly noteworthy. At the same time, a combination of lower labor costs and more high-speed equipment has made imports from Europe, and especially from Asia, formidable competitors. This industry, therefore is affected by the kind of broad-gauge competition that straddles the entire product line from the highest quality to the cheapest items.

Machinery, Except Electrical (SIC 35, Except 357)

This entire major group still showed an export surplus in 1984, with an apparent consumption of its product below domestic production, specifically with an A/S ratio the third lowest of all industry groups (Table 6). However, the EIR ratios tell a different story. As Table 5 indicates, the EIR fell from 3.00 in 1977 to 1.20 in 1985 (i.e., in only eight years). A more detailed set of data appears in Table 4, in which all categories of machinery are shown to have EIR ratios denoting a sharp deterioration in the export-import balance. It is of particular interest that in the period 1967–80, two major categories, those of special machinery and of metalworking machinery, became net importers; machine tools actually went into the net import column in 1979. Further sharp declines in the U.S. trade situation are shown by the EIR ratios in 1980–85.

In spite of its overall situation, this is a deeply troubled industry group in all its leading sectors. The reasons were reviewed in chapter 2 in connection with its general product mix and the troubles it has had. In chapter 3, the particular case of robots was discussed, as an illustration of the difficulties the industry faces in its products and in the ways it could change its production systems so as to become more competitive with foreign producers. Many once famous American firms have lagged badly in product innovation and design, in understanding the needs of the customers, and in product quality. Worst of all, perhaps, has been a tendency of the managements involved to give up on an independent existence, seeking refuge instead in some forms of disinvestment or dealerships for foreign makers. This is clearly an industry in dire need of extensive therapy; an often observed tendency on its part to coast along on memories of past glory simply will not be enough in the changed conditions in which this group now finds itself.

Instead, parts of it at least have turned sharply protectionist; the voice of this industry group is not, however, united in this, illustrating the problems and inconsistencies that protectionists often face. Conventionally protectionist sentiment becomes somewhat inhibited when one relies on one's own foreign subsidiaries to support third country markets and becomes an agent for foreign machinery instead of producing one's own.

Electrical Machinery, Except Electronics (SIC 361–364)

Major group 36 as a whole shows a relatively poor A/S ratio, but that is probably largely due to electronic equipment. As to the EIR's, however, two categories in this group, power generation equipment and electrical machinery, both show deterioration of their EIR's in the study period, with EIR ratios from 1967 to 1980 at 0.80 and 0.71

respectively (Table 4). These industries have also shown secular declines as the rapid pace of expansion of the electric power industry has come to a halt after the energy crises of 1973 and subsequently. The impact on the domestic industry was thus twofold; there was less business altogether, and exports played a much bigger part in it.

As to the other large industries in this group, the major appliance industry of the United States is fortunate that its products are too heavy and bulky to be convenient import products. Thus, pending the arrival of branch plants of foreign makers, the U.S. manufacturers have the American market largely to themselves and are also in a position to let foreign subsidiaries supply other markets. In small appliances, however, the situation is much different; there, major incursions of foreign appliances have occurred that are again broad gauge in nature. There are imports both at the cheap end—made abroad for American labels—and at the high end of the scale—special items and advanced designs from foreign suppliers.

Electronic Products (SIC 357, 365–369)

The problems created for these industries by imports are so grave and so central that they necessarily affect all discussion of their products and manufacturing. Chapters 2 and 3, therefore, dealt with certain aspects of the problem in much detail. As Table 4 indicates, the EIR ratio for office machines and computers (SIC 357) showed only a small deterioration between 1967 and 1980 (i.e., approximately during the study period). Thereafter, however, the drop was rapid. The EIR ratio from 1980 to 1985 was only 0.38, the export advantage being cut to a little over one-third of what it had been. Imports of small computers especially, as well as Japanese and other imported copying machines, were major factors in this decline.

Telecommunications equipment (SIC 366) likewise showed a very sharp decline; its EIR ratio for 1967–85 is 0.25, reflecting a reduction of the export-import balance to a quarter of what it had been at the beginning of the period.

The accounts of other classes of equipment, especially in consumer electronics, are, if anything, even more daunting. In 1960, 95 percent of all radios were produced domestically; in 1980, half the market was supplied by imports. By then, 87 percent of black-and-white sets were imported, as were all tape recorders and dictation machines.[8]

The situation has strongly deteriorated since then, because even American brand names are generally found on equipment with major imported components or are increasingly imported as finished products, thus completing the transformation of the U.S. electronics business from originator and pioneer to distributor of imports.[9]

Finally, as noted in chapter 2, one of the comforting rationalizations and illusions in this issue was always that the simple stuff could be safely left to foreigners. It was, of course, always questionable that an industry could subsist or even advance on the pioneering activities that are generally the most risky and show little profit. In earlier times, such work was considered the entry ticket to mass production of staple products which would provide a sound basis for major industries; yet that part of the market was lightly abandoned to the imports.

Such a concentration also is inherently unstable. These doubts were strongly confirmed in a report to the Joint Economic Committee of the U.S. Congress that high-tech trade had itself moved into a net trade deficit.[10] As defined, high-tech is an activity involving an industry whose research spending is more than twice the industrial average. Though not exclusively electronic, electronic products are by far its largest component. This, in a sense, is the ultimate judgment on the difficulties that now face these industries, in that not even so-called advanced products can have markets adequate to counterbalance the imports and that the once prevalent skills in the commercial development of technically and scientifically sophisticated products have fallen on bad times.

Motor Vehicles (SIC 371, 3751, and 379)

The export problems of the automobile industry are so well known that only an outline is required here. Extensive reference was made to them in earlier discussions of this industry. As Table 4 shows, road vehicles still had a favorable export balance in 1967. By 1980, exports were 57 percent of imports and fell further to 43 percent in 1985. These statistics are the principal reason why major SIC group 37 taken together has the rather poor A/S ratio of 107.9 (Table 6). This group, after all, also includes passenger aircraft, in which the United States still has an export surplus, albeit a rapidly shrinking one.

Imports of cars are holding steady at close to 30 percent, and the competition is again what in this volume has been called broad gauge; that is, it covers the entire range of vehicles, from subcompacts to luxury cars. There are now also potent Japanese entries in the latter segment where the imports had typically been European.

During the study period, quotas were imposed once the proportion of imports rose to 25 percent of the market. One aspect of the competition that was most disastrous to the American makers was that it concentrated on small cars and small trucks, both of which were in great demand after the oil crisis. It took the American industry some years to respond, and it did so in part by importing cars itself from foreign subsidiaries, through joint ventures or as agents.

The Japanese car industry responded to the numerical quotas by importing the more expensive ("loaded") models and thus was propelled into the luxury market; prior to that, it had made expensive models mainly for its home market. In short, what had been billed as a way of protecting American prosperity exacted a considerable toll from American car buyers.

Meanwhile a real cheap generation of subcompacts came on the scene. One of them, the Korean Hyundai, is manifestly a formidable competitor. Though rated below the Japanese cars in quality, its price is so much less that it has made major inroads in the market for small cars. Another challenger, the Yugo, a Yugoslav version of an earlier Fiat model, was much less well received, but cars from other countries are waiting to make their entry, including other Korean makes. American industry executives estimate that there will soon be a global excess capacity of at least three million cars a year. This is reminiscent of the overcapacity in steel, and for a similar reason. Having a car industry is something of a national status symbol as well as a way of making money. Furthermore, as noted in the last chapter, the Japanese car industry has been moving to the United States, lured by a totally distorted devaluation of the dollar and lower interest costs. This move also distorts the whole protectionist picture, with the prospect of "Japanese" cars made in the U.S.A. and "American" cars made in the Far East, Mexico, or Brazil.[11]

The U.S. industry has done much to respond to the problem, as noted before. However, there has been no real product innovation, such as a new propulsion system, even though greatly reduced fuel consumption is technically feasible. The study period also witnessed an increase in the time people kept their cars. From an average age of 5.7 years in 1972, cars were kept an average of 7.2 years in 1982; the premium placed on the reliability of Japanese cars suggests that this trend will continue, and indeed, the economics suggest that it is advisable to keep a car until it literally will not run any more.[12]

This complex situation raises the question of what the American industry could and should have done better. A number of books have chronicled the hidebound methods of management of American firms, as compared to those of their Japanese rivals, particularly their penchant for ignoring innovation other than styling.[13] Worst of all was the complacent belief that the large auto makers would always be around no matter what they sold. The resultant quality collapse gave the imports a bigger boost than prices, which were identical or higher for most of the imports. Good reputation, once lost, is very hard to recapture. Beyond that, it will, as noted, soon be difficult to classify many cars as domestic or foreign.

In another related industry, the situation in motorcycles was almost as bad, with predominantly Japanese imports like Kawasaki, Honda, Yamaha, and Suzuki reducing American makers to Harley Davidson as sole survivor. Again, it was a matter of not innovating and of ignoring a demand for smaller units.

As to tanks, the number of participants in the international arms game has grown steadily, and where any sort of competition with real money changing hands is involved, rather than being part of military aid, the United States has not fared well. The frequent news reports on troubled products like the M-1 tank and Bradley vehicle are not exactly helpful to the sales effort.

Other Transportation Equipment (SIC 372, 373, 374, 376)

Aircraft are, as noted, still something of a bright spot, but the arrival of Airbus Industrie as an effective competitor has demolished what had once been an American monopoly. As to rail equipment, only diesel locomotives and freight cars are still made in the United States.

Rapid transit equipment and electric traction generally are, for practical purposes, no longer available from U.S. makers, except for units made under foreign license. The United States has not participated significantly except as a minor player and late entrant in such technologies as traction using commercial frequencies or AC traction motors. It is not active at all in magnetic levitation technology or in high speed rail traffic generally, even though it keeps being talked about. Several cities have built extremely expensive new systems, and some have gone into "light rail," meaning trolley cars. The equipment must now be imported, however, in the country where first invented.

As to shipbuilding, the fact that it is virtually extinct, except for naval shipyards, can be set against the fact that ever fewer vessels fly the American flag, flying instead flags of convenience.

Instruments and Related Products (SIC 38)

This industry group might be regarded as favorably situated in the total export-import balance, having an A/S ratio of less than 100 percent, as shown in Table 6. That, however, was in 1984. In 1985, as Table 5 indicates, the EIR had shifted to a net import balance, albeit a small one. The table shows a long-term deterioration, for an industry group that as recently as 1977 had exports almost two-thirds greater than imports. The culprit is probably the increasing electronic content of instruments, since the problems faced by that industry quickly spread to other users of their products.

To be sure, some industries in this group, such as medical instruments, have always had a substantial imported component of specialized items, but even so, the decline in only eight years must be considered quite startling. This group also includes photographic equipment, another industry that, though the mass product had been pioneered in the United States, has been reduced to a maker of supplies rather than cameras. Even granted that the better ones have long been imported, that is yet another troublesome case. It is probably responsible, to an important extent, for the move of this group into the net import column.

Miscellaneous Manufactures (SIC 39)

This group had the second worst A/S ratio of all major industry groups, showing that the United States consumed about 28 percent more of its products than it makes domestically. The group includes several areas in which quality products from abroad have sharply reduced the markets for American products. Optical goods like binoculars and telescopes are cases in point. Other items are again broad gauge, like toys in which both some of the most expensive and some of the cheapest items are imported. Foreign sourcing or manufacturing arrangements are common in that industry. In spite of occasional contrary trends that mostly involve novelties or temporary crazes, the EIR ratios show a steady decline; by 1985, exports had fallen to one-sixth of imports, from a little less than half only eight years before.

A LONG ROAD BACK

The discussion of industrial troubles in this volume has revealed a set of difficulties that stretches over every major industry group and most of the constituent industries. There can be no doubt that the decline has gone very far indeed and that urgent attention must be paid to the possibility of recovery. How this is to be done must obviously depend on the situation in each industry. Nevertheless, declining industries appear to share the following features:

1. A sense of complacency that what American manufacturers turn out is best for the American market and that people will buy the product, no matter how unsuitable or how poor the quality

2. A belief that American industry is always at the conceptual, scientific, or technological forefront and that where it is not, it can always buy what it needs from others

3. A sense of isolationism that leads managements to ignore the international dimensions that have been taken on by virtually all major industries

4. A preoccupation with short-run returns and a lack of long-term planning, not so much of a financial nature but of products and related research

5. A tendency to ignore the central role of good production design, which is not the same as piling on overhead in celebration of the "information age"—a concept that now demands some cold reassessment of cost effectiveness

6. Sustained, ideologically determined opposition by managements to governmental regulation of products and workplaces but not to subsidies, protectionism, or currency manipulation, thus continuing to rely on governmental remedies for managerial folly

7. In the advanced scientific products, a failure to recognize the dysfunctions created by the military preemption of scientific and technical talent and the resultant misdirection of industrial effort away from commercially viable products

8. A failure, above all, to enlist the cooperation of employees at all levels, choosing instead further elaboration of an already far too hierarchical mode of organization and of confrontational policies generally

It might be objected that the foregoing problems are hardly novel and that indeed they are familiar in many industrial contexts. What is new, however, is their simultaneous spread over almost the entire industrial spectrum, rather than just being troubles of individual firms. This is clear from the discussion of the various industry groups in this volume.

It is also important to view in perspective what appears to be something of a resurgence in manufacturing in 1987. There was a 19 percent increase in exports of manufactured goods in 1987, but as the year ended the trade gap was as wide as ever, in part because, as noted, the devaluation of the dollar had largely exempted the major Asian exporters other than Japan.[14] However Japan has not fared badly; although the yen has doubled in value against the U.S. dollar since 1985, Japan has been able to compensate for a fall in auto exports by exporting machinery and office equipment. It has become doubtful that the 1988 Japanese trade surplus with the United States will be much reduced from its previous high levels, despite a decline early in the year.[15]

Even more serious was the fact that so much manufacturing capacity had been eliminated, or had never been built, that American ability to take advantage of what amounted to an international subsidy for the dollar was sharply constrained on that score alone.[16] Many managements had become used to congratulating themselves on the plants they had shut down and the number of jobs they had slashed and were unable to reverse themselves at anything remotely resembling short notice. Most serious of all, in addition to the lack of skills and facilities, the products that might have fueled a true reversal no longer existed in many potentially fruitful areas.

American firms have, in fact, spent record amounts on expanding their foreign facilities. One news report quoted some executives who seemed to find it almost bizarre that products should actually be exported from the United States rather than made in their foreign branches. Also evident was the desire to have "access" to foreign technology.[17] There is therefore the danger that with the current research lag in many industries, "access" will turn into "dependence," and an independent American industrial recovery will fade far into the future.

It appeared to be a more realistic sign of the times that in December 1987 the city of Chicago decided to create a new kind of zoning, that of the Protected Manufacturing District, in which factory buildings were to be preserved for their original purposes rather than converted into apartment lofts, trendy shops, and restaurants.[18] This kind of change had become increasingly widespread, especially near waterfronts.

In a sense, this trend showed a double industrial decline: Manufacturing industry had perished, at least in the locality affected, and the construction industry was no longer able to provide even the relatively affluent customers attracted by the redevelopers of factories with spacious residences having such amenities as high ceilings and floor load capacities. Even "luxury" apartments had become small, constricted, and poorly built—what the architectural critic Lewis Mumford once called "superslums."

These issues and many others must be addressed in what will be a long road back to industrial competence. Neither ideological posturing nor slogans will provide shortcuts to a restoration of the kind of industrial strength that can avoid a sustained decline in the standard of life to which Americans have been taught to aspire and which seems essential to their civil peace and social cohesion.

NOTES

1. W. Cline, *The Future of World Trade in Textiles and Apparel* (Washington, D.C.: Institute for International Economics, 1987).

2. Ibid.

3. "Why Cheap Fuel Isn't Such Good News," *Business Week*, April 8, 1985, 122.

4. "Oil and Gas: More Bad News Is in the Pipeline," *Business Week*, March 22, 1985, 241.

5. T. C. Hayes, "An Industry Where U.S. Prospers," *New York Times*, March 10, 1988.

6. "Rubber and Plastics Products," in U.S. Department of Commerce, *U.S. Industrial Outlook 1985* (Washington, D.C.: Government Printing Office, 1985), 18-3.

7. "Innovative R&D Gone with the Wind?" *Chemical Engineering*, September 1978, 73.

8. The Business Week Team, *The Reindustrialization of America* (New York: McGraw-Hill, 1982), 14.

9. "America's High Tech Crisis," *Business Week*, March 11, 1985, 62.

10. U.S. Congress, Joint Economic Committee, *The U.S. Trade Position in High Technology, 1980-1986* (Washington, D.C.: Government Printing Office 1986).

11. "Will the Auto Glut Choke Detroit?" *Business Week*, March 7, 1988, 54.

12. Shell Oil Company, *The Longer Life Car Book* (New York: Shell Oil Co., 1983).

13. See, for instance, D. Halberstam, *The Reckoning* (New York: Morrow, 1986).

14. C. H. Farnsworth, "4 Asian Economies Assailed," *New York Times*, November 27, 1987.

15. "More Than Ever, the World Is Buying Japanese," *Business Week*, May 30, 1988, 44-45.

16. B. J. Feder, "What the Dollar's Drop Won't Do," *New York Times*, December 6, 1987.

17. L. Uchitelle, "Overseas Spending by U.S. Companies Sets Record Pace," *New York Times*, May 20, 1988.

18. W. E. Schmidt, "Chicago Plan Aims to Curb Factory Losses," *New York Times*, December 10, 1987.

APPENDIX

Rates of Change in Constant Dollar
Value Added and Capital Spending
per Employee (CDVAM/E and CDCS/E), 1967–82,
by SIC Four-Digit Industries

SIC	NAME	CDVAM/E	CDCS/E
		percent per year	
20	Food and Kindred Products		
2011	Meatpacking plants	0.7	1.4
2013	Sausages and other prepared foods	2.0	2.6
2015	Poultry and small game dressing, packaging, wholesale	0.2	2.5
2021	Creamery butter	0.0	2.3
2022	Cheese, natural and processed	3.5	5.0
2023	Condensed and evaporated milk	1.4	6.1
2024	Ice cream and frozen desserts	0.3	-0.3
2026	Fluid milk	2.4	3.4
2032	Canned specialties	0.3	0.8
2033	Canned fruits and vegetables	1.9	1.9
2034	Dehydrated fruits, vegetables, soups	2.3	4.2
2035	Pickles, sauces, salad dressings	3.2	1.9
2037	Frozen fruits and vegetables including frozen specialties	1.8	0.3
2041	Flour, other grain mill products	1.1	2.2
2043	Cereal breakfast foods	2.2	6.2
2044	Rice milling	2.7	9.4
2045	Blended and prepared flour	-2.4	-1.5
2046	Wet corn milling	5.1	13.1
2047	Dog, cat, and other pet food; prepared feeds, etc.	1.6	0.4
2051	Bread, cake, and related products	n.a.	n.a.
2052	Cookies and crackers	1.3	5.3
2061	Raw cane sugar	1.7	5.2
2062	Cane sugar refining	-0.2	0.3
2063	Beet sugar	-1.5	-0.1
2065	Confectionery products	3.5	2.6
2066	Chocolate and cocoa products	3.0	3.1
2067	Chewing gum	-0.1	-0.9
2074	Cottonseed oil mills	4.3	6.9
2075	Soybean oil mills	-1.0	2.9
2076	Vegetable oil mills, n.e.c.	-0.2	9.3

SIC	Name	CDVAM/E	CDCS/E
		percent per year	
2077	Animal and marine fats and oils	0.4	0.9
2079	Shortening and cooking oils	1.4	3.0
2082	Malt beverages	1.4	7.4
2083	Malt	2.6	13.9
2084	Wines, brandy, and brandy spirits	-0.2	1.8
2085	Distilled liquor, except brandy	1.4	-1.3
2086	Bottled and canned soft drinks	2.9	5.0
2087	Flavoring extracts, syrups, n.e.c.	1.1	0.6
2091	Canned and cured seafoods	2.3	4.0
2092	Fresh or frozen packaged fish	-0.1	3.2
2095	Roasted coffee	3.2	-0.4
2097	Manufactured ice	0.4	4.3
2098	Macaroni and spaghetti	3.0	9.5
2099	Food preparations, n.e.c.	1.8	1.4
21	Tobacco Products		
2111	Cigarettes	1.5	10.8
2121	Cigars	1.9	-1.5
2131	Chewing and smoking tobacco	4.9	10.6
2141	Tobacco stemming and redrying	1.6	9.8
22	Textile Mill Products		
2211	Broad-woven fabric mills, cotton	3.2	3.6
2221	Broad-woven fabric mills, man-made fiber and silk	3.3	0.0
2231	Broad-woven fabric mills, wool	3.2	-0.7
2241	Narrow fabrics	2.2	0.8
2251	Women's full-length and knee-length hosiery	3.8	-3.7
2252	Hosiery, other	2.4	-1.7
2253	Knit outerwear mills	2.7	-3.4
2254	Knit underwear mills	1.7	3.7
2257	Circular knit fabric mills	n.a.	n.a.
2258	Warp knit fabric mills	2.1	-6.7
2259	Knitting mills, n.e.c.	-1.5	-7.1
2261	Finishers of broad-woven fabrics of cotton	2.4	-1.1
2262	Finishers of broad-woven fabrics of man-made fiber and silk	2.9	0.3

SIC	Name	CDVAM/E	CDCS/E
		percent per year	
2269	Finishers of textiles, n.e.c.	2.2	-2.2
2271	Woven carpets and rugs	1.8	-5.5
2272	Tufted carpets and rugs	1.6	-3.5
2279	Carpets and rugs, n.e.c.	-1.5	-17.4
2281	Yarn spinning mills: cotton, man-made fibers, and silk	3.0	-1.6
2282	Throwing and winding mills	0.7	-4.8
2283	Yarn mills, wool, including carpet and rug yarn	2.1	-4.1
2284	Thread mills	1.2	-1.9
2291	Felt goods, except hats	1.9	6.6
2292	Lace goods	0.6	-4.9
2293	Paddings and upholstery filling	0.7	0.6
2294	Processed waste and recovered fibers and flock	5.6	0.2
2295	Coated fabrics, not rubberized	0.6	-0.8
2296	Tire cord and fabric	3.2	-14.2
2297	Nonwoven fabrics	n.a.	n.a.
2298	Cordage and twine	2.4	2.6
2299	Textile goods, n.e.c.	n.a.	n.a.
23	Apparel and Fabricated Textile Products		
2311	Men's and boys' suits and coats	1.1	-1.1
2321	Men's and boys' shirts	1.6	1.4
2322	Men's and boys' underwear	n.a.	n.a.
2323	Men's and boys' neckwear	2.0	0.7
2327	Men's and boys' separate trousers	3.5	-2.6
2328	Men's and boys' work clothes	2.5	4.0
2329	Men's and boys' clothing, n.e.c.	1.1	-0.7
2331	Women's and misses' blouses and waists	2.6	0.3
2335	Women's and misses' dresses	0.1	2.0
2337	Women's and misses' suits and coats	2.0	-2.0
2339	Women's and misses' outerwear, n.e.c.	2.3	1.8
2341	Women's and children's underwear	2.0	0.0
2342	Brassieres and allied garments	1.9	0.1
2351	Millinery	n.a.	n.a.
2352	Hats and caps, except millinery	1.7	8.0
2361	Children's dresses and blouses	1.8	-3.4
2363	Children's coats and suits	-0.3	0.9

SIC	Name	CDVAM/E	CDCS/E
		percent per year	
2369	Children's outerwear, n.e.c.	1.3	-0.3
2371	Fur goods	2.8	-7.6
2381	Fabric dress and work gloves	-0.4	1.6
2384	Robes and dressing gowns	2.2	6.8
2385	Waterproof outer garments	n.a.	n.a.
2386	Leather and sheep-lined clothing	-3.3	-1.4
2387	Apparel belts	2.7	0.0
2389	Apparel and accessories, n.e.c.	1.5	-3.8
2391	Curtains and draperies	1.9	-1.5
2392	House furnishings, n.e.c.	3.4	-6.5
2393	Textile bags	3.0	5.7
2394	Canvas and related products	4.0	1.4
2395	Pleating and stitching	4.7	9.2
2396	Automotive and apparel trimmings	4.7	7.3
2397	Schiffli machine embroideries	-0.5	7.8
2399	Fabricated textile products, n.e.c.	2.2	-7.0
24	Lumber and Wood Products, except Furniture		
2411	Logging camps and contractors	1.5	5.8
2421	Sawmills and planning mills, general	0.2	7.2
2426	Hardwood dimension and flooring mills	-0.3	-4.8
2429	Special product sawmills, n.e.c.	1.1	4.2
2431	Millwork	n.a.	n.a.
2434	Wood kitchen cabinets	n.a.	n.a.
2435	Hardwood veneer and plywood	-3.1	-1.4
2436	Softwood veneer and plywood	0.4	5.4
2439	Structural wood member, n.e.c.	n.a.	n.a.
2441	Nailed and lock corner wood boxes	-0.2	-2.8
2448	Wood pallets and skids	n.a.	n.a.
2449	Wood containers, not elsewhere classified	-2.3	2.1
2451	Mobile homes	n.a.	n.a.

SIC	Name	CDVAM/E	CDCS/E
		percent per year	
2452	Prefabricated wood buildings and components	n.a.	n.a.
2491	Wood preserving	1.0	5.3
2492	Particle board	n.a.	n.a.
2499	Wood products, n.e.c.	n.a.	n.a.
25	Furniture and Fixtures		
2511	Wood household furniture, except upholstered	n.a.	n.a.
2512	Wood household furniture, upholstered	-2.1	0.9
2514	Metal household furniture	1.9	1.2
2515	Mattresses and bedsprings	4.0	-1.7
2517	Wood television, radio, phonograph, and sewing machine cabinets	n.a.	n.a.
2519	Household furniture, n.e.c.	2.8	7.2
2521	Wood office furniture	1.7	6.0
2522	Metal office furniture	-0.2	2.5
2531	Public building and related furniture	-1.2	2.1
2541	Wood partitions, shelving, lockers, and office and store fixtures	-2.2	-0.8
2542	Metal partitions, shelving, lockers, and office and store fixtures	-0.6	0.5
2591	Drapery hardware and window blinds and shades	-0.1	3.0
2599	Furniture and fixtures, n.e.c.	0.2	2.6
26	Pulp and Paper		
2611	Pulp mills	2.3	1.9
2621	Paper mills, except building paper mills	3.2	6.0
2631	Paperboard mills	0.6	8.7
2641	Paper coating and glazing	-2.2	0.4
2642	Envelopes	-0.4	-0.5
2643	Bags, except textile bags	1.3	1.7
2645	Die-cut paper and paperboard and cardboard	0.5	1.0

SIC	Name	CDVAM/E	CDCS/E
		percent per year	
2646	Pressed and molded pulp goods	-1.6	-7.8
2647	Sanitary paper products	0.6	1.6
2648	Stationery, tablets, and related products	n.a.	n.a.
2649	Converted paper and paperboard products, n.e.c.	n.a.	n.a.
2651	Folding paperboard boxes	0.4	0.8
2652	Set-up paperboard boxes	0.4	n.a.
2653	Corrugated and solid fiber boxes	0.6	0.6
2654	Sanitary food containers	0.4	-1.6
2655	Fiber cans, tubes, drums, and similar products	0.9	0.5
2661	Building paper and building board mills	-1.6.	1.2
27	Printing, Publishing, and Allied Industries		
2711	Newspapers: publishing and printing	-0.2	1.9
2721	Periodicals: publishing and printing	1.4	-1.7
2731	Books: publishing and printing	0.1	0.4
2732	Book printing	-0.8	-0.5
2741	Miscellaneous publishing	1.1	4.2
2751	Commercial printing, letterpress and screen	n.a.	n.a.
2752	Commercial printing, lithographic	1.0	1.5
2753	Engraving and plate printing	-1.6	0.7
2754	Commercial printing, gravure	n.a.	n.a.
2761	Manifold business forms	0.6	-0.1
2771	Greeting card publishing	2.5	2.9
2782	Blankbooks, looseleaf binders and devices	1.0	3.0
2789	Bookbinding and related work	-0.8	-0.5
2791	Typesetting	-1.8	5.9
2793	Photoengraving	-1.0	13.3
2794	Electrotyping and stereotyping	*	*
2795	Lithographic platemaking and related services	n.a.	n.a.

*Included in SIC 2793

SIC	Name	CDVAM/E percent per year	CDCS/E
28	Chemicals and Allied Products	3.9	5.5
2812	Alkalies and chlorine	-0.6	2.7
2813	Industrial gases	-0.9	3.5
2816	Inorganic pigments	-0.4	1.0
2819	Industrial inorganic chemicals		
2821	Plastics materials, synthetic resins, and nonvulcanizable elastomers	n.a.	n.a.
2822	Synthetic rubber (vulcanizable elastomers).	-2.2	-3.1
2823	Cellulosic manmade fibers	-4.7	0.2
2824	Synthetic organic fibers, except cellulosic	4.4	-2.7
2831	Biologicals	0.1	-1.7
2833	Medicinals and botanicals	3.1	3.6
2834	Pharmaceutical preparations	-1.6	0.9
2841	Soap and other detergents	0.6	2.8
2842	Polishes and sanitation products	1.6	1.2
2843	Surface active agents	3.5	8.8
2844	Toilet preparations	-1.0	0.4
2851	Paints and allied products	0.3	2.7
2861	Gum and wood chemicals	0.2	4.9
2865	Cyclic crudes and intermediates	1.1	1.8
2869	Industrial organic chemicals	2.6	6.0
2873	Nitrogenous fertilizers	n.a.	n.a.
2874	Phosphatic fertilizers	-1.9	5.5
2875	Fertilizers, mixing only	4.4	9.8
2879	Agricultural chemicals	3.6	4.0
2891	Adhesives and gelatin	0.2	-2.1
2892	Explosives	3.2	5.2
2893	Printing ink	0.1	0.8
2895	Carbon black	-3.0	0.0
2899	Chemical preparations, n.e.c.	1.6	3.4

SIC	Name	CDVAM/E	CDCS/E
		percent per year	
29	Petroleum Refining and Related Industries		
2911	Petroleum refining	-1.7	4.1
2951	Paving mixtures and blocks	-3.1	-0.9
2952	Asphalt felts and coatings	-2.5	7.7
2992	Lubricating oils and greases	-7.6	3.4
2999	Products of petroleum and coal, n.e.c.	0.7	17.4
30	Rubber and Miscellaneous Plastics Products		
3011	Tires and inner tubes	0.7	-4.4
3021	Rubber and plastics footwear	n.a.	n.a.
3031	Reclaimed rubber	2.6	-7.6
3041	Rubber and plastics hose and belting	n.a.	n.a.
3069	Fabricated rubber products, n.e.c.	n.a.	n.a.
3079	Miscellaneous plastics products	n.a.	n.a.
31	Leather Goods and Shoes		
3111	Leather tanning and finishing	0.9	5.9
3131	Boot and shoe cut stock and findings	-1.3	-0.7
3142	House slippers	-0.5	0.2
3143	Men's footwear, except athletic	n.a.	n.a.
3144	Women's footwear, except athletic	n.a.	n.a.
3149	Footwear, except rubber, n.e.c.	n.a.	n.a.
3151	Leather gloves and mittens	-1.9	0.1
3161	Luggage	0.7	-1.6
3171	Women's handbags and purses	-1.4	0.6
3172	Personal leather goods	0.7	0.6
3199	Leather goods, n.e.c.	n.a.	n.a.

SIC	Name	CDVAM/E	CDCS/E
		percent per year	
32	Stone, Clay, and Glass Products		
3211	Flat glass	1.0	0.0
3221	Glass containers	0.4	3.1
3229	Pressed and blown glass	-0.2	1.7
3231	Purchased glass	-1.6	2.5
3241	Hydraulic cement	-0.2	5.9
3251	Brick and structural clay tile	0.6	4.3
3253	Ceramic wall and floor tile	1.1	3.0
3255	Clay refractories	0.6	1.0
3259	Structural clay products	0.3	3.1
3261	Vitreous plumbing fixtures	1.0	0.4
3262	Vitreous china food utensils	0.4	4.0
3263	Fine earthenware food utensils	0.5	2.3
3264	Porcelain electrical supplies	1.8	1.6
3269	Pottery products	-1.4	3.3
3271	Concrete block and brick	0.3	2.9
3272	Concrete products	1.2	1.1
3273	Ready-mixed concrete	0.5	1.7
3274	Lime	0.9	2.6
3275	Gypsum	0.7	6.8
3281	Cut stone and stone products	0.5	1.3
3291	Abrasive products	0.5	3.3
3292	Asbestos products	0.5	4.9
3293	Gaskets, packing, and sealing devices	n.a	n.a.
3295	Minerals, ground or treated	1.5	2.1
3296	Mineral wool	1.0	1.1
3297	Non-clay refractories	0.9	-15.3
3299	Non metallic mineral products	0.7	11.6

SIC	Name	CDVAM/E	CDCS/E
		percent per year	
33	Primary Metal Industries		
3312	Blast furnaces, steel works, and rolling mills	-0.9	-3.6
3313	Electrometallurgical products	-1.4	-0.6
3315	Steel wire drawing and steel nails and spikes	-1.1	-9.8
3316	Cold rolled steel sheet, strip and bars	0.1	-5.5
3317	Steel pipe and tubes	1.0	1.1
3321	Gray iron foundries	-0.4	1.0
3322	Malleable iron foundries	-0.4	-1.1
3324	Steel investment foundries	n.a.	n.a.
3325	Steel foundries, n.e.c.	n.a.	n.a.
3331	Primary smelting and refining of copper	0.8	-1.6
3332	Primary smelting and refining of lead	3.1	1.3
3333	Primary smelting and refining of zinc	-2.6	1.2
3334	Primary production of aluminum	-1.2	-3.8
3339	Primary smelting and refining of nonferrous metals	-3.6	-1.7
3341	Secondary smelting and refining of nonferrous metals	n.a.	n.a.
3351	Rolling, drawing, and extruding of copper	0.8	-1.3
3353	Aluminum sheet, plate and foil	n.a.	n.a.
3354	Aluminum extruded products	-1.2	1.4
3355	Aluminum rolling and drawing, n.e.c.	4.0	-1.2
3356	Rolling, drawing, and extruding of nonferrous metals, except copper and aluminum	2.4	-3.3
3357	Drawing and insulating of nonferrous wire	-1.2	-5.2
3361	Aluminum foundries (castings)	-1.0	1.2
3362	Brass, bronze, copper, copper base alloy foundries	-1.3	0.5
3369	Nonferrous foundries, n.e.c.	1.0	1.6
3398	Metal heat treating	0.9	-0.8
3399	Primary metal products, n.e.c.	0.6	-4.9
34	Fabricated Metal Products, except Machinery and Transportation Equipment		
3411	Metal Cans	2.3	0.5
3412	Metal shipping barrels, drums, kegs, and pails	0.3	2.4

SIC	Name	CDVAM/E	CDCS/E
		percent per year	
3421	Cutlery	-2.5	2.0
3423	Hand and edge tools, except machine tools and handsaws	-0.4	1.7
3425	Handsaws and saw blades	-1.4	7.2
3429	Hardware, n.e.c.	-1.0	3.0
3431	Enameled iron and metal sanitary ware	0.6	6.2
3432	Plumbing fixtures, fittings, and trim (brass goods)	-0.5	2.4
3433	Heating equipment, except electric and warm air furnaces	n.a.	n.a.
3441	Fabricated structural metal	1.1	5.0
3442	Metal doors, sash, frames, molding, and trim	-0.9	2.5
3443	Fabricated platework (boiler shops)	0.1	0.3
3444	Sheet metalwork	-1.2	2.0
3446	Architectural and ornamental metalwork	1.1	-0.5
3448	Prefabricated metal buildings and components	-2.2	3.1
3449	Miscellaneous metalwork	1.2	-1.3
3451	Screw machine products	-1.9	-1.1
3452	Bolts, nuts, screws, rivets, and washers	-0.8	0.3
3462	Iron and steel forgings	0.4	6.5
3463	Nonferrous forgings	3.0	1.0
3465	Automotive stampings	-0.2	8.1
3466	Crowns and closures	0.9	3.7
3469	Metal stampings, n.e.c.	-0.7	0.4
3471	Electroplating	-1.6	2.1
3479	Coating, engraving, and allied services, n.e.c.	0.4	2.6
3482	Small arms ammunition	0.9	4.0
3483	Ammunition, except for small arms, n.e.c.	0.4	0.8
3484	Small arms	-0.3	3.9
3489	Ordnance and accessories, n.e.c.	0.6	-5.0
3493	Steel springs, except wire	0.5	3.3
3494	Valve and pipe fittings, except plumbers' brass goods	0.2	2.6
3495	Wire springs	-0.6	1.7
3496	Miscellaneous fabricated and wire products	-0.8	2.8

SIC	Name	CDVAM/E	CDCS/E
		percent per year	
3497	Metal foil and leaf	-1.2	-1.8
3498	Fabricated pipe and fabricated pipe fittings	0.0	3.1
3499	Fabricated metal products, n.e.c.	-1.1	0.9
35	Machinery, except Electrical		
3511	Turbines and turbine generator sets	-7.8	2.3
3519	Internal combustion engines	3.7	1.0
3523	Farm machinery and equipment	n.a.	n.a.
3524	Lawn and garden equipment	n.a.	n.a.
3531	Construction machinery	4.6	2.3
3532	Mining machinery	4.6	1.8
3533	Oil field machinery	10.5	1.7
3534	Elevators and moving stairways	5.9	-1.9
3535	Conveyors and conveyor equipment	2.4	0.5
3536	Hoists, cranes, and monorails	0.8	1.4
3537	Industrial trucks and tractors	2.5	0.2
3541	Machine tools, metal cutting types	2.7	1.9
3542	Machine tools, metal forming types	1.8	0.9
3544	Special dies, tools, jigs and fixtures	0.7	-0.5
3545	Machine tool accessories	3.2	1.0
3546	Power-driven hand tools	n.a.	n.a.
3547	Rolling mill machinery	n.a.	n.a.
3549	Metal working machinery	n.a.	n.a.
3551	Food products machinery	0.1	0.1
3552	Textile machinery	1.1	0.8
3553	Woodworking machinery	0.3	0.1
3554	Paper industries machinery	3.3	0.4
3555	Printing trades machinery	5.2	0.4
3559	Special industry machinery	-0.3	0.3
3561	Pumps and pumping equipment	2.8	1.5
3562	Ball and roller bearings	0.8	1.4
3564	Blowers and fans	-1.1	-0.3

SIC	Name	CDVAM/E percent per year	CDCS/E percent per year
3565	Industrial patterns	-1.6	-0.4
3566	Speed changers, drives, and gears	2.2	1.2
3567	Industrial furnaces, and ovens	0.6	-0.3
3569	General industrial machinery	1.6	0.7
3572	Typewriters	2.7	7.7
3573	Electronic computing equipment	2.4	4.6
3574	Calculating and accounting machines	2.0	6.8
3576	Scales and balances, except laboratory	3.4	1.7
3579	Office machines, n.e.c.	inc. in 3572	inc. in 3572
3581	Automatic merchandising machinery	4.2	-1.6
3582	Commercial laundry equipment	n.a.	n.a.
3585	Refrigeration & heating equipment	n.a.	n.a.
3586	Measuring & dispensing pumps	1.4	1.6
3589	Service industry machinery	2.2	-0.3
3592	Carburetors, pistons, rings, and valves	n.a.	n.a.
3599	Machinery, except electrical, n.e.c.	n.a.	n.a.
36	Electrical and Electronic Machinery, Equipment, and Supplies		
3612	Power, distribution, and specialty transformers	1.0	-2.0
3613	Switchgear and switchboard apparatus	2.3	1.6
3621	Motors and generators	2.5	0.8
3622	Industrial controls	2.4	0.7
3623	Welding apparatus, electric	1.2	1.6
3624	Carbon and graphite products	4.0	2.8
3629	Electrical industrial apparatus, n.e.c.	3.3	3.7
3631	Household cooking equipment	2.7	0.1
3632	Household refrigerators and home and farm freezers	1.1	1.1
3633	Household laundry equipment	2.2	-2.2
3634	Electric housewares and fans	1.8	1.8
3635	Household vacuum cleaners	2.3	-0.4

SIC	Name	CDVAM/E percent per year	CDCS/E percent per year
3636	Sewing machines	-0.3	-2.3
3639	Household appliances, n.e.c.	2.3	-2.2
3641	Electric lamps	0.6	-1.6
3643	Current-carrying wiring devices	1.1	1.5
3644	Noncurrent-carrying wiring devices	2.0	-0.3
3645	Residential electric lighting fixtures	n.a.	n.a.
3646	Commercial, industrial, and institutional electric lighting	n.a.	n.a.
3647	Vehicular lighting equipment	n.a.	n.a.
3648	Lighting equipment, n.e.c.	n.a.	n.a.
3651	Radio and television receiving sets, except communication types	3.5	6.9
3652	Phonograph records and pre-recorded tape	4.6	3.5
3661	Telephone and telegraph apparatus	3.4	1.7
3662	Radio and television communication equipment	2.9	4.5
3671	Electron tubes, all types	-0.7	1.8
3674	Semiconductors and related devices	n.a.	n.a.
3675	Electronic capacitors	n.a.	n.a.
3676	Electronic resistors	n.a.	n.a.
3677	Electronic coils, transformers, and other inductors	n.a.	n.a.
3678	Electronic connectors	n.a.	n.a.
3679	Electronic components, n.e.c.	n.a.	n.a.
3691	Storage batteries	4.3	6.5
3692	Primary batteries, dry and wet	1.2	7.8
3693	Flectromedical and electrotherapeutic apparatus	2.1	6.1
3694	Engine electrical equipment	1.6	3.7
3699	Electrical equipment and supplies, n.e.c.	0.7	-5.8

SIC	Name	CDVAM/E percent per year	CDCS/E
37	Transportation Equipment		
3711	Motor vehicles and passenger car bodies	13.2	0.1
3713	Truck and bus bodies	2.8	2.1
3714	Motor vehicle parts and accessories	8.2	1.7
3715	Truck trailers	-1.0	2.1
3721	Aircraft	3.5	3.0
3724	Aircraft engines and engine parts	n.a.	n.a.
3728	Aircraft parts and auxiliary equipment, n.e.c.	n.a.	n.a.
3731	Shipbuilding and repairing	3.2	3.2
3732	Boat Building and repairing	1.6	1.1
3743	Railroad Equipment	0.2	2.2
3751	Motorcycles, bicycles, and parts	2.6	4.2
3761	Guided missiles and space vehicles	3.3	5.2
3764	Guided missiles and space propulsion units and propulsion unit parts	n.a.	n.a.
3769	Space vehicles equipment, n.e.c.	n.a.	n.a.
3792	Travel trailers and campers	-2.2	0.6
3795	Tanks and tank components	11.4	0.4
3799	Transportion equipment, n.e.c.	3.9	-0.2
38	Instruments and Related Products		
3811	Engineering and scientific instrumentation	5.7	2.2
3822	Environmental controls	3.3	-0.9
3823	Process control instruments	n.a.	n.a.
3824	Fluid meters and counting devices	n.a.	n.a.
3825	Instruments to measure electricity	3.2	1.1
3829	Measuring and controlling devices, n.e.c.	2.7	-1.5
3832	Optical instruments and lenses	5.2	1.7
3841	Surgical and medical instruments	2.7	0.5
3842	Surgical appliances and supplies	1.3	-0.1
3843	Dental equipment and supplies	-1.0	0.4
3851	Ophthalmic goods	-0.4	0.0

SIC	Name	CDVAM/E	CDCS/E
		percent per year	
3861	Photographic equipment and supplies	-0.3	1.8
3873	Watches, clocks, and watch cases	1.1	-0.2
39	Miscellaneous Manufactures		
3911	Jewelry, precious metal	-1.6	1.8
3914	Jewelry, silverware, and plated ware	-0.6	-5.0
3915	Jeweler's material and lapidary work	-0.3	-1.9
3931	Musical instruments	-2.6	-1.8
3942	Dolls	3.8	7.2
3944	Games, toys, and children's vehicles	4.8	3.7
3949	Sporting, amusement, and athletic goods	2.5	2.8
3951	Pens, mechanical pencils, and parts	0.3	2.4
3952	Lead pencils, crayons, and artists' materials	0.2	0.4
3953	Marking devices	-1.6	2.2
3955	Carbon paper and inked ribbons	-0.6	-1.0
3961	Costume jewelry, novelties	-2.3	0.1
3962	Feathers, plumes, artificial flowers	2.3	0.0
3963	Buttons	0.0	-1.1
3964	Needles, pins, notions	0.0	0.5
3991	Brooms and brushes	-1.8	-2.0
3993	Signs and advertising displays	-2.3	-1.3
3995	Burial caskets	-0.7	3.6
3996	Linoleum and related floor coverings	3.5	-2.1
3999	Manufacturers, n.e.c.	-0.5	2.7

Source: 1982 U.S. Census of Manufactures (Washington, D.C.: Government Printing Office, 1982).

INDEX

About the Author

JOHN E. ULLMANN, Professor of Management and Quantitative Methods at Hofstra University in Hempstead, New York, holds degrees in civil, mechanical, and industrial engineering. He is the author of more than sixty books, monographs, and articles on industrial and community development, technological innovation, and production management. His previous books include *The Prospects of American Industrial Recovery* and *Social Costs in Modern Society*, both published by Quorum Books.